Non-Governmental Organizations in Contemporary China

The development of non-governmental organizations (NGOs) and the evolution of a civil society in China emerged in the aftermath of the 1978 reforms, creating for the first time new institutions and organizations outside of the state system. This book analyzes how the rapid growth of NGOs was a measure of the profound social change and political tensions occurring within China from the 1980s to the present day.

As the first comprehensive volume on Chinese NGOs, it covers crucial aspects of the subject including governmental NGO policy, roles of the grassroots organizations, features of people's associational behavior and involvement from international NGOs. Qiusha Ma draws on a wealth of primary material from interviews with key Chinese figures to detailed case studies on NGO organizations and individuals. Her in-depth research highlights the environmental protection movement, advocacy for victims of AIDS and drugs, organizations for women's rights and the activities of the HOPE project for children in deprived rural regions.

By taking into account China's history, its current political system and the influence of the global revolution in associational activity, *Non-Governmental Organizations in Contemporary China* challenges and revises the very concepts of civil society and non-governmental organization in the study of contemporary China.

Qiusha Ma is Associate Professor of Chinese at Oberlin College, USA. She is an authority on NGOs in China and has published numerous articles on the subject.

Routledge Contemporary China Series

1 **Nationalism, Democracy and National Integration in China**
   Leong Liew and Wang Shaoguang

2 **Hong Kong's Tortuous Democratization**
   A comparative analysis
   Ming Sing

3 **China's Business Reforms**
   Institutional challenges in a globalised economy
   Edited by Russell Smyth and Cherrie Zhu

4 **Challenges for China's Development**
   An enterprise perspective
   Edited by David H. Brown and Alasdair MacBean

5 **New Crime in China**
   Public order and human rights
   Ron Keith and Zhiqiu Lin

6 **Non-Governmental Organizations in Contemporary China**
   Paving the way to civil society?
   Qiusha Ma

7 **Globalization and the Chinese City**
   Fulong Wu

8 **The Politics of China's Accession to the World Trade Organization**
   The dragon goes global
   Hui Feng

9 **Narrating China**
   Jia Pingwa and his fictional world
   Yiyan Wang

10 **Sex, Science and Morality in China**
    Joanne McMillan

Non-Governmental Organizations in Contemporary China
Paving the way to civil society?

Qiusha Ma

Routledge
Taylor & Francis Group
LONDON AND NEW YORK

First published 2006
by Routledge
2 Park Square, Milton Park, Abingdon, Oxon OX14 4RN

Simultaneously published in the USA and Canada
by Routledge
270 Madison Ave, New York, NY 10016

Routledge is an imprint of the Taylor & Francis Group

© 2006 Qiusha Ma

Typeset in Times New Roman
by Graphicraft Limited, Hong Kong
Printed and bound in Great Britain
by Antony Rowe Ltd, Chippenham, Wiltshire

All rights reserved. No part of this book may be reprinted or reproduced or utilized in any form or by any electronic, mechanical, or other means, now known or hereafter invented, including photocopying and recording, or in any information storage or retrieval system, without permission in writing from the publishers.

British Library Cataloguing in Publication Data
A catalogue record for this book is available from the British Library

Library of Congress Cataloging in Publication Data
Ma, Qiusha.
Non-governmental organizations in contemporary China : paving the way to a civil society? / by Qiusha Ma.
p. cm. – (Routledge contemporary China series)
Includes bibliographical references and index.
ISBN 0-415-36919-3 (hardback : alk. paper)
1. Non-governmental organizations – China.
2. Civil society – China. I. Title. II. Series.

HS81.C5A22 2005
361.7′7′0951–dc22
2005004672

ISBN 10: 0-415-36919-3
ISBN 13: 9-78-0-415-36919-0

For Nengli and Linda, with love and gratitude

Contents

List of Figures ix
List of Tables x
Acknowledgements xi
List of Abbreviations xiii

Introduction 1

Western theories vs Chinese reality 4
NGOs with Chinese characteristics 8
Chapter outlines and methodology 12

1 In search of civil society in China: theoretical and historical discourses 16

Chinese intellectuals' debates over civil society in the 1990s 17
Evolution of civil society in late Qing and early Republican China 33

2 "Small government, big society": the Chinese government's NGO policy and its dilemma 47

The government's motives for promoting NGOs 48
Major features of China's registration-regulation of NGOs since the late 1970s 61
Contradictions in the government's NGO policy 69

3 NGO landscape in China: classification, scope, and autonomy 76

Defining NGOs in China: classification and terminology 77
Analyses of Chinese NGO growth 86
NGO–government relations in China: how much autonomy? 95

4 Social capital: the significance and dynamics of grassroots NGOs and social networks — 105

The concept of social capital and its application in China 107
The significance of grassroots organizations 111
Dynamics and leadership of grassroots NGOs: the role of Chinese intellectuals 121

5 Corporatism vs civil society: NGOs in the economic realm — 136

Simultaneous development of corporatism and civil society 137
Four categories of top-down associations 145
Bottom-up pattern: the chambers of commerce in Wenzhou 159

6 "It takes two to tangle": international NGOs in China and their impacts — 167

The impact of globalization and global civil society on China 168
Chinese government policy towards INGOs 171
The current state of international NGOs in China 176
The role of international NGOs in China 180
Limitations of INGOs' efforts in China 195

Conclusion — 201

The major forces promoting Chinese NGOs 201
Changes in associational landscapes in China 204
Do NGOs facilitate civil society in China? 206

Notes — 209
Bibliography — 219
Index — 237

Figures

2.1	The official administrative structure over the NGOs	63
3.1	Hierarchy of Chinese NGOs	80
3.2	Social organizations nationwide (1993–2003)	89
3.3	National social organizations (1978–2003)	89
3.4	Decline of social organizations in provinces since 1996	89
3.5	Numbers of social organizations: coastal vs inland	90
3.6	Social organizations in minority autonomous regions	90
3.7	Social organizations by type (1994)	93
3.8	Social organizations by type (2003)	93
3.9	Non-governmental and non-commercial enterprises by type (2000)	94
5.1	The managerial system of trade associations in the machine industry	140
5.2	Self-employed laborers in urban China (1949–93)	150
5.3	The organizational structure of the Self-employed Laborers' Association	152
5.4	Growth and decline of national social organizations (1994–2003)	157
5.5	Decline of all types of social organizations nationwide (1996–2001)	158
5.6	Growth of national trade associations (1988–99)	158
5.7	Growth of trade associations nationwide (1992–2001)	158

Tables

2.1	The industrial GNP (%) divided by ownership	54
2.2	The development of individually owned businesses	54
2.3	Relevant official documents on NGOs in the People's Republic of China	64
3.1	Six equivalents of social organizations	81
3.2	Formation of national SOs (1950–94)	88
3.3	Comparison of provincial SOs by population (2003)	91
3.4	SOs and population ratio in minority autonomous regions	91
3.5	SOs and population ratio in China's four largest cities	91
6.1	Number of INGOs entering China since 1978	178
6.2	Country origins of INGOs currently in China	179
6.3	INGOs' organizational status in China	179
6.4	Major foci of INGOs in China, by organization	180
6.5	Largest US funders of charitable activities relating to or in China (1994–96)	190
6.6	The Ford Foundation-funded China-related programs (1986–2001)	191
6.7	A comparison of giving foci between China's CANGO and US foundations	192
6.8	Geographical distribution of Ford Foundation's funding in China (2000)	193
6.9	The Ford Foundation's grants to different types of organization (1989–2000)	194

Acknowledgements

I began studying Chinese non-governmental organizations (NGOs) and civil society in 1996, at a time when not only few scholars, Chinese or international, were pursuing this topic, but also the subject itself was politically sensitive in China. There were not comprehensive and consistent official statistics on NGOs open to the public. With few existing studies and sufficient data to build upon, it has been a long and difficult journey during which I received immeasurable help and support without which I could never have completed this endeavor.

First and foremost, to make up for the absence of statistical data and independent research, this book relied heavily upon personal interviews. I am deeply indebted to those I interviewed, including NGO activists, scholars, and government officials; though not all their names are mentioned in this book in order to protect their identities, they are all very much appreciated. These people generously provided their information, knowledge, and insights on the development of Chinese NGOs, and some shared their time and thoughts again and again over the years. From those honest conversations I learned many NGO people's personal experiences and sacrifice, and their courage, spirits and devotion inspired me to write this book, which is based upon their stories and those of their organizations.

This book has gone through several drafts, and I have received help at every step. Many colleagues and friends have been incredibly supportive and generous with their time, knowledge, and opinions, and I have benefited from them immeasurably. I appreciate their help and friendship from the bottom of my heart. When I started my doctoral program, I had no idea what non-government organizations were. It was my advisor David C. Hammack at Case Western Reserve University, a renowned scholar of the non-profit sector, who led me to this fascinating field and guided me at every step. His knowledge, insights, encouragement and generosity have been, even after I obtained my doctorate, an important resource of my research. Eve Sandbuger read the first couple of chapters in the early stages of this project and gave me crucial guidance to the structure of the book. Sami Hasson read quite a few chapters, and not only provided valuable comments but also carefully corrected errors in my writing. Roger DesForges read through the entire manuscript, including all the endnotes, and his comments and corrections were very helpful and sincerely appreciated. My deep gratitude also goes to the anonymous reviewer whose ten pages of suggestion and critiques proved very valuable to the final revision of the account. David Kelley kindly read my work and offered me comments as well as his knowledge and thoughts on contemporary Chinese history. Marc Blecher generously gave me advice when I needed. Elisabeth Koll, Sheila Jagar, and Pauline Chen not only spent time on my work but also gave me much appreciated encouragement and advice.

I would like to use this opportunity to thank the Aspen Institute's Nonprofit Research Fund and Oberlin College's Powers Travel Funds and grants-in-aid. Without this generous research and travel support, my many trips to work in the field would have been impossible.

Finally, I cannot thank enough my father, husband and daughter, for the enormous love, support, understanding and encouragement they have given me; I cannot imagine how I would have completed this book without them. My special appreciation to my daughter, Linda, for her sincere interest in the project, candid opinions, and countless time spent on editing my writing.

List of Abbreviations

ACFIC	The All-China Federation of Industry and Commerce
ACFTU	The All-China Federation of Trade Unions
ACWF	The All-China Women's Federation
ASMI	Association of Shanghai Material Industry
BFIC	Beijing Federation of Industry and Commerce
BIC	Bureau of Industry and Commerce
BMNGO	Bureau of Management of NGOs (under the Ministry of Civil Affairs)
BOCA	Bureau of Civil Affairs
CANGO	The China Association for NGO Cooperation
CASS	China Academy of Social Science
CBIK	Center for Biodiversity and Indigenous Knowledge
CCA	China Customers' Association
CCF	China Charity Federation
CCP	Chinese Communist Party
CCYL	Chinese Communist Youth League
CFPA	China Foundation for Poverty Alleviation
CGCPA	China Grouping Companies Promotion Association
CPPCC	Chinese People's Political Consultative Conference
CSELA	China Self-employed Laborers' Association
CSWA	China Social Workers' Association
CTCF	The China Teenagers' and Children Foundation
CYDF	China Youth Development Foundation
DSO	Division of Social Organizations
ENGO	Environmental Non-governmental Organization
FFCC	Federation of Foreign Chambers of Commerce
FIC	Federation of Industry and Commerce
FON	Friends of Nature
GEV	Green Earth Volunteers
GONGO	Government Organized Non-governmental Organization
GVB	Global Village of Beijing
INGO	International Non-governmental Organization
MFET	Ministry of Foreign Economy and Trade

List of Abbreviations

MOCA	Ministry of Civil Affairs
MOIA	Ministry of Internal Affairs
NFA	Ningbo Fellows' Association
NGNCEs	Non-governmental and Non-commercial Enterprises
NGO/NPO	Non-governmental and Non-profit Organization
OCA	Organizational Capacity Assessment
PEA	Private Entrepreneurs' Association
PINGOS	Provincial International Non-governmental Organization Society
PRA	Participatory Rural Appraisal
PRC	People's Republic of China
RC	Residents' Committee
RMB	Renmin Bi (the currency of the PRC)
SDFC	Sina Drivers' Friendship Club
SEL	Self-employed Laborers
SELA	Self-employed Laborers' Association
SFIE	Shanghai Federation of Industrial Economy
SO	Social Organization
SOE	State-owned Enterprise
WCC	Wenzhou Chambers of Commerce
WCW	World Conference for Women
WGCC	Wenzhou Garment Chamber of Commerce
WFIC	Wenzhou Federation of Industry and Commerce
WOICC	Wenzhou Optical Industry Chamber of Commerce
WTO	World Trade Organization

Introduction

In the aftermath of the 1978 reforms that created a market economy and diversified public interests and social life in China, new institutions and organizations outside of the state system increased dramatically in number, size, and influence. According to the 2001 edition of China's official statistics, the Ministry of Civil Affairs (MOCA) and its local branches had registered as many as 136,841 social organizations (SOs) nationwide as well as almost 700,000 non-governmental and non-commercial enterprises (NGNCEs) (Liao 2000: 31). Furthermore, the number of non-registered, self-organized social and cultural groups in urban neighborhood communities may well exceed that of registered social organizations.[1] These organizations, which barely existed before the reforms began in the late 1970s, assist the government in many social, economic, and cultural tasks. In addition, they carry out programs that address social issues neglected by the government, from establishing centers for abused women and children to organizing community recycling programs.

This study uses the term non-governmental organizations (NGOs) to refer to all organizations classified by the Chinese government as SOs and NGNCEs, whether registered or not. As it traces their development from the late 1970s to the early 2000s, the study attempts to make sense of two over-arching questions. First, under China's one-party state, is it possible for NGOs to thrive and play important economic, social, and even political functions? Second, are these NGOs facilitating the formation of a civil society in China? These questions lead, in turn, to other issues: what are the economic and social dynamics behind the emergence of Chinese NGOs? What are the major characteristics of these organizations, and what is their strategy for sustainable development? What is the government's attitude towards NGOs, and how has this official NGO policy shaped the growth patterns of these new organizations? What is the impact of globalization in general and global civil society in particular on the evolving civil society in China? These are the fundamental questions that the following chapters seek to answer.

Profound changes in social and economic structures have created public as well as private spheres that have allowed NGOs to emerge and

2   *Introduction*

survive. This study argues that legally and institutionally, Chinese SOs and NGNCEs no longer exist within the state system, and that such a status carries substantial importance to the long-term development of the non-governmental sector in China. According to Chinese official regulations, all registered SOs and NGNCEs are non-governmental and not-for-profit. These organizations' staff members are not civil servants (government employees), and a large proportion of organizations are becoming self-sufficient, with their day-to-day operations independent of government control. It is true that Chinese NGOs have a long way to go to achieve autonomy on political matters; yet, the degree of autonomy they have gradually obtained during the past twenty-odd years is one of the most meaningful changes in China's institutional landscape. The key issue to our understanding of Chinese NGOs is not whether they are still closely aligned with the government, but whether they carry out missions and roles that differ from those of state institutions.

This study further argues that NGOs are becoming increasingly powerful instruments through which the Chinese people participate in public affairs, develop personal interests, express themselves, and collectively form a more active and engaged citizenry. In the ensuing chapters, the substantial effects of NGOs on societal functions and people's behavior will be elaborated in detail. In so many important matters in China, from securing the 2008 Olympics to combating SARS, the government has called on NGOs for help. One may argue that these are simply service functions; nevertheless, this study is convinced that, as NGOs deliver their services, they are going to have – and some have already had, as the environmental NGOs demonstrated – an influential voice in many social and economic concerns. At this stage, Chinese NGOs do not have a substantial effect on government policy-making and political matters. They do, however, present a clear and undeniable political statement: people are gaining control of their lives in a heretofore unseen fashion.

This study concludes that NGO development since the late 1970s has been a crucial step in the emergence of a new state–society relationship, and that non-governmental institutions are indeed facilitating the formation of civil society in China. As the country's social transformation continues under the direct influence of globalization, a Chinese civil society as understood internationally is irreversibly evolving. Nevertheless, the preliminary nature of the current state of NGOs must be recognized. The vulnerability of NGOs may be attributed to a number of factors: the inadequate practice of associational life in the past, limited resources, lack of a visionary and inspiring NGO leadership, and, most of all, the persistence of a harsh political environment. In addition, NGO growth in China is highly unbalanced, with the non-governmental sector playing an increasingly active role in economic and social development while possessing almost no voice in political and religious issues. Moreover, Chinese NGOs are not yet integrated into a dynamic third sector able to exert a strong role in balancing or supervising governmental behavior. This situation has hampered the healthy growth of civil society in China.

The idea of civil society provides a conceptual framework that assesses the state–society relationships in a given political culture. This study emphasizes the necessity of applying this approach according to China's circumstances. The presence of a continuously strong state inhibits the development of factors crucial to civil society such as the public sphere, forms of public communication, citizen participation, and interaction between the state and economy. Thus, while the emerging Chinese civil society presents an expanding sphere for individuals, associations, and businesses to represent and develop their own and public interests, the relationship between the state and civil society is, and will be in the foreseeable future, a state-dominated interaction. Could the state–society relationship in China ever resemble the models described by Western civil society theoreticians? Considering China's historical tradition and current political system, the answer remains open-ended.

As one of the most significant events in post-Mao China, the upsurge of these new institutions as a whole requires close attention and poses a great challenge to students of modern China. Despite recent efforts to understand China's state–society relationships, we know very little about these organizations' distinct values, roles, operations, and forms of management. We also lack much documentation on the domestic and international forces promoting and forming these organizations. Decentralization and the rise of a market economy in China have directed scholarly attention mainly towards the rapidly expanding business sector along with the changes in power structure between central and local governments. Helmut Anheier raised the concern that conventional social science theory typically considers either the business firm or public agency, while "little attention has been paid to non-state and non-market forms" (Anheier 2001: 4). This is very much the case in the studies of modern institutional changes in China.

In an effort to enhance comprehension of China's new institutional landscape and its significance, this book focuses entirely on the most important issues pertaining to NGO development, most of them new concerns. These include mapping NGOs by type, mission, nature, and locality; clarifying how NGOs are classified and regulated; analyzing NGO dynamics, leadership, sustaining strategies, and operating mechanisms; and examining the mutually interactive relations with international NGOs within China. This book approaches NGOs from both governmental and organizational perspectives, with their respective political, economic, and social agendas. Most of all, this study places Chinese NGOs in the context of China's present political and economic realities as well as the history behind current circumstances. It then tests the applicability of Western theories of NGOs and civil society to the state of NGOs in China.

Western theories vs Chinese reality

To study the current state of Chinese NGOs and their roles in facilitating civil society, the Western concepts of NGOs adopted here must first be clarified. A vast array of Western theories and ideas were introduced into Chinese academia following the reforms and open policy of the late 1970s. Not until the late 1980s, however, did the dramatic changes in China's institutional landscape and power structures attract considerable scholarly interest. The consequence is an impressive body of recent literature that relies on a set of Western political theories to try to understand China's reforms, the new state–society relationship, and the growing role of NGOs in China's public sphere. Around this time, concepts such as corporatism, civil society, and state–society relationship came to be applied by Western and Chinese students of China, indicating a new generation of scholarship that was shifting away from Cold War or Cultural Revolution approaches (Perry 1994: 704).

Today, the concepts of NGOs, civil society, corporatism, and the third sector have become a part of Chinese political vocabulary, and Chinese scholars find these Western theories helpful in their interpretation of what is happening in China (Chapter 1). The insights of Western academics have inspired Chinese scholars in their search for a civil society in China and in their study of non-governmental behavior. The discourse on these theories among Chinese intellectuals has extended beyond a purely scholarly discussion to application. Indeed, their work has been a necessary step in the emergence and growth of NGOs. The birth of this rapidly expanding area of study in China has directly affected NGO behavior and, to a certain degree, government policy on NGOs.

Models of civil society and non-profit sectors in other cultures also provide valuable examples for our analysis of China's new institutions; thus, students of China have a foundation from which to compare China's developments with models and practices in other countries. Furthermore, analyses based on such theoretical frameworks allow the international NGO society to assess the state of Chinese organizations in a familiar terminology. By the same token, the introduction of this common language connects the Chinese NGO community with their counterparts abroad.

The adoption of these concepts is not without controversy and inevitably leads to the question of the applicability of Western political theories to the Chinese situation. It is always risky and controversial to assume Western theoretical frameworks in the study of non-Western cultures, histories, or politics. Furthermore, the discourse on these concepts among Western scholars, especially on civil society, has left a profusion of philosophical and political interpretations and models, and the debate continues today. Many interpretations may be too broad or confusing, even controversial, to apply to a specific cultural or socio-economic system, and scholars need to clarify their definition of the terms employed in their research. Gideon Baker, a

British political scientist, once said that the crux of the problem arises "when the idea of civil society is applied uniformly outside of the West." Cultural and historical specificity must be taken into account:

> Though most theorists of civil society will not do this explicitly, their account of civil society, contained as it is within a wider normative democratic theory, is implicitly universalized. A problem then emerges which is that the underlying structures necessary to the realization of liberal politics – to the autonomy or negative liberty of civil society on which these theorists want to build a democratizing project – are actually particular in important ways to the historical experiences of the West, experiences which are not directly applicable elsewhere.
> (Baker 1998: 83)

Heeding this caveat, this study will carefully define the terms being adopted. Given that Western studies form the core body of theory behind NGOs, and that they are widely incorporated into the research of Chinese scholars on the topic, I believe that the use of these ideas will prove beneficial to this study.

As the following chapters will discuss, many previous studies of Chinese non-governmental institutions have debated whether civil society or corporatism best describes the role of the new organizations and their relations with the state (Chapter 1). Others have raised serious doubts concerning the legitimacy of Chinese NGOs (Chapter 3). The divergence in their interpretations of the current state of Chinese NGOs reflects the difficulty in evaluating these new institutions according to popular Western concepts given the actual conditions in China. In my study of the subject, I, too, face this serious challenge. Yet having grown up under the Chinese Communist Party (CCP)'s total political control, I am greatly struck by the enormous and fundamental changes that have occurred in the lives of the Chinese and in the nature of social space. I am convinced that the key here is not to generalize or simplify issues specific to China and overlook their complex reality while trying to interpret events through a Western lens. Therefore, while Western theories of NGOs and civil society guide this book, they are subsumed under China's context.

What is the political condition, then, that Chinese NGOs are facing? After twenty years of reforms and open policy, China's one-party state apparatus remains almost unchanged. The government is still controlled by a CCP that continues to affirm Marxism and Leninism as its ideological basis and the foundation of its authority. Although the Constitution guarantees the people's right of association, the party-state still suppresses politically oriented organizations that do not conform to the party's position. The CCP and the government remain the most decisive factors in NGO growth, which can be frustrating since the official attitude towards NGOs often shifts between encouragement and restraint. A prerequisite of government promotion of NGOs is its confidence in its ultimate control of NGOs. Politically sensitive issues may heighten the government and party's concern over the political risk posed by NGOs, and the leadership may believe that certain organizations form a threat to national interests and security. In such cases, the state does not hesitate to suppress these organizations and their voices.

Another related problem facing Chinese NGOs involves the legal environment. China is not yet a country that upholds the rule of law, although it is moving in that direction. On the one hand, China still does not have a social organization law to protect NGOs from the abuse of power by official agencies and office holders. The governmental regulatory system is based on official executive documents, and these stipulations are not only subject to change according to state political interests and interpretations, but they are also inconsistent and often contradictory. On the other hand, the state lacks the means necessary to implement existing laws or regulations to effectively prevent or punish illegal actions on the part of non-profit organizations or counterfeit NGOs. A climate of uncertainty and the possibility of grave consequences raise serious doubts as to whether legitimate NGOs can thrive in China's political atmosphere.

Despite these unfavorable conditions, official Chinese NGO policy since the late 1970s has had a positive impact on China's NGOs; without it, they would not have been able to progress as far as they have. After the Cultural Revolution (1966–76), a series of economic and political crises seriously challenged the legitimacy of the CCP and government. The vital issue to the CCP was and still is how to stay in power, and the top leaders were convinced that their regime needed to spur economic development and improve the general standard of living. With its own interests in mind, the government found that NGOs, with support from society and the international non-profit sector, could provide vital social and professional services as well as intermediary mechanisms for economic and social transformations. For the first time since the inauguration of the CCP regime, the government adopted a policy that legalized a broad range of NGOs initiated and operated by the people. Especially since the 1990s, the government has consistently promoted certain types of non-governmental and non-profit organizations as indispensable steps in its reform agenda.

Furthermore, the Chinese government is not, to use a Chinese phrase, "a solid iron board" (*tieban yikuai*). Namely, the official NGO policy varies greatly from the central to local governments as well as among different departments in the government. The decentralization of political and economic power has intensified diverse interests among cities, provinces, and regions, and some local governments hold much more open attitudes towards NGOs, domestic or international, than do other local governments or the national government. Thus, a given local government's attitude towards the non-profits is not necessarily in line with the CCP's opinion. For example, the government in Yunnan Province has been more open to international

NGOs (Mas 1999), and officials in Wenzhou actively supported private chambers of commerce in the early 1990s when the central government had not yet approved these organizations (Chapter 5). Meanwhile, conflicts of interest among different divisions of the government, often related to the downsizing of administrative bodies, also has had a mixed influence on official policy-making concerning NGOs. The expansion of official support of NGOs inevitably fuels intra-governmental power struggles. For example, when the Ministry of Civil Affairs pushes policies that favor NGO development, the Ministries of Treasury and Taxation react negatively because they see no particular benefit to their own sphere of power.[2] Such situations no doubt complicate the NGO environment in general; yet, they often give NGOs space to grow or opportunities to influence official policy.

The pressure of the international community on China's reforms has also affected the government's NGO policy. Examples of this include the requirement by the International Olympic Committee that NGO representatives be part of the Beijing Committee for Hosting the 2008 Olympics, and the roundtable meeting that Chinese environmental NGO leaders held with the then President of the United States, Bill Clinton, when he visited China in 1998. As will be discussed in Chapter 6, large amounts of international aid and other forms of assistance from the private sector have motivated the Chinese government to create NGOs to attract such support and to improve the climate for both foreign and domestic NGOs.

The social pressures that contribute to the government's policy decisions are equally important and complex. Since the late 1970s, the substantial growth of a market economy and the loosening of political control have fostered conditions favorable to non-governmental activities. At the same time, these rapid transformations have spurred a massive relocation of workers and peasants, thus creating a daunting social agenda. Governments at all levels lack the means to adequately meet these urgent needs, so they have turned to the private sector for help. With economic development and social stability as their number one priority, the state has had to relax its reins and let society expand. In this context, the government came up with the reform slogan of "Small Government, Big Society."

To a great extent, China is no longer a society as tightly controlled by the party-state as it was before the reforms. As the state gradually withdrew – in part by design, in part by default – from many economic and social responsibilities, the Chinese people responded to this new situation with great energy and creativity. The appearance of voluntary organizations, private non-profit institutions, and all kinds of civil associations reflected a serious effort to address social needs, economic and social injustice, disadvantaged groups, and environmental degradation. In addition, economic development produced a rapidly enlarging middle class, especially in cities and coastal regions, whose members vigorously pursued associative actions to represent their economic and political voices. Lastly, the increasing social and cultural multiplicity, along with the expansion of private space, time, and monetary resources, led to the flourishing of all kinds of cultural and spiritual activities, social networks, and self-help groups. These collective activities have quietly transformed ordinary people's lifestyles and their views of themselves and their communities.

China is a country that treasures its history and tradition. At the same time, with the exception of the CCP's first thirty years (1949–78), China has also been strongly influenced by the West since the Opium War of 1840. The confrontation and interaction between China's traditional culture and Western science, technology, political ideas, and democratic systems are at the heart of reform movements in contemporary Chinese history. One can hardly exaggerate the impact since the 1980s of globalization and the technological revolution on Chinese society and culture. In his study of globalization and China's state transformation, Yongnian Zheng points out that

> while economic globalization and the IT revolution have contributed directly to China's economic transformation, they have also provided an important medium for a new form of associational activity to rise . . . Citizens are now able to express their own political views, regardless of whether the government sanctions it or not. In other words, the IT revolution has created a new tool for political participation.
>
> (Zheng 2004: 13)

Chinese NGO behavior clearly reveals the influence of both tradition and the West. On the one hand, this study applies civil society and NGO theories against China's historical reality and sees how deep-rooted traditional Chinese understandings of government (*guan*), public (*gong*), private (*si*) and the roles of private associations in the early twentieth century have given modern NGOs inextricably Chinese characteristics. It highlights the shadow of the past on China's NGO development. On the other hand, this study examines the direct international influence on the emergence of new institutional forms and approaches. It argues that the global civil society movement has not simply pressed the government to be more open to the non-governmental sector; foreign and international NGOs have also assisted and promoted this growth, especially that of autonomous and grassroots organizations, through methodological, technical, monetary, and personal assistance. Their influence is growing impressively in depth and breadth. The surge of global civil society and China's entrance to the World Trade Organization (WTO) has further pushed both the government and NGOs to catch up to international standards. Only when we recognize that the state, society, China's traditions, and Western ideas are working hand in hand to shape China's new third sector can we make sense of the unique evolution of Chinese NGOs.

NGOs with Chinese characteristics

The CCP's control of policy and the state of human rights in China cast serious doubt on the autonomous nature of China's "non-governmental organizations." In a 1994 study of non-profits in Asia, Isagani R. Serrano asserts that the Chinese government "has been omnipresent and overbearing for four decades and has left virtually no room for private voluntary organizations" (Serrano 1994: 276). In her *Non Governments: NGOs and the Political Development of the Third World*, Julie Fisher takes autonomy as a key feature of the non-governmental sector, and she believes that China has only a handful of NGOs (Fisher 1998: 48). Kang Xiaoguang, a Chinese political scientist, concludes in his study of Chinese social organizations that very few Chinese organizations meet the Western conceptions of NGOs (Kang 1999). A 2003 study of Chinese NGOs by three Chinese scholars shares this opinion (Wang *et al.* 64).

Lester Salamon and Helmut Anheier, two leading scholars of international NGOs, put forth a definition of NGOs in a widely cited article. In their explanation, non-governmental organizations are not only formal, private, and non-profit-distributing, they are also self-governing and voluntary (Salamon and Anheier 1992: 134). This study agrees with Salamon and Anheier's definition, and it recognizes the fact that Chinese NGOs as a whole are not yet the type of organizations they describe. Chinese NGOs do not command the degree of organizational autonomy that NGOs in democratic countries do. Nonetheless, this study argues that our examination of the importance and role of these new organizations should not be confined by a narrow interpretation of NGO criteria. The distinctively Chinese characteristics of modern institutions reflect weaknesses these organizations have inherited under China's historical and current socio-political culture; yet, the same characteristics also demonstrate the ability of Chinese NGOs to survive the party-state system, thus indicating their potential. While the following chapters will discuss specific features of different types of NGOs, several general characteristics of Chinese NGOs will be highlighted here to begin an understanding of the real roles that these organizations play.

To begin, unlike independent organizations or third sectors in many countries with a long history of civil society, China's NGOs in general have yet to establish a clear ideology of their political and social roles outside of what the state has determined for them. In re-emerging under the socio-political culture that began in the late 1970s, these institutions and associations represented a social response to profound changes and pressing needs rather than a clear ideological position. As Chapter 1 will discuss, China never had a full-fledged civil society, nor does its present political system allow a third sector to be truly independent from the state. Finally, an overarching concern is that the state–society relationship is perceived differently in Chinese culture than in Western civil society theory.

Against such a broad context, Chinese NGOs do not consider themselves as the vanguards of society battling state intrusion or as an independent sector with distinct functions. Rather, the great majority of Chinese NGOs see their roles as complementing and assisting the state.[3] Furthermore, there is a great array of organizational autonomy, and Chinese NGOs with different backgrounds hold a variety of attitudes toward the issue of autonomy. For example, while newly founded grassroots NGOs consider organizational autonomy as a crucial issue, many governmentally organized NGOs (GONGOs) see the benefits of continuing close relations with the state. It is true that Western theories about civil society and NGOs have been rapidly introduced into China in the past decade; nevertheless, the Chinese will need time to embrace ideas such as NGOs and civil society and harmonize them with the existing culture. It is not difficult to understand that obtaining independence is not the top priority for most Chinese NGOs (Chapter 3).

Having said this, the organizational autonomy enjoyed by NGOs in China is much greater than may appear on the surface. The state needs NGOs to carry out responsibilities it can no longer meet, and, as a result, it is relinquishing certain kinds of authority to society and NGOs. At the same time, the government simply lacks the resources necessary to control all NGO activities. Chinese people call it "not enough police force" (*jingli buzu*). As Tony Saich, a China expert, notes, "There is a significant gap between rhetoric and practice and between the expressed intent of the party-state authorities, a system that is itself deeply conflicted, and what can actually be enforced for any significant period throughout the entire country" (Saich 2000: 125).

NGO activists have exploited this governmental weakness in order to grow. As survivors of countless political movements, many of them know how to play political games under China's CCP-state. For instance, self-censorship of NGOs is a useful strategy to stay out of political trouble. NGOs understand well what they can and cannot do, and they behave accordingly. Thus, NGOs must compromise, sometimes painfully, and yet they consider the sacrifice a necessary cost that allows them to continue to serve society and those in need.[4] NGOs try to avoid confronting the government directly, nor do they touch issues seen as politically taboo. They know that as long as they do not overtly challenge official rules, the government will leave them alone. As a Chinese saying goes, the officials keep "one eye open, the other closed" (*zheng yizhi yan, bi yizhi yan*).

One of the most interesting features of China's NGO–government relations is the ability of organizations to obtain official power and resources for their own purposes. Living in the crevice, as some describe their situation, NGOs maintain good relations with the government as a basic survival tactic. In other words, in China, a close relationship with the government is not always a sign of state control; it may just as well be NGO manipulation of the government. In many cases, this complicated "study" of relationships (*guanxixue*) works in the NGOs' favor. Having close ties with governmental organizations or high officials helps NGOs obtain approval for registration, gain protection from all kinds of trouble, and often win access to state financial, personnel, and information resources. It is not uncommon for NGOs, of their own accord, to invite retired or even current high officials to head the board of trustees or executive board, or to give credit to the governmental organizations that supervise them.[5] Therefore, although the state holds ultimate power over NGOs, the latter are not passive partners. Those who doubt the legitimacy of Chinese NGOs because of their close relations with the state see only one side of the coin.

In fact, in many countries, the government and the non-profit sector maintain a cooperative rather than a conflicting relationship. In 1981, Salamon coined the term "third party government" to depict the fundamental pattern of relationships between government and the private sector in the delivery of public services in the United States. As Dennis Young explains, "In this model, private, nonprofit organizations serve as partners with government in the provision of public services rather than as substitutes or gap fillers. In this view, government typically provides the finances and influences service policies, while nonprofits deliver the services" (Young 2001: 365). In China, by contrast, the government finds that financial self-sufficiency is a sign of NGO autonomy, one that the government is willing to permit. The government does not provide any financial assistance to the independent NGOs, but the NGOs need to use their relations with the government to obtain the support they should receive in their delivery of public services. The Chinese official interpretation of NGO autonomy and the denial of funding to NGOs certainly strains government–NGO relations.

The starkest contradiction in the matter of NGO autonomy, however, is the conflict between the rapid growth of autonomous NGOs and the state's still tight political control. Especially since the mid-1990s, the number of self-managing and self-sufficient NGOs and grassroots organizations has mushroomed. These organizations represent the most vibrant and meaningful progress toward a civil society in China, and they completely fit the NGO criteria popular internationally. Yet, under China's macro-political reality, these organizations are not fully autonomous. The biggest obstacle to Chinese NGO independence is that all NGOs must follow the CCP's political ideology in order to exist, and all are subject to suppression if they cross the political line. Under government pressure, for example, in 2002 one of the best-known independent environmental organizations in China had to fire one of its founders because this person expressed opinions contrary to the view of the CCP.[6] In this sense, there are no truly autonomous non-governmental organizations in China.

In the past two decades, new Chinese organizations have developed in various forms, evolving simultaneously along lines of civil society and corporatism. This unique feature of NGO development has caused students of modern China to draw strikingly different conclusions on the state–NGO relationship. The stark imbalances in China's surging economic and social development have caused great diversity in the evolution of NGOs and civil society across the country. On the one hand, the private sector – for profit or not-for-profit – in major cities and economically prosperous regions has become increasingly active and influential. In such areas, new civic

12 *Introduction*

associations and social networks, whether formally registered or loosely extant, are facilitating civil society impressively. On the other hand, modern forms of organizations rarely exist in most rural areas. In the countryside, the kinship and clan system, traditional cultural and entertaining groups, and folk religious activities have flourished (Gao 2000; Jiang 2002). The uneven growth of NGOs is also evident in the range of NGO types and activities. Whereas NGOs and civil associations are strongly engaged in economic development, poverty alleviation, and community development, the political, religious, and advocacy groups play an insignificant role in the overall rise of NGOs.

Chapter outlines and methodology

Chapter 1 summarizes the discourse of civil society in China to provide the theoretical and historical context of this study. From the mid-1980s to mid-1990s, intense debates among Chinese and international scholars took place around the following questions: whether a civil society existed in the late Qing Dynasty (1890s to 1911) and early Republic (1911–37); the possibility of building a civil society in China, considering the country's history and current party-state regime; and the applicability of Western political theories in general and civil society in particular to the study of China. In discussing these debates, Chapter 1 first explains how Chinese scholars perceive civil society and NGO ideas as well as why the theoretical discourse has become integral to the evolution of NGOs and civil society in China. Then, drawing on the rich Chinese and English literature on gentry-merchants, intellectual associations, and religious institutions during the late Qing and early Republic, the chapter highlights the significant role of the private sector in China's modernization movement and suggests that civil society in its preliminary form indeed emerged in certain regions of China during that time. An examination of some basic features of these organizations, including their close relations with the state, shows a striking similarity with modern NGOs and thus offers a valuable historical background for an understanding of the latter.

Chapter 2 discusses the government's NGO policy and the motives behind it. To further its own interests, the Chinese government has legalized and promoted NGOs since 1978. The chapter elaborates on the political, economic, and social considerations that prompted the state to allow opportunities for people to organize and associate, and it shows that the government's realization of the role of NGOs became clearer as the reforms deepened. At the same time, however, the fear of political challenges has repeatedly driven the government to tighten its control over NGOs. This chapter outlines the major features of official NGO policy since the 1980s; it also explains the contradictory nature of official policy and the dilemma the state faces in struggling between restraining and releasing NGOs. It argues that even as the party-state remains the most decisive component in the development of NGOs in China, its capacity to control the growth of non-governmental organizations is declining.

Chapter 3 presents an outline of China's NGO landscape and follows a threefold purpose: to clarify the current terminology and typology used to classify Chinese NGOs, to map the landscape of Chinese NGOs, and to discuss the autonomous status of the organizations. The chapter explains the historical origins and political implications of NGO terminology according to contemporary Chinese political language and notes how the lingering use of some old terms indicates the inconsistency in official NGO policy. Based on available official statistics, the chapter goes on to offer a more concrete description of the present content of China's non-profit sector. Case studies demonstrate the complicated and even contradictory situation of NGO relations with the government and address the importance of China's circumstances in understanding them. The argument is made that autonomy is not the only or even the most pertinent criterion for evaluating the non-governmental nature of those organizations. Instead of discussing how GONGOs are not autonomous NGOs, this study examines how NGOs differ from governmental organizations and even from their own predecessors and how they have changed China's state–society relationship.

Chapter 4 focuses on the role of civic associations in the evolution of civil society in China and discusses two aspects of the issue: the significance of associational activities, and the dynamics and leadership characteristic of NGOs. By examining different types of associations, formal or informal, for individual interests or the public good, Chapter 4 shows how civic engagement increases the social capital of China's citizens and nourishes some of the most important elements in civil society. This chapter also discusses the important contributions of Chinese intellectuals to the emergence of grassroots NGOs. With a close look at particular NGO leaders, the chapter argues that the values and ideas of these intellectuals have shaped the vision and unique roles of NGOs. It concludes that their leadership indicates a promising future for China's NGO development.

Chapter 5 deals with trade and professional associations in the economic realm. Immediately after the end of the Cultural Revolution (1966–76), these organizations were among the earliest to be revitalized and organized, and they have since become the most rapidly rising type of NGO. The official promotion of trade associations, professional associations, and chambers of commerce since the late 1980s has proven to be a primary factor in both the transformation of economic institutions and the reform of the administrative apparatus. Meanwhile, private entrepreneurs are also actively organizing trade associations to represent their interests. To test the civil society and corporatism approaches, this chapter examines two distinctive growth patterns of these associations: top-down and bottom-up.

Chapter 6 studies the role of international non-governmental organizations (INGOs) in China's NGO development. The chapter focuses on three aspects of INGOs in China. First, it looks at INGO involvement in China as an arm of globalization and a sign of an emergent global civil society. Second, it approaches the Chinese government's attitude towards foreign NGOs in light of China's economic and social transformation and its policy towards domestic organizations. Third and foremost, it analyzes the impacts and limitations of INGO operations in China given current conditions of local NGO development. The chapter provides an overall review of international organizations and their crucial role in China's NGO development as well as case studies of the operations of some well-established foreign foundations and NGOs.

A major theoretical point of this study is that under different cultural contexts civil society evolves to produce culturally distinct characteristics. In order to address the specific conditions under which Chinese NGOs have developed and to identify their unique features, this book adopts a comparative approach. It evaluates the current state of NGOs and civil society against Western theories and definitions, and it analyzes the debate over civil society among Chinese scholars in light of Western interpretations. The book compares the major features of Chinese NGOs today with those of the scholarly and gentry-merchants' associations in the late Qing Dynasty and early Republican period, as well as with the total state control of all associations in the first thirty years of the CCP regime. It distinguishes and compares official NGO policies in different periods and towards different types of NGOs. Most importantly, this study addresses the distinct and diverging forms of autonomy, operation, and governance among various types of NGOs.

This is an empirical study. This book uses the available official statistics and other data to sketch the landscape of Chinese NGOs. It also depends heavily on empirical data I collected in the field from 1996 to 2004 to portray individual SOs and NGNCEs in depth. The study recognizes its serious limitations due to the lack of consistent and comprehensive data on domestic and foreign organizations and their operations. The complex and rapidly changing nature of government NGO regulations, the sensitivity of NGO matters, and the impossibility of conducting independent surveys of NGOs in China – especially by foreign scholars (MOCA 2000a: 1) – in ways that have become standard in the United States and other Western countries make the study of Chinese non-governmental behavior a daunting task.

The inconsistency and deficiency of published official statistics, as well as the lack of transparency of most NGOs, have made any comprehensive quantitative analysis of Chinese NGOs impossible. Government agencies provide only general statistics that cannot be independently verified. The operations of government bodies are not transparent, nor are the management of most SOs and NGNCEs. The recent literature reflects efforts to understand the growing role of NGOs in the Chinese public sphere, but the absence of agreement on definitions and the uncertainty about facts leave the overall picture of the Chinese non-governmental sector unclear. Thus, I depend on isolated bits of information gleaned from a wide variety of sources, including official documents and interviews with officials, NGO activists, and NGO scholars as well as daily newspapers. Despite the handicaps, this book uses many case studies as prisms to display the spectrum of complicated and highly diverse non-profit organizations and their relations with the state and the for-profit sector.

On a hot summer day in 2001, I interviewed a well-known Chinese environmental NGO leader. Exhausted from too much work and frustrated by having obtained neither government support nor appreciation, she asked me a question I will never forget: "What can you do for us?" I have always wished that I could do something for Chinese NGOs, and this book is about them and for them, the Chinese NGO pioneers, with the sincere hope that the portraits sketched here will help others outside of China better understand how much these people have accomplished and how determined they are to travel the great distance ahead.

1 In search of civil society in China
Theoretical and historical discourses

From the mid-1980s to the late 1990s, a series of debates over civil society in China took place among Chinese scholars and China scholars in the West. The earliest attempts to understand Chinese institutions and practices in terms of Western notions such as "civil society" or the "public sphere" appeared in the mid-1980s in histories of the late Qing Dynasty (1890s to 1911) and early Republic (1911–37) (Rowe 1984, 1989; Rankin 1986).[1] Simultaneously, China scholars in the West were increasingly interested in whether "civil society" was emerging in mainland China in the late 1980s as evident in the student democratic movement at the time (Gold 1990a; Sullivan 1990; Whyte 1992; Solinger 1992; Brook 1992; White 1993; Nevitt 1996; White *et al.* 1996; He, B. 1997; Frolic 1997; O'Brien 1998). The dramatic changes in Eastern Europe, the 1989 student democratic movement, and the Western conceptions of civil society sparked a heated debate among Chinese intellectuals. In the early 1990s, discussions on the applicability of Western ideas of civil society to China's ongoing reforms and to understanding China's state–society relationship attracted an impressive number of scholars.[2]

These discourses provide the theoretical and historical context for my study of NGOs in China today. The scholarly debates fueled intellectual inquiry in mainland China by introducing a host of Western ideas and concepts on civil society, corporatism, the third sector, and NGOs. Moreover, these discussions brought new perspectives to understanding events in post-reform China and opened new research fields in Chinese academia. As later chapters will elaborate, many Chinese intellectuals are actively involved in China's NGO activities, and ideas about civil society have thus spread among NGO practitioners. Since the mid-1990s, the new phrases and terms such as civil society, NGO, public sphere, social capital, empowerment, and citizen participation have become catchwords in China's new political lexicon, and the influence of theoretical discussions has gone far beyond the academic circle.

This scholarship is also important because, to a great extent, the search by Chinese intellectuals for civil society in the 1990s represents their answer to "the challenge of the reform reality" and their attempt "to originate a theory of a unique pattern for China's modernization" (Jing 1994: 29–30; Yang

1995: 37). As Jing Yuejin, a leading scholar in the debate, clearly states, "if the government's 'small government and big society' policy represents a top-down approach of dealing with the new state–society relationship, then the study of civil society can be seen as a bottom-up effort" (Jing: 30). In China, discussions about civil society and NGOs have never been purely academic, and one definite, pragmatic purpose of Chinese intellectuals especially is to establish a theoretical system to guide China's future political reforms. As Jude Howell and Jenny Pearce point out, the contestation of different normative views of civil society underlines the politics of civil society: "Different social actors use the language of civil society, appropriate and adjust its meanings and empirical referents as part of a broader process of negotiating, and challenge power relations" (Howell and Pearce 2001: 231).

To those intellectuals, "establishing civil society is not only a means to achieve political modernization; establishing civil society itself is also their goal" (Deng 1994: 25). The wide array of different opinions among Chinese scholars overall reveals the complex nature of the subject and the continuing impact of Chinese tradition on the state–society relationship and the role of the private sector. Arguments on how to translate Western terms into Chinese and how to apply them under China's cultural and political contexts should be seen not merely as scholarship but rather as how Chinese intellectuals envision China's future state–society relations and power arrangements.

Finally, the exploration by American historians into whether a civil society existed in the late Qing and early Republic is juxtaposed with studies by Chinese scholars on chambers of commerce and scholars' associations during the same period. To a certain degree, the former inspired the latter with a new approach and theory, while the latter's research relied on rich first-hand material to conclude that a preliminary civil society was evolving in some coastal cities and lower Yangzi valleys. The Chinese research also provided full accounts of the major features of early modern organizations as well as their close yet conflicting relations with the government.

Previous studies and debates offer a valuable reference for our understanding of the emergence of civic associations in the post-reform era and their relations with the state. A comparison in this study of organizations past and present shows a continuity of certain features as well as substantial changes. In considering prior studies, this chapter highlights how Chinese NGO scholars have approached the major issues concerning civil society; it also discusses certain key aspects of civic associations in the early twentieth century as a historical background of NGOs today.

Chinese intellectuals' debates over civil society in the 1990s

In the wake of the fall of the Berlin Wall and the Tiananmen student movement, the search for civil society in China reflects the desire for a democratic China. This search has brought knowledge and insight to our understanding of China's state–society relationship past and present. Most

18 *In search of civil society in China*

importantly, by analyzing views of Chinese intellectuals on the subject, this study argues that the discourse of civil society itself has become an indispensable and even crucial step in the emergence of a civil society in China. Thus, scholars have played an important role in China's political and social reforms. Their debates represent a theoretical breakthrough against the Chinese Communist Party's (CCP) ideological taboos, and, with the exchange of opinions among international and Chinese scholars as well as the interaction between Chinese intellectuals and NGO practitioners, new civic associations are starting to have as never before a clear mission of promoting civil society and the rule of law in China.

Translating the term "civil society" into the Chinese political lexicon

To discuss civil society in the Chinese language, Chinese scholars first needed a Chinese phrase for this concept. Chinese has no precisely equivalent term for *civil society*. The English term has been rendered into several distinctive Chinese translations, and it is an open question as to which best conveys the meaning of civil society. The debate reflects Chinese scholars' different understandings of this concept and their various purposes in introducing it to China. Discussions among Chinese scholars on the appropriate translation illustrate the complications of "transplanting" a Western political idea into a strikingly different cultural and political system. The problem here derives not only from the absence of traditional thoughts on civility, citizenship, or civil society in Chinese history; the rich connotations and controversial nature of the concept of civil society itself also make translation difficult. The debate also reveals how political situations on the mainland and on Taiwan differ with regard to the evolution of civil society.

American anthropologist Robert Weller once said that Confucianism in China left little ideological room for a distinction between state and society, "except in the way that fathers can be distinguished from sons." According to Weller, as late as the nineteenth century "civil society" could not plausibly be translated into Chinese. Even today, the term is translated through a variety of, as Weller puts it, "awkward neologisms."[3] Robert Hefner uses Weller's observation to try to illustrate the complexity and difficulty of cultural globalization and the cross-cultural prospects for civil society ideals (Hefner 1998: 22). However, Weller's conclusion is rather stereotypical. It does not demonstrate a deep understanding of the complex cultural background behind the Chinese translations, nor does it recognize the relevance of these Chinese terms to attempts to preserve the original meaning of civil society while serving the purpose of China's political reforms.

The term *civil society* has been translated into Chinese as follows: "*gongmin shehui*" (*gongmin*: citizen, *shehui*: society), "*shimin shehui*" (*shimin*: townspeople, or bourgeoisie), "*minjian shehui*" (*minjian*: literally people and their space, so it can be translated as popular society). In Chinese translations of Marx's works, this term is "*zichanjieji shehui*" (bourgeois society), and a few scholars also use *"wenming shehui"* (civilized society) for this term (Forges 1997: 68–95). The first three translations are the most popular and are alternately used by scholars and NGO activists in both mainland China and Taiwan. The differences in translation indicate the rich connotations of the word "civil" and the complex origin of the term civil society.

It is interesting to see how Chinese scholars choose certain words to emphasize or imply a specific connotation of "civil society." These Chinese terms have different cultural origins and convey obvious or subtle distinctive meanings and purposes of adoption. *"Gongmin"* is a modern political term adopted from European political thought in the early twentieth century by Chinese reformers. The character *"gong"* means public, and *"min"* is people; together this word stands for citizenry or citizenship. Ironically, the Chinese conceptual interpretations have been rather different from Western common understandings of this political term.[4] Created in the early twentieth-century cultural movement, *"gongmin"* represents a new image of Chinese people who take responsibility for the public good and behave accordingly, in comparison to the Western notion of citizen as a signifier of individual rights for property, political power, and social or economic welfare (Perry 1994: 704–13). In the People's Republic of China (PRC), the "citizen" status indicates the people's right to vote; nevertheless, the CCP's real concern is that citizens follow "good behavior" according to party standards.

The first time Chinese scholars adopted the term *"gongmin shehui"* (civil society) was to challenge the CCP's interpretation of citizen. As early as 1988, Liu Zhiguang and Wang Suli argued in their study of China's social reforms that although the PRC Constitution adopted the words "citizenry" and "citizens' rights," Chinese people rarely understood the real meaning of the term and often confused it with the word *"qunzhong"* (masses) (Liu and Wang 1988: 9–12). The word "masses" carries a great deal of political freight in the CCP vocabulary. Mao Zedong and the CCP used the term to refer to those core groups the party purported to represent, in particular the workers and peasants. Mass movement politics is also especially associated with Maoism and the rise of communist political power. This usage continued after the establishment of the PRC. Indeed, mobilizing "the masses" as a powerful force in all kinds of political movements was a hallmark of Mao's rule. Liu and Wang carefully distinguish "mass society" from the idea of "civil society." For them, "the concept of mass cannot replace the legal status of 'citizenship' because citizenry is related to democratic polity . . . The transition from 'mass' to 'citizen' indicates the transition from rule of men to rule of law, and this is a process of moving towards a lawful and egalitarian democratic polity" (Liu and Wang: 10–2).

Later, the discussion of Western origins of civil society further rationalized the adoption of *"gongmin shehui"* for its political connotation. Fang Zhaohui, a philosophy scholar, carefully illustrates two rather different Western linguistic origins of this concept, and his work sheds light on the considerations behind the Chinese translation of "civil society." Linguistically and culturally, as

Fang elucidates, the word "civil society" or "société civile" (French) derives from the Latin "civilis societas." By the eighteenth century in England and France, according to Fang, civil society as an important political idea stood for:

1   a civilized, progressive, and moral society;
2   a lawful society where citizens' private rights were protected; and
3   a political society in which citizens participated in public affairs (Fang 1994: 85).

This is the political origin of civil society. Many Chinese intellectuals first learned the term "civil society" from the East European political movements in the late 1980s, and that understanding of "civil society" was as a politicized society arrayed against the state. In that context, *"gongmin shehui"* became an appropriate translation for this term and for Chinese intellectuals' search for a democratic China (Wang, S. 1991: 102–3).

"Shimin," on the other hand, is an ancient and authentic Chinese word for townspeople or urban residents, and it originally had no particular political implications. Yet, historical research demonstrates the emergence of a political urban consciousness in the later nineteenth century (Rowe 1984 and 1989). Since the early twentieth century, urban residents have become increasingly important in China's political movements, from the May 4 movement in 1919 to the student democratic movement in 1989. However, unlike the term *"gongmin," "shimen"* does not carry the notion of political rights. Wang Shaoguang, a political scientist, believes that people are *"shimin"* in the private sphere and become *"gongmin"* when they enter the public sphere (Wang, S. 1991: 105).

Again, the adoption of *"shimin shehui"* as the equivalence of civil society indicates an attempt to challenge the orthodox interpretation of Marxism and advocate for people's rights and the value of civil society. Shen Yue was the first Chinese scholar to address the importance of using "townspeople's society" or civil society to translate the term "bürgerliche Gesellschaft" in the works of Marx and Engels. Shen points out the mistranslation of the term townspeople's right as bourgeois right and of townspeople's society as bourgeois society (Shen 1990: 44–51). According to Shen, Marx's works contain important distinctions between townspeople's right and bourgeois right and between townspeople's society and bourgeois society. The townspeople's right refers to the right of equal exchange of commodities; "however, since the term has been mistranslated into 'bourgeois right' in Chinese it has been equated with the improper privileges of the bourgeois. Consequently, it has been denied to Chinese townspeople" (Shen 1986).[5] Shen highlights Marx's major theory on the dual economic nature of modern Western societies: a townspeople's society of free and equal citizens in a realm of commodity circulation and a bourgeois society composed of two major classes, bourgeois and proletarian, in realm of production. According to Marx and Engels, townspeople's society or civil society therefore becomes the economic foundation of human societies. Shen also believes that the misinterpretation of "bürgerliche Gesellschaft" is a major reason why many Chinese scholars have overlooked Marx's idea of civil society (Shen 1990: 44). By reinterpreting Marxism, Shen thus makes new theoretical or political claims.

"*Minjian shehui*" is also an ancient Chinese term. This phrase indicates a popular society separated from the space of official control. As Liang Zhiping, a scholar of law, explains, this popular society is the world of ordinary people: "It is in this world that people live their familiar life style and pursue their respective interests; also, it is associated with this or that kind of social organization such as clans, trade associations, village organizations, religious groups and secret societies" (Liang 2001: 67–8). In fact, Liang argues that "popular society may be the only concept we can find in the traditional vocabulary that is very close to the concept of civil society" (67). Because the term "*minjian shehui*" has a clear traditional Chinese connotation, Liang and other scholars argue that it should be the standard translation of civil society.

Yet, in Chinese culture, the concept "*min*" (people) contrasts with "*guan*" (officials or government). Some Chinese scholars argue that popular society clearly connotes opposition to governments and officials. Gan Yang, a political scientist, thus disagrees with adopting popular society as a Chinese version of civil society. In Gan's view, civil society should not set society against the state, but rather indicate a constructive interactive relationship, and yet the Chinese term popular society implies a deep-rooted tradition of a dichotomous structure of "society against officials" or "popular society opposes or even confronts the officials." He is convinced that adoption of this term would only undermine the real meaning of civil society, namely, one which assumes mutually dependent and constructive relations between the state and society (Gan 1998: 24–35).

Taiwan's advocates for political reform and civil society intentionally chose this term in their civil society movement in the late 1980s because they understood "popular society" as implying an anti-government orientation. Deng Zhenglai, a leading scholar in this debate, believes that what the Taiwan theorists wanted most was "anti *Guomindong* (the Nationalist Party)" or "society confronting the state." If civil society had been translated as "townspeople society," he argues, it would not have had the same political resonance as "popular society" (Deng 1997: 72). This translation suggests, according to Deng, that Taiwanese civil society theory simplified the concept into a dichotomous model of society vs the state. These advocates purposely applied this Western liberal idea in a transformative manner for their political agenda, which is, as Deng puts it, to stand in opposition to the state in order to establish a bottom-up people's democratic confrontation in Taiwan (48–85).

Indeed, in Chinese history leaders of peasant rebellions usually were portrayed as *minjian* heroes; and *minjian* organizations, especially *minjian* religious groups and secret societies, have always been considered a dangerous threat to the state.[6] Quite a few well-known proverbs and fables in Chinese describe the relations between people and officials, such as "the people rebel when suppressed by officials" and "people are water and officials are the boat; water can carry the boat as well as overturn it." These sayings reflect a tradition of peasant rebellions. However, the questions here are: can this anti-official tradition represent the main character of state–society relations in traditional China? Was this popular society a clearly defined and relatively autonomous social sphere that protected society from state control? Many studies of Chinese culture and tradition since the start of the twentieth century have revealed a much more complicated and even contradictory relationship between the state and society and between the people and officials in traditional China, and these relations have changed over time (Liang 2000: 18–67).[7] The reappearance of the term popular society, as Liang argues, does not suggest the return of China today to the traditional social structure; rather, it indicates that the connotation of the term popular society has changed but is still vital (Liang 2001: 82).

In short, the contest over terminology is not just about which translation is better. More importantly, it reveals different understandings of state–society relations in China. The Chinese translations of *civil society* reflect the preferences of translators and users in choosing certain interpretations of this idea for their own political or social opinions and agendas. In this sense, Chinese scholars are doing what their international colleagues have been doing for decades: namely, to define or redefine this concept in light of their own cultural and political circumstances. Most scholars in Taiwan use *minjian shehui* with the intention of preserving China's tradition and making a strong political statement. In mainland China, on the other hand, their counterparts choose a more neutral term, *gongmin shehui* or *shimin shehui*, because they are seeking "the constructive and interactive relationship between state and society."

Introducing civil society to China and reinterpreting Marxism

Deng Zhenglai sees the discourse of Chinese intellectuals on civil society as a reflection of favored political theories in the 1980s such as "the new authoritarianism" and "democracy-led reform" (*minzhu xiandao lun*) that advocated top-down, elite-led political reforms (Deng 1997: 94–5). Around that time, some prominent Chinese intellectuals started to promote a political theory called "the new authoritarianism." In 1986, Wang Huning – then a professor of international politics at Shanghai Fudan University and since 1995 head of the Political Section of the CCP's Central Committee's Policy Research Office under Jiang Zemin – discussed the need for "a necessary concentration" of central authority in the course of reform (Fewsmith 2001: 76).

Xiao Gongqin, another well-known advocate of the new authoritarianism, described neo-authoritarianism as "emphasizing increment, stability, and order," and "advocating resorting to enlightened authoritarianism to lead modernization." In Xiao's opinion, political stability is a precondition for economic development because the multiplication of interests and contractual relationships between interest groups forms the social foundation of democratic politics (Xiao 2002: 84). The new authoritarianism, as these intellectuals intended, did affect China's reform policy in the 1980s even as it encountered serious criticism from liberals who believed that advocating authoritarianism was dangerous when China had not yet eliminated the influence of autocracy (Xiao: 85).

The repression of the 1989 Tiananmen demonstrations interrupted the debate and forced all Chinese intellectuals to rethink their perspectives on the reforms. Deng Xiaoping's South Tour speeches in early 1992 reaffirmed the economic reform policy; consequently, the political and ideological control that had been tightened since the 1989 student movement began to relax, and ideas of political reform resurfaced. The exploration of Western ideas of civil society in the 1990s was in large measure a continuation of the debate of the late 1980s; yet, the impact of intervening events redirected the debate to civil society. In particular, the rifts exposed between social forces and state power in the wake of the 1989 events presented new problems for those debating civil society's place in China. As Deng Zhenglai later recalled, the key meaning of the discussion over civil society in the early 1990s was the effort by Chinese intellectuals to shake off "the state-centered" top-down reform approach and seek the social structural transformations that would lead to the incremental development of a democratic polity (Deng 1994: 94–5).

The theoretical exploitation of Western ideas of civil society has proven a great challenge to Chinese intellectuals. Prior to the reforms and open policy in 1978, political science, sociology, and anthropology had been dismissed by the CCP as "pseudosciences"; indeed, these disciplines had vanished from Chinese universities for three decades. Even now, political science occupies a precarious position within the academy. At the start of the discourse on civil society, Chinese academia and political scientists knew little about this concept and related theories. Understandably, the first step was to introduce classical and modern Western literature on the subject. The great bulk of recent research by scholars outside of China was not easily accessible to Chinese scholars, however, and very few of the works had Chinese translations at the time.[8]

The earliest effort to introduce Western ideas on civil society to Chinese academia started in the early 1990s, and within a few years some Hong Kong and mainland journals systematically presented the works and thoughts of many classical Western thinkers on the subject, including Locke, Hobbes, Rousseau, Montesquieu, Kant, Adam Ferguson, Hegel, Marx, Paine, Tocqueville, and Talcott Parsons, among others. Some important post-Marxist and contemporary theorists such as Antonio Gramsci, Jürgen Habermas, Jean L. Cohen, and Andrew Arato also attracted much attention.

The introduction of works of these thinkers provided the knowledge necessary for Chinese scholars to carry on further discussion.

The greater challenge to Chinese intellectuals, however, was to break the existing theoretical and ideological constraints and find a battleground for their fight. Scholars in mainland China first discovered civil society in Marx's works and reinterpreted Marxism. This was indeed a smart move, because at that time Marxism was the most familiar of all Western theories and the works of Marx and Engels had been translated into Chinese and were widely available. Moreover, scholars needed to find support in the writings of Marx to secure political (and in a sense intellectual) legitimacy for their arguments on civil society. Reinterpreting Marxism, including correcting some existing translations, proved to be a necessary theoretical and political battle for civil society to obtain a place in China's political thought. These arguments are particularly meaningful to Chinese intellectuals, because exploration of civil society is not simply an academic issue; it carries political weight. Not only have Chinese scholars been able to discuss Marxism in a more open and objective manner; their points of view aim directly at the reconstruction of state–society relationships in order to redirect China's future toward a more open civil society.

The debates on civil society began in Hong Kong. Not until 1993 and 1994, when a group of articles on civil society appeared in a prestigious mainland China journal, *Chinese Social Science*, did the political atmosphere there allow scholars to discuss these topics openly. These studies focus on Marx's civil society theory and reinterpret Marxism from new perspectives distinct from those of the old generation of scholars.[9] Although Marxism formed the foundation of the CCP's ideology, prior to the 1980s, scholars in mainland China had never discussed this term, let alone its importance in Marx's theory, even though "bürgerliche Gesellschaft" appears frequently in Marx's works. Even after the 1980s, some still dismissed this subject. They argued, for example, that "civil society" is an inaccurate concept that Marx borrowed from Hegel, and, in addition, in his mature works Marx replaced "bürgerliche Gesellschaft" with other more accurate and rational concepts such as "economic structure," "economic basis," and "all relations of production." Others believed that to Marx civil society equaled bourgeois society (Yu, K. 1993: 65).

Yu Keping, a scholar of Marxism, was the first to counter certain assumptions that deny the importance of Marx's civil society theory. He argues that "Marx started his historical materialist theory from the study of civil society and its relationship with the political society," and that "bürgerliche Gesellschaft" is the most important and frequently used term in his works (Yu: 67–8). In his study of the origins of civil society in the West, Fang Zhaohui concludes that although Kant was the first German philosopher to employ "bürgerliche Gesellschaft" as an important concept, it was Hegel and Marx who separated the concept of "state" from "bürgerliche Gesellschaft" and gave civil society an entirely new meaning:

an economic society (Fang 1994: 86).[10] Some Chinese scholars concluded that "the modern concept of civil society started from Hegel but was completed by Marx" (He 1994b: 70), and that "Hegel and Marx gave the civil society theory an unprecedented depth" (Chen 1998: 89).

These scholars are familiar with Marx's well-known definition of civil society:

> The form of relations determined by the existing productive forces at all previous historical stages, and in its turn determining these, is *civil society* . . . Civil Society embraces all the material relations of individuals within a definite stage of the development of productive forces.
> (Marx 1973: 38, 76)

Marxist political economy is one of the few bodies of knowledge that most Chinese political scientists know well, and in the new perception of this theory they believe that Marx's major contribution was to describe a civil society separate from the political system (Yu, K. 1993; He 1994b).

Unmistakably, many Chinese scholars accept the notion of civil society as the antithesis of state versus society, in which society is not only independent from the state but also more decisive and essential than the state. Yu repeatedly cites Engels' famous passage: "the state, the political order, is the subordinate, and civil society, the realm of economic relations, the decisive element." And also, "it is not the State which conditions and regulates civil society, but it is civil society which conditions and regulates the State" (Engels 1973a: 178, 1973b: 369). Yu stresses the importance of separating civil society from political society as the precondition for representative democracy (Yu: 62–3).

Another attraction of Marx's civil society is that he took economic activities and production relations as the core of civil society. Yu argues that Marx did not – as Norberto Bobbio, John Keane and some other Western scholars have assumed – exclude social organizations, social system, individual interests, or family life from civil society (Yu: 67–8).[11] Some Chinese scholars think that Marx and Engels included everything not in the state into civil society. "Our concept of civil society," He Zengke, a political scientist, announces, "starts with the separation of state and society, and we insist on the dichotomous model of political society and civil society, based on which Hegel and Marx built their civil society definition" (He 1994a: 46). According to the Chinese publications I surveyed, Chinese scholars interpret Marx's idea of civil society as a dichotomous model, state versus civil society. Many Chinese scholars consider this model the Western concept of civil society.

Civil society in light of China's history and culture

In their efforts to build a political reform model formulated primarily by Western ideals or theories, Chinese intellectuals inevitably need to answer a serious question: is such a model possible in a country where history and tradition remain influential? Indeed, whereas some Western historians and political scientists have adopted "civil society" or "public sphere" in studying China's state–society relationship during the late Qing/early Republican period, others have cast doubt on the usefulness of the state–society dichotomy in interpreting China's power structures in the past and present. For example, Philip Huang, an American China scholar, concludes that "[t]he binary opposition between state and society is an ideal abstracted from early modern and modern Western experience that is inappropriate for China." And "contrary to the vision of the public sphere/civil society models," Huang argues, "actual sociopolitical change in China has really never come from any lasting assertion of societal autonomy against the state, but rather from the workings out of state–society relations in the third realm" (Huang 1993: 216–38).

The debate among China scholars in the West has influenced Chinese intellectuals, many of whom have argued against adopting Western concepts unchanged to China's situation. Some have cited Huang's opinion questioning the applicability of civil society to the study of China as well as to reform. As the following shows, these contestations reflect the Chinese intellectuals' view of civil society as an alien theory, their understanding of Chinese culture and state–society relations, and, most of all, their vision of China's future polity.

In addressing the uniqueness of Chinese culture, much attention has focused on China's classical thought and its traditional pattern of state–society relations (Yuzo 1994; Yang 1995; Gan 1998; Liang 2001: 68). Some Chinese and Japanese studies have pointed out that in classical Chinese philosophy or culture, the understanding of antitheses such as state – society, public (*gong*) – private (*si*), and people (*min*) – officials (*guan*) diverges sharply from Western political thought based on natural rights and the rule of law. In general, the concept of people (*min*) in Chinese culture has a dual connotation. As the origin of public, people are seen as the foundation of the state and the legitimacy of the regime; yet, in real life, people are often subjected to the will of authority. Zhang Jing, a political scientist, asserts that

> The manifestation of order in Chinese culture starts from "integration," favoring a unity that you contain me and I contain you. This is also the essential condition of the establishment of order. The separation of power is not the prerequisite of order, and it may even be seen as against order.
>
> (Zhang 1998: 3)

To a great extent, such an understanding of the state–society relationship has strongly influenced the way Chinese people see and deal with the government, even today.

During the debates, a group of scholars has shown serious reservations about the applicability of civil society to China's future political reforms. Xiao Gongqin advocates new authoritarianism and expresses doubts about a civil society in China today. He insists that in China's history there was no such concept as society independent from the state. Xiao emphasizes that China's traditional patriarchal clan system and its underdeveloped market economy created a social sphere with a strong patriarchal nature. Since the nineteenth century, he argues, the deepening crises of state authority disabled the state's capacity to nourish a normal civil society; thus, as the state political power grew weak with corruption, civil society, parallel with secret society, expanded abnormally. This twisted situation, according to Xiao, forced modern Chinese intellectuals to split into either emphasizing strengthening state power and its control and intervention over society or advocating expanding societal autonomy to achieve modernity. Therefore, he concludes, the Chinese historical experience of civil society has created major obstacles to its contemporary growth (Xiao 1993: 183–70).

Meanwhile, quite a few scholars emphasize so-called "oriental totalitarianism" and its most distinctive feature: state monopoly of power. "In oriental countries, there had been a constant historical development of political state annexing civil society" (Ma 2001: 21–2). One study declares, "The most outstanding feature of China's feudal society was the highly developed and long lasting centralized autocracy. Under this polity, the state, via national and local institutions, conveyed its comprehensive and strict control." It concludes that a strong anti-civil society tradition in China's history has had, and will continue to have, a tremendous influence on China's current politics and society. Consequently, this scholar states, it is very difficult, if not impossible, to build a civil society in China (Xia 1993: 176–82).

In fact, the over-simplifying and generalizing of China's history and culture are evident in many arguments that address impediments to building civil society in China today. For example, some Chinese scholars imagine that China was a purely agricultural economy, even though China had a highly developed market economy, beginning in the Song and becoming fully developed by the Qing period. Shi Yuankang, a scholar of philosophy, examines how in Confucianism the emphasis on agriculture and restraint of commerce had become decisive in preventing China from becoming an industrial and commercial society. He is convinced that China still is an agricultural country and therefore has a long way to go before it becomes a modern state with civil society (Shi 1991: 105–20). Another scholar believes that Confucian culture is the rich resource that must provide the positive dynamics for building civil society in China: "to build a Western style civil society [in China] is impossible and inappropriate, and Chinese civil society will be a civil society with Confucian style" (Jiang 1993: 170).

It is important to recognize the impact of history and culture on China's modernization movement as these influences differentiate China's political structure and evolution towards democracy from that of Western countries.

However, it is worth noting that some Chinese scholars have overlooked certain crucial issues that have shaped China's unique state–society relations. Key among these, modern studies fail to discuss the fact that both Western and Chinese scholars had conducted research on civic associations and civil society evolution during the late Qing and early Republic. These developments counter the stereotype that civil society cannot develop in countries with strong Confucian roots. Nor do studies touch upon contemporary influences such as Mao Zedong's political theory on proletarian dictatorship and the CCP's political ideology. While this is understandable given China's current political climate, these bodies of thought have affected and will continue to affect the modern Chinese polity and civil society's future in China.

Furthermore, although Confucianism still influences the lifestyles and ways of thinking of Chinese people today, some studies tend to overemphasize its influence on China's politics and culture. Unlike many Asian countries where officials still resort to Confucian values to integrate society, since the May 4 movement in 1919, China's modernization movement and communist revolution have explicitly rejected many Confucian values. Even though many old traditions and values have revived in post-reform China, Chinese culture has been profoundly changed by the embrace of Western ideas and lifestyles, especially in cities and among young people. Cultural globalization and the technological revolution has rapidly spread information about what is happening outside of China, and this is the context under which civil society is evolving.

A civil society model for China

To Chinese intellectuals, from the very beginning the discourse of civil society has signified a strong sense of mission or purpose. Yu Keping articulates the political meaning of these discussions clearly: "The study of civil society is not just a theoretical subject, it is more a practical matter" (Yu 1993: 74). It is the ultimate concern of Chinese intellectuals to establish a workable theory for China's political reforms. The difficulty is in applying Western concepts or theories to their understanding of China's history and current events, and, most of all, to their efforts to reform China's political system. This mixture of theoretical discourse and pragmatic consideration has brought obvious problems and controversy to their efforts. The scholars have their own opinions on many current political and social issues, and since their search for civil society is so closely tied up with the reform agendas, political considerations may color their approach to Western theories and especially to the application of these ideas to practical issues. Thus, the search for a theoretical notion of a Chinese civil society is not merely an academic exercise; it is an integral part of the evolution of civil society in China.

During the debates, intellectuals discussed intensely how to establish a civil society model for China. The most significant contribution from those efforts is the notion of a "constructive interaction" (*liangxing hudong*) between the state and civil society, published in 1992 in a widely cited article by Deng Zhenglai and Jing Yuejin. Deng and Jing define Chinese civil society in this way:

> It is a private sphere where members of society engage in economic and social activities following the rule of contract and voluntary principle as well as based on autonomous governance, and it is also a non-governmental public sphere for participating in policy discussions and decision-making.
>
> (Deng and Jing 1992: 6)

Accordingly, under a constructive interaction relationship, the state recognizes the autonomy of civil society and provides legal protection and space for it; meanwhile, it also interferes with and regulates civil society when necessary. Conversely, civil society balances the state and nourishes plural interests that will eventually become the foundation for China's democracy. More importantly, this proposition addresses the limitation of the state's intervention in social matters and the rationale of implementing state policy through legal and economic means rather than political power (Deng and Jing: 12–3). Compared to the "new-authoritarianism" theory popular before 1989, "constructive interaction" signals a substantial shift from focusing on a state-led or an elite-led political reform to addressing society's crucial role in the reforms.

The "constructive interaction" idea has become one of the most influential articulations on the subject of civil society in Chinese academia, and many participants in the discussion agree with the notion. To these intellectuals, it is particularly important to address the non-confrontational model of civil society for China. He Zengke asserts that obtaining societal space by confronting the state not only will not benefit a constructive interaction between the state and society, but will also lead to anarchism and totalitarianism. Moreover, he argues that challenging the state and prompting it to act will lead to social turmoil and interrupt the democratization process. He emphasizes that the "constructive interaction" notion is a more appropriate model for developing countries (He 1994a: 42–4).

Yet, most Chinese scholars insist that the "constructive interaction" relationship between the state and civil society is a uniquely Chinese feature, and they think that Western ideas of civil society posit a dichotomous model of state and society based on antagonism, emphasizing either a state-dominated or a society-dominated model (Deng 1997: 23–47; Ma 2001: 11). Some also believe that capitalism prevents Western countries from establishing a constructively interactive relationship between the state and civil society (Ma 2001: 19–41). In actuality, since the 1980s, especially in developed countries, interdependence and cooperation between the government and nongovernmental sectors has become a new trend of NGO development. This trend is reflected in a Western scholar's argument that "there is no zero-sum opposition between civil society and the state" (Hefner 1998: 21). Unaware of most recent theoretical revisions in Western concepts of civil society, Chinese scholars have made assumptions that over-simplify a complex theory.

Another change vital to the development of Chinese civil society, as some Chinese scholars have stressed, is reforming China's legal system and establishing a polity based on the rule of law. Some Chinese intellectuals are convinced that civil society can be an essential factor in this cause. The concept of the "rule of law" and a Western-style legal system were imported to China in the late Qing Dynasty as a part of the court's efforts to reinvent its power. The problem, as Liang Zhiping explains, has been the lack of people's involvement.

> In all the reforms of law and legal system since the early twentieth century, the state has always been solely a promoter: it designs the entire plan, makes the law, establishes the institution, implements the law, leads and puts forward the plan. Now one should point out that the state itself is also the object of reform.
>
> (Liang 2000: 42)

Liang argues that "the establishment of the rule of law definitely requires people's participation and a multi-interests society outside of the state" (52).

Ma Changshan, a law professor, considers the interaction of state and civil society as the precondition for the rule of law in China. He believes that "it is the interactive development of civil society and the political state that has built the social foundation for the rule of law." In Ma's opinion, an autonomous civil society is an underpinning for a rational arrangement of power, rights, and responsibility, for plural societal rights, for authority of public power and good law, and for checks and balances. Nevertheless, he also emphasizes that the essential aspect for the rule of law in China "is to build a constructive interaction relationship between the state and civil society" (Ma 2001: 23, 40–1). Recalling the short life of democratic movements and political reforms in modern Chinese history, one realizes how significant and sometimes contestable these arguments are.

To most Chinese scholars, the civil society model for China should be a dichotomy of the state and civil society, with the latter including the economy and economic associations. This contestation derives from the influence of classical Western ideas of civil society represented by Hegel and Marx and the understanding of current Chinese economic transformation. Charles Taylor once described the conceptual history of civil society as consisting mainly of two streams, economic and political: society as an "economy," "where the self-regulating, entrepreneurial economy is given a central place," or as a political society, where public opinion is what matters most (Taylor 1991: 117–36). The classical writings on this concept have clearly inclined toward one or the other stream, and their opinions have influenced scholars in the current debate significantly. Yet, the classical dichotomous model that Taylor described has yielded to a modern three-part model, based on the experiences and crises in Western democratic countries following World War I.

A series of efforts has been made to adjust classical interpretations of civil society to twentieth-century political culture. Jean L. Cohen and Andrew Arato, two American political scientists, argue that

> Only a concept of civil society that is properly differentiated from the economy (and therefore from "bourgeois society") could become the center of a critical political and social theory in societies where the market economy has already developed, or is in the process of developing, its own autonomous logic. Otherwise, after successful transitions from dictatorship to democracy, the undifferentiated version of the concept embedded in the slogan "society vs the state" would lose its critical potential.
>
> (Cohen and Arato 1994: viii–ix)

In separating the economy from civil society, they suggest "a reconstruction involving a three-part model that distinguishes civil society from both state and economy" (Cohen and Arato: ix). Such a civil society, according to Cohen and Arato, is a sphere of social interaction between economy and state, composed of the intimate sphere (especially the family) and associations (especially voluntary associations), social movements, and forms of public communication (ix). As a fundamental argument in their conception, they criticize the dichotomous model of state and society still used by some Marxists and particularly by neoliberals, neoconservatives, and present-day heirs of utopian socialism as representing a quintessentially nineteenth-century figure of thought. They are convinced that the dichotomous model can no longer describe either the forces behind its transformation or the new structure of society in today's world (423–4).

The three-part model goes back to Gramsci's idea of civil society as the non-state and non-economic area of social interaction (Anheier *et al.* 2001: 13–4). Cohen's and Arato's arguments are especially inspired by Habermas.[12] Both Habermas and Cohen/Arato are seeking solutions for political, social, and cultural crises that arose in Western countries since the two world wars. For example, Habermas, in his later works in particular, focuses on the profound changes in civil society in the post-WWI world, and the criticism of the welfare state leads him to his theory of a crisis of legitimation. According to Daniel Bell, Habermas "locates the legitimation problem primarily in the conflict between a capitalism founded on private, individual motives, and one which inexorably becomes a state capitalist society where the individual cannot be motivated or rewarded in individual terms" (Bell 1976: 249).

Thus, Habermas's major concern is to show that the bureaucratization of life under late capitalist conditions is a highly "irrational" process. What

Habermas worries about is that "formal democracy could just as easily be replaced by a variant – a conservative, authoritarian welfare state that reduces the political participation of the citizens to a harmless level; or a Fascist authoritarian state that keeps the population toeing the mark on a relatively high level of permanent mobilization" (Habermas 1973: 643–67). Obviously the crises that are discussed by Habermas and Cohen/Arato are issues in late capitalist societies (Cohen and Arato: viii–ix). Contemporary Western scholars are trying to establish theories that best interpret changes in twentieth-century European countries and the United States and to suggest solutions to preserve the democratic features and liberal traditions of civil society from the penetrations of both the state and capital.

In disagreeing with the three-part model, some Chinese scholars address the usefulness of a dichotomous model that includes the economy in civil society. He Zengke thinks that the dichotomous model is not out of date at all in developing countries where the state and society were for a long time strongly united and where their separation has just begun. Thus, defining the bounds between state and society is a more realistic and urgent task in those countries (He 1994a: 43). The independence of economic life from state control is the precondition of the independence of social and cultural life, He further argues, because the separation between the state and society usually begins in the economic realm and then gradually extends to other realms (47). Other scholars consider the crucial role of new economic forces in the development of China's civil society. Deng and Jing believe that the entrepreneurial stratum and the intellectuals are the backbones of civil society because entrepreneurs are the main dynamic force behind the growth and perfection of a market economy in China. They contend that entrepreneurs not only are the supporters of market order, equal contract, and freedom from outer forces' interruption of economic activities, but that their economic status and financial resources also confer on them a leading role in organizing and sponsoring civic associations and interest groups (Deng and Jing 1992: 6–7).

The important contribution of these insights is to make clear the need for distinctive models of civil society in countries with different economic systems and political cultures. Furthermore, these scholars cogently conclude that the study of Chinese civil society should include economic activities, forces, and associations as major dynamic elements. Indeed, the problems facing Chinese reforms are quite different from problems in the contemporary West. Chinese intellectuals need a workable theoretical framework that addresses China's situation and crises. China is undergoing a transition that delivers society from the rigorous control of the party-state, a process launched just two decades ago. On the one hand, society is extending its autonomous space because of the growth of the market economy and the multiple interests the market has brought in tow. On the other hand, the state still regulates or interferes in many matters in the private and social spheres, and therefore the separation is far from completed. Chinese society has not yet developed institutional means or collective actions sufficient to balance the state. Fundamental changes in the economic realm not only explain why civil society is evolving in China in spite of the party-state's control of political matters; they also reveal a future trend.

Thus, the rise of the market and private economy has given vitality to new interests and strata outside of the state. The increasingly pluralized economy and social life have created enormous needs and possibilities that did not exist before the reforms. As Chapter 5 elaborates, the entrepreneurs and economic associations are the most substantial driving forces in changing China's institutional landscapes and the differentiation of civil society from political society. To ignore what is happening in the economic realm would leave the study of Chinese NGOs and the evolution of civil society incomplete.

In short, the open discussion of civil society among Chinese intellectuals has significant political consequences. It has opened up a theoretical subject that is critical to China's future political reforms, and the debate presents itself as a political statement by intellectuals on their role in the reforms. Since the outset of the reforms and open policy, three major debates have taken place at crucial moments in China's economic transitions (1978, 1992, and 1997).[13] These debates were over key reform policies, and both sides sought theoretical rationales from Marxist and Maoist thought. High party officials have been involved in the debates as much as the political theorists, and on each occasion speeches from the top leaders of the CCP, first Deng Xiaoping and then Jiang Zemin, concluded the discussions. The Chinese officials call these confrontations "the great emancipating of mind," and, indeed, they have helped in overcoming obstacles in the way of economic reforms.

In contrast to these debates, the discussion of civil society was initiated entirely by Chinese scholars. Rather than party officials, they involved themselves in one of the most sensitive yet crucial issues in China: political reform. More importantly, unlike the three debates that focused on economic issues, the study of civil society is directly aimed at reconstructing China's political system. One should also not overlook the fact that, as late as 1996, the discussion of civil society was still very sensitive politically.[14] The constant flux in the political atmosphere has restricted study in serious ways; yet, many Chinese scholars have taken risks in organizing and participating in the debates.

Evolution of civil society in late Qing and early Republican China

Associations and institutions that engaged in political, social, or cultural activities outside of state control had deep roots prior to the establishment of the People's Republic of China in 1949. This section discusses early modern civic associations in the late Qing and early Republic, and it highlights three points: chambers of commerce and intellectuals' associations increased impressively in that period and played substantial roles in China's economic and political life; certain features displayed by these organizations are strikingly similar to those of NGOs today; and a civil society in its early stage was indeed evolving in some of the regions. Thus, the experience of the early associations provides a pertinent historical context for the study of current NGOs.

In the mid-1980s, to challenge Max Weber's assertion that the absence of urban political autonomy accounted for China's failure to develop capitalism, American historians William Rowe and Mary Rankin, among others, stressed that in the late nineteenth century, led by the activities of the Qing landowning and merchant elite, a "public sphere" of activity outside the bureaucracy expanded rapidly. Using Hankow as a case study, Rowe describes "the steady development of organized, corporate-style civic action and the proliferation of a wide range of philanthropic and public-service institutions" (Rowe 1989: 3). Rankin, meanwhile, emphasizes the key role of the expansion of elite public-management and the emergence of oppositional public opinion in the Lower Yangzi region (Rankin 1986: 15, 19). Rankin and David Strand further conclude that by the beginning of the twentieth century an "incipient civil society" existed in China (Rankin 1986 and Strand 1990). Political scientist Lucian Pye put the point this way: between the official, government sphere and the private, family and clan sphere, "there was a fairly clearly defined third and public sphere that consisted of the collective actions of the gentry in the countryside and the merchant guilds in the cities" (Pye 2001: 390).

Some historians, however, disagree with these views and criticize the use of such Western notions as "public sphere" and "civil society" in attempting to understand China. Philip Kuhn does not consider Habermas's concepts applicable to Chinese local elite and urban merchant-managers during the Ming and the Qing periods. Kuhn argues that "'Public Sphere' for Habermas is like 'Protestant Ethic' for Weber: it is a social philosopher's ideal type, not a social historian's description of reality" (Kuhn 1991).[15] Frederick Wakeman finds "poignant" the effort to apply Habermas's concepts to China because, although the public realm has expanded continually since 1900, this has not led to the assertion of civic power against the state. According to Wakeman, state coercive power has grown steadily, and most Chinese citizens appear to conceive of social existence mainly in terms of obligation and interdependence rather than rights and responsibilities (Wakeman 1993: 133–4).

Yet, in the late 1980s, a group of Chinese scholars started to study chambers of commerce, students' and scholars' associations, and other associations during the late Qing and early Republic, without awareness of the debate among the China scholars in the West until some time in the mid-1990s.[16] An impressive amount of publications not only shed new light on state–society relations during that time, but also provide valuable references for the study of NGOs today (Xu and Qian 1991; Zhu 1991 and 1997; Zhang and Liu 1992; He 1992; Yu Heping 1993; Ma and Zhu 1993; Ma 1995; Sang 1995 a and b; Chen 1996; Zhang, Ma and Zhu 2000 a and b; Wang 2001; Zhao 2002). Substantial case studies on China's modern bourgeoisie and intellectuals in coastal cities as well as in the upper valley of the Yangzi River have provided a picture of an active and influential private sector centered on chambers of commerce and intellectual associations.

A major contribution of these studies is the work on chambers of commerce. Zhu Yin, a leading scholar of chambers of commerce, points out that most studies by Western scholars neglect the chambers of commerce. Disagreeing with Philip Huang's conclusion that "the new chambers of commerce illustrate well the simultaneous involvement of state and society in the new institutions of the third realm," Zhu is convinced that "the gentry-merchants and the chambers of commerce were the most symbolic social force of civil society in China" (Huang 1993: 230; Zhu 1997: 11–12, 112–13). Addressing variations of civil society under different cultures, some Chinese historians conclude that an early stage of civil society did evolve in China's coastal cities and some economically developed areas during that historical period (Ma 1995: 281–92; Zhu 1997: 105–13).

New social forces and the rise of chambers of commerce and intellectual associations

The emergence of a large number of modern civic organizations during the late Qing and the early Republican years gives the most convincing evidence for the evolution of civil society. This could not have occurred if new social forces had not begun to reshape traditional society. The modern bourgeoisie and intelligentsia came into being largely from similar backgrounds and around the same historical moment, and associational life was a crucial part of their progression. Historically, the predecessor of the modern bourgeoisie was "gentry-merchants," a social stratum that had gone through profound economic and social changes during the late nineteenth century. Gentrymen and merchants had been two distinct social classes in traditional China; the former attained a prestigious status when they passed the imperial examinations and became eligible for official appointment, while the latter had the lowest status among four traditional professional categories in agricultural China (gentry, peasants, craftsmen, and merchants). Yet, in reality, many merchants became socially influential by purchasing degrees or official ranks or resorting to their connections with officials.

Following the Opium War in 1840, under the influence of Western political and economic power, China's industries and market economy grew and urbanization spread. However, the most decisive factor was the swift conversion of the Qing government to the cause of reformation. Starting with the 1901 "New Policies," the Qing government launched a series of reforms towards constitutionalism as well as educational reforms, and these efforts led directly to the dynasty's fall. During the New Policies, new economic policy was also issued in an effort to invigorate industry and business.

The Qing court's new policies dramatically reoriented the traditional emphasis on the agricultural economy to an emphasis on business and industrial development, and this accelerated the confluence of gentry and merchants. "The replacement of feudalist ethics by modern utilitarianism . . . is an important symbol of the development of capitalism" (Zhang et al. 2000b: 617). In the late nineteenth century, especially after the Sino-Japanese War of 1894–95, many members of the literate elite, even officials, began to run businesses, a trend that recurred in the 1980s and the 1990s. The most famous late nineteenth century example was Zhang Jian, recipient of the highest examination rank (*jinshi*), who founded and supervised an early textile factory (Zhang et al. 2000b: 221–2; Koll 2003).

The abolition of the imperial civil service examinations in 1905 ended the traditional path to wealth, status, and power as an official, and it was a significant factor in turning the literate class toward new pursuits, including commerce and industry. By the turn of the twentieth century, gentry-merchants had become the most powerful political, economic, and social class. This mixed gentry-merchant class carried with it Confucian influence, merchant roots, official ties, and Western business connections. Its multiple character and origins in fact gave it a unique position among all political and economic forces. This was why gentry-merchants, and later on the bourgeoisie, played such a central role in social transformation at the time. Yet, such characters, sometimes self-contradicting and controversial, were also the main reason that modern Chinese bourgeois and their associations had close and yet conflicting relations with the government and Western businesses in China.

Modern Chinese intellectuals shared a similar social background with the gentry-merchants. In pre-modern China, all officials got their starts as scholars who had passed the imperial examinations. Generally, scholars who obtained officials' ranks became "*shen*" (gentry), and those who did not were still "*shi*" (scholar). As a status, *shenshi* might go back 2,500 years, and yet the literate, landowning class that became a social elite and provided the majority of government officials appeared in the Song dynasty. To a great extent, *shi* and the rich connotation it embraces represents the essential spirit of Chinese culture, and modern Chinese intellectuals come from this tradition that sees the educated man as one who has a responsibility to act on behalf of the public good, serve the state when it acts in the common interest, and remonstrate the powerful when it does not.[17]

During the institutional transformation of gentry-merchants' and scholars' associations, traditional merchants, craftsmen, landlords, scholars, and officials became the Chinese bourgeoisie. During this process, not only did they capitalize their business and become real bourgeoisie themselves, but the Chinese merchant-bourgeoisie also became better organized with a national and even cosmopolitan perspective, as evident in the development of the chambers of commerce (Yu, H. 1993: 28–90). Zhang Kaiyuan, a scholar of China's modern bourgeoisie, points out that only after the establishment of the chambers of commerce did the bourgeoisie have social organizations that spoke out and worked in their interests. From then on, they no longer dealt with the government or other social forces individually or as lowly tradesmen, but as legal corporations (Zhang 1985: 181).

Modern social organizations made their debut around the Reform Movement of 1898 when at least seventy associations were founded and assumed missions of political and social reform (Min 1995: 39–76). The founding of the Shanghai Chamber of Commerce in 1904 signaled the birth of the gentry-merchants' modern institutions (Zhu 1997: 113). The two decades that followed witnessed the blooming of merchants' organizations and intellectuals' associations. By the early twentieth century, more than two thousand merchants', intellectuals', and peasants' organizations had appeared, and many formerly secret groups surfaced (Sang 1995a: 274–5). Led by educated and wealthy women, the earliest women's association formed in 1906 in Beijing, and early women's organizations for charity, women's equality, education, foot-binding abolition, and political participation pioneered the women's movement in China (Liu 1994: 1–26).

The 1911 Revolution overthrew the Qing Dynasty and gave civic associations and chambers of commerce a new boost. The years right after the revolution were the golden age for chambers of commerce. In 1912, the China National Federation of Chambers of Commerce finally obtained approval from the government. By 1915, a total of 1,242 chambers of commerce were registered nationwide. Some historians believe that "the early Republican period was the most active time in contemporary Chinese history for the civic associations." The great majority of those organizations appeared after the May 4 Movement in 1919, and their mainstays were young intellectuals (Zhang and Liu 1992: 232–3, 250–3).

Major features of modern Chinese associations

Many features of today's NGOs and their relations with the state echo the experience of chambers of commerce and intellectuals' associations in the late Qing and early Republic. To begin, the chambers of commerce and scholars' associations in the late nineteenth and early twentieth centuries clearly presented features of modern civic associations, even though many traditions did continue. For instance, unlike traditional craftsmen's or trade associations that organized informally and depended largely on master–apprentice relations, family ties, and native-place connections, the modern chambers of commerce were formally established and professionally managed. Their charters enunciated a well-defined organizational mission, structure, membership requirements, and managerial principles. The old craftsmen's associations were limited to a single trade, usually organized on a native-place basis. By contrast, the chambers of commerce cut across family, locality, and trade boundaries. Their members came from different regions and businesses, all based in the same urban center. These modern institutions thus could represent broader urban interests and eventually play a major role in local and national economics and politics.

Furthermore, the new institutions demonstrated a certain degree of democratic and voluntary nature. In the old clan associations or craftsmen's guilds, for example, membership was mandatory, and the management was very much patriarchal. In comparison, the membership of chambers of commerce was voluntary. Trades often joined the chambers of commerce collectively, but if some merchants or craftsmen did not want to participate, they could decline to do so. During that time, merchants and intellectuals were learning to run their associations democratically. The managerial structures, similar to many associations today, usually included boards of trustees, committees, and staff in charge of financial, accounting, secretarial and other matters (Ma 2004: 27–36). All the leaders in chambers of commerce were elected, and every member over 20 years old had the right to vote. Moreover, mechanisms existed to supervise or impeach the chambers' leaders. A charter of one chamber of commerce states: "Whether matters big or small, they require discussions among members to reach decisions. Everyone has the responsibility of participating, and nobody should make arbitrary decisions" (Zhang *et al.* 2000a: 352–5). In practice, patriarchal leadership often continued and the leaders of chambers of commerce usually were the wealthy and powerful who could exert their will. Many traditional forms and practices persisted in these "modern" associations (Goodman 1995). Compared to the chambers of commerce, the scholars' associations were more democratic in their governance, since many of them were organized by students who had returned from overseas.

Another feature of the modern Chinese associations is the influence of the West. While Chapter 6 will discuss the impact of the ideas and resources of international NGOs on the upsurge of civic associations in the post-reform era, it is interesting to see a Western influence on China's first generation of modern institutions. The Western invasions since 1840 had opened China to modern science, technology, and Western political and educational systems. Various Western institutions, including chambers of commerce, missionary schools, and hospitals, brought Western notions of associational life to China. Students returned from overseas served as another channel of learning. The Chinese gradually adopted these new forms of organizations and managerial mechanisms. The development of chambers of commerce is a good example of such an influence.

From 1840 to 1894, Western powers opened 857 businesses in China's coastal cities. As early as 1834, the British established a British chamber of commerce in Guangzhou (Canton). In 1861, the first federation of foreign chambers of commerce (FFCC) opened in Hong Kong, and by 1904 six similar federations had appeared in major cities in China (Yu, H. 1993: 62–4). Zheng Guanyin, a famous gentry-merchant in Shanghai, was the first

Chinese to introduce this institutional form to China by addressing the necessity of the chamber of commerce in promoting and protecting the merchants' interests. Later, Kang Youwei, the leader of intellectual reformers, proposed to Emperor Guang Xu the idea of establishing Chinese chambers of commerce (Yu: 65–70). The merchants and bourgeoisie in Shanghai were the first to break the traditional trade boundaries, and in 1902 they founded China's first chamber of commerce. The constitution of the Shanghai chamber of commerce that later became the model for other chambers of commerce imitated the constitution of the FFCC in Shanghai.

In the same year, the Qing court sent an observation group headed by Prince Zaizhen to Europe, the United States, and Japan. Right after his return, Zaizhen proposed a Department of Commerce, which later became the second most important department in the Qing government. The new department soon passed the "Company Law" and the "Regulations of Merchants," which closely copied German and Japanese commercial laws. Under pressure from merchants who asked for a comprehensive commercial law based on other countries' experiences, the government invited a Japanese jurist to draft a comprehensive commercial law in 1906 for the department of commerce (Ma and Zhu 1993: 36–7).

In contrast with gentry-merchants, the modern intellectuals did not become an influential political force until the late nineteenth and early twentieth century. The rapid extension of Western-style schools after 1860 was the most important factor in nourishing modern Chinese intellectuals. Around the turn of the century, over 2,000 Protestant or Catholic missionary schools, eighty percent of them American, enrolled over 40,000 students, from elementary schools to universities (Chen 1979: 74–5). The Chinese officially ran Western-style schools opened in the 1860s, and when in 1906 the Qing court abolished the imperial examination, it ordered that all types of traditional schools should be transformed into new schools. One study estimates that by the end of the early Republican era, China had about one million intellectuals, thirty thousand of whom had studied abroad (Zhang and Liu 1992: 212–13).

Students with a Western education formed an extraordinary pro-modern and pro-reform force, and from them came the leadership for the upsurge of social organizations during the 1900s to 1920s. Immediately following the 1911 Revolution, Lord Cecil, an acknowledged expert on China, wrote a long article for the *Daily Mail*. He said: "no country in China had exerted the moral influence that the Americans had, and that anyone might say unhesitatingly that nine-tenths of the men responsible for the revolution of 1911 were educated in American mission schools." He employed that as the basis of a plea to ask the British to do more in furthering education (RF 1914: 60).

With Western schools, hospitals, newspapers, translation bureaus, and, most of all, Western technology and products pouring into China, the Chinese people's comprehension of Western learning changed substantially. By the turn of the twentieth century, the term "new learning" gradually replaced "Western learning," indicating that the Chinese had connected Western knowledge and ideas with reform, and that new politics and new style of citizenry were superseding the old (Xiong 1994: 729–30). The growth of Western education after the turmoil of the Boxer Movement in 1900 reflected both the missionaries' determination to return to China and the acceptance of Western ideas by China's newly rising social forces: bourgeoisie and new intellectuals. If in the nineteenth century missionary education was still excluded by China's social elites, by the early twentieth century universities run by missionaries and Western private institutions had become centers of young elite intellectuals. The so-called "Johns Hopkins in China," the Rockefeller Foundation's Peking Union Medical College (PUMC, 1915–51), presented the most advanced medical education and research model for China and Asia to follow, and it attracted students from some of the most famous elite families (Ma 2002b: 159–83).

As these institutions became the dynamic force behind the development of modern education and medicine in China, they created an environment for the growth of modern private institutions in general. Many Chinese academic and charitable organizations adopted the Western model. For instance, the Chinese Red Cross (1904) was a copy of the International Red Cross. The Chinese Medical Association (1910) followed the examples of the Medical Missionaries Association in China (1886), the China Pharmaceutical Association in Japan (1907), and the China Nurses Association (1909, organized by European and American nurses in China). The first Chinese women's organization, the China Women Association, was inspired by the Red Cross. Students returned from abroad founded the first group of Chinese associations in the natural sciences.

The involvement of Western influences in China's education and other modern movements was an extremely controversial matter during the late Qing and early Republic. It took almost half a century for the Qing court to value or at least accept Western learning. As later discussions will explain, this issue is not only historical. The portrayal of Western institutions and their role in China's modernization directly affects people's perspective of a similar involvement today, and, inevitably, the ambivalent attitude is reflected in current official policies. While the government would like to invite foreign NGOs and private sectors to support China's charitable, educational, or environmental organizations, it expresses clearly the suspicion of any foreign influence on Chinese NGOs. Consequently, it prohibits any foreign connection with political or other sensitive issues.

The most noticeable and controversial feature of China's civic associations, past and present, however, is their close and interdependent relations with the government. This relationship is a complicated and important issue because it characterizes the powers and limitations of these organizations. In 1901, when the Qing court restored some measures of the short-lived Reform of 1898, most of the prohibitions against associations became invalid.

The founding of a chamber of commerce in Shanghai (1902) was in fact under the encouragement of the Qing government. The Department of Commerce (1903) and the official regulatory document *A Brief Regulation of Chambers of Commerce* (1904) in many ways served as powerful vehicles to promote private businesses and chambers of commerce. The new policy reduced official regulations in commercial activities and left more opportunity for private business while improving merchants' social status, and, to a certain degree, protecting Chinese businesses from foreign competition. Soon after the 1911 Revolution, the Northern Warlords' government in Beijing adopted the Chambers of Commerce Law. Thus, the government completed, in a very preliminary way, its regulatory system over the chambers of commerce.

Some Chinese historians call the relationship between the government and chambers of commerce during this period somewhat "constructively interactive" (Zhang et al. 2000b: 486–513), a term similar to that advocated by scholars today as an ideal state–society relationship. No doubt, both the Qing court and later the Northern Warlords' government had some mutual interest, political and economic, in the development of chambers of commerce. The Qing court saw rapid economic growth as its last hope to restoring power, leading some Chinese scholars conclude that "the strong state promotion of industry and business in the late Qing was unprecedented in China's history" (Zhang et al. 2000a: 119). Beyond economic considerations, the Qing court also depended heavily on the gentry-merchants' local networks to stabilize local social order. Conversely, without favorable official policies, the gentry-merchants could not have become the most powerful economic and political class in the late Qing, and indeed the merchants readily extended their political and economic power into the space vacated by the Qing government.

Fundamental conflicts of interest occurred, however, between the gentry-merchants and the Qing court as well as between the bourgeoisie and the warlords' government. As the strength and influence of chambers of commerce grew, their confrontations with the state worsened (Yu, H. 1993: 84–92). Neither the Qing court nor the Northern Warlords' regime actually gave up control over chambers of commerce, and they never ceased to repress students' and scholars' organizations. One major issue between the government and the bourgeoisie involved the autonomy of chambers of commerce, as evident in the struggle over the establishment of a national federation of chambers of commerce that lasted from the final years of the Qing Dynasty until the early years of the Northern Warlords' regime.

Some scholars, Chinese and Western, question the autonomous nature of chambers of commerce because of official control and the lack of complete independence. For example, in the early 1980s, some Chinese scholars called chambers of commerce "semi-official" (Zhang and Liu 1980: 399). Marie-Claire Bergere, a French scholar of the Chinese bourgeoisie, argues that the bourgeoisie were not the opposing class against the Qing Empire; at a certain point, their organizations, especially the chambers of commerce, could be seen as subordinate agencies under the imperial government.[18] Some Japanese scholars concluded that the Chinese chambers of commerce during the Qing Dynasty were the product of the government's powerful leadership and strong support and thus governmental (Zhu 1991: 64).

The most recent Chinese works, however, conclude otherwise. According to some accounts, "the chambers of commerce during the late Qing and early Republican period had ties with the officials, but they were not official organizations, and they were not even semi-official organizations. They were new popular social organizations run by merchants" (Zhang et al. 2000a: 343). These studies argue that the gentry-merchants voluntarily founded chambers of commerce, even though they did have the government's encouragement. These organizations maintained relative independence in finance and leadership to protect merchants' interests. With some exceptions, the majority of chambers of commerce had their own financial resources. Moreover, their operation and governance, including fundraising, financial management, and auditing procedure, were independent (Zhu 1991: 65–6; Yu, H. 1993: 80; Zhang et al. 2000a: 342–8). The respective chambers of commerce elected their leaders, mostly successful and powerful businessmen. These leaders were subject to official approval, but they were not officials nor were they appointed by the government.

The government took a harder line toward the new intellectuals' associations than toward the chambers of commerce. For example, unlike its policy towards merchants, the Qing court never removed its prohibitions against scholars' and especially students' associations. The surge of over two thousand intellectuals' organizations during 1901–04 did not result from the Qing government's reform, but rather from the indomitable efforts for growth and self-expression exhibited by intellectuals under a rapidly weakening government. In his study of intellectuals' organizations during the late Qing, Sang Bing argues that these organizations, in comparison with the government-approved merchants' organizations, demonstrated more independence politically. While the chambers of commerce had to depend on the government in their struggles with foreign economic intrusion and focused mostly on the interests of their own class, intellectual associations embraced a broader range of interests and sought to consider the national welfare as a whole. Their criticism usually directly pointed to the Qing court, which in turn often moved to suppress them (Sang 1995a: 289).

Compared to the associations in the early twentieth century, the Chinese NGOs now face a very different political context. The late Qing and early Republican states were weak, and the patriotic nationalism of the earlier associations was aimed at resisting imperialism, building a new Chinese society, and "saving the nation." Under such circumstances, both chambers of commerce and intellectuals' associations were very active and influential politically, and they played a major role in promoting reform and modernization. According to *The Encyclopedia of Chinese Social Organizations*, among

578 listed social organizations before 1949, 388 were political organizations, and many others were academic or educational associations also active in political matters (Fan 1995).

In contrast, today's NGOs face a much stronger state. From the CCP's perspective, the NGOs' efforts in building a powerful and wealthy China can mean strengthening the state as a means of ensuring the conditions of stability and international position that modern economic development demands. As later chapters will elaborate, under China's party-state, NGOs cannot engage in political matters freely, nor can they directly confront the government as those early associations did. In this sense, the current development of NGOs has not yet reached the political height of their predecessors.

The evolution of civil society in early twentieth-century China

As discussed earlier, some Chinese scholars assert that civil society cannot evolve in China today because of the nation's history and tradition. Yet, studies on the development of new institutions of bourgeoisie and intellectuals during the early twentieth century suggest otherwise. These associations seized the opportunity provided by weak states in the late Qing and early Republic to extend their influence in political and economic arenas. Never in China's history had private organizations and their activities enjoyed as much power and autonomy as they did in this period. For example, since 1905, chambers of commerce, student associations, and other social organizations had organized political and economic movements protesting unequal treaties and economic invasions by the Western powers and Japan. These actions peaked with the May 4 Movement. Chambers of commerce also played a major role in the constitutionalism movement in the late Qing and early Republican period. Holding the strength gained during the 1911 Revolution, the chambers of commerce pushed the Beijing warlords' government to pass the Chambers of Commerce Law vigorously and on the founding of the national federation of chambers of commerce.

During these political struggles, the new social forces established themselves politically and institutionally. Some scholars point out that, unlike craftsmen's guilds, chambers of commerce were well organized and operated; moreover, they had complicated networks of connections with other organizations on a large scale. Merchants and intellectuals extended their local organizations vertically into cross-regional or even national federations (Zhang et al. 2000b: 327). Since the late Qing, chambers of commerce had established an extensive organizational system with three tiers: chambers of commerce (*shangwu zhonghui*) at the municipal level, their branches (*shangwu fenhui*) in mid-cities, and lower branches (*shangwu fensuo*) at the township level. Zhu Ying points out that never before in China's history were there such extended non-governmental social networks from the metropolis to the town (Zhu 1997: 114–15).

44 In search of civil society in China

Robert Putnam emphasizes the crucial role of horizontal networks among civic associations in generating social capital and promoting democracy. By the early twentieth century, in some cities in coastal areas and in the upper areas of the Yangzi River, social organizations at the municipal level had built the power networks outside of government. These organizations, centered around and led by chambers of commerce, had achieved an impressive amount of control over municipal affairs. A parallel political movement for local autonomy that evolved in the late nineteenth century reached its peak in 1909, and chambers of commerce were the most dynamic force in the fight for local power. This movement had strengthened the bourgeoisie's political influence considerably.

Suzhou, a prosperous city in the heart of the Yangzi delta, offers a convincing example (Ma and Zhu 1993). Around the early twentieth century, Suzhou's chambers of commerce established a comprehensive system with a general chamber of commerce on top and two levels of local branches. The chambers of commerce further recruited two other non-governmental networks under their influence: Merchants' Physical Education Association, an autonomous militia organization, and Townspeople Communes (*shimin gongshe*), organizations pursuing local autonomous governance. Through the personnel overlap and participation in decision-making, the chambers of commerce became an authoritative voice of the communes, and the commune networks assisted the chambers of commerce in further extending their influence on the city's life.

Around 1909, some twenty new-style social organizations in the Suzhou area were all centripetal to the chambers of commerce. An important cooperation started between gentry-merchants and intellectuals in creating a non-official municipal board of education for new schools. Thus, the two most powerful private entities joined forces. Later on, a similar coalition extended to the peasants' association and other organizations. In Suzhou, as elsewhere at this time, merchants and bourgeoisie actively devoted their money and time to education, charities, and other efforts for the public good. Eventually, a complex and autonomous power network outside of the Suzhou municipal government reached into almost every aspect of city life: economic, political, public welfare, city security, fire control, judicial matters, education, and hygiene. This unofficial power network effectively manipulated the governance of municipal affairs. The complete historical records of Suzhou chambers of commerce allow historians to fully examine such a network; nevertheless, Suzhou is not the only case of such development. By the end of the Qing Dynasty, 60 to 70 percent of the administrative districts and counties had established "self-government bureaus" (*zizhi gongsuo*), agencies that the bourgeoisie used for comprehensive municipal autonomy (Zhang *et al.* 2000b: 329).

At that time, the chambers of commerce, intellectual associations and political organizations also resorted to newspapers and other publications to agitate public opinion. In his *The Structural Transformation of the Public*

Sphere, Habermas (1989: 31–43) highlights the role of coffee shops and the increase in readers and publications in the formative stage of the public sphere. Although the situation in late nineteenth and early twentieth-century China was quite different, one can hardly overestimate the crucial function of newspapers and other publications at that time. One of the earliest newspapers in China was *Wan Guo Gongbao* (Review of the Times), published monthly between 1868 and 1907 and edited by an influential missionary, Young Allen. The earliest Chinese merchants' newspaper, *Craftsmen and Merchants' Newspaper*, appeared in Shanghai in 1898. In the early twentieth century, the merchants' national newspapers, *Chinese Merchants' Federation Newspaper* and *The Newspaper of All China Federation of Chambers of Commerce*, became powerful tools in the bourgeoisie's political and economic struggles.

The blooming of newspapers, journals, and books – including translations of Western and Japanese books – as well as libraries and reading rooms gave a powerful impetus to the promotion of reforms. This was particularly true in big cities. By the end of the nineteenth century, there were over a hundred newspapers nationwide; after the 1911 Revolution, this number suddenly jumped to five hundred with 42,000,000 subscriptions (Zhang and Liu 1992: 155). According to a list of all periodicals in Beiping's libraries, published by Beiping (Beijing) Library Association in 1929, over a hundred periodicals, mostly academic and political, were issued from 1912 to 1918. The first modern publishing house, Shangwu Publishing House, opened in Shanghai in 1897, and by 1930 it had published a total of 18,708 periodicals and books (Zhang and Liu: 115–65). As early as 1904, at least 116 libraries and reading rooms provided newspapers and books to the public (Sang 1995a: 282). Never before could ordinary people learn of domestic and international news this quickly and pervasively, and these newspapers and journals also provided forums for public opinions and ideas.

By the early twentieth century, with a considerable amount of autonomy in associative matters and a wide range of activities in the public sphere, the new organizations of merchants, intellectuals, workers, and peasants in some prosperous cities developed significant features of civil society. Yet, some scholars have distinguished Chinese civil society from the classical Western concept of a civil society opposing state power. Ma Min, a historian of chambers of commerce, points out,

> The purpose of early Chinese civil society was not to confront the government, but rather to harmonize the relations between society and the government, providing autonomy to assist government. This point was mutually accepted by both the government and society.
> (Ma 1995: 287)

China's civil society did not want to contend with the state. Thus the civil society was always extremely cautious and sought political balance in the hope of gaining recognition and protection from the government (Zhang et al. 2000a: 332).

Such a development in early twentieth-century China was very uneven geographically, however, and the merchants' and intellectuals' organizations were concentrated mostly in coastal areas and major cities. Politically, the existence and growth of these private organizations became possible largely because of the extremely shaky condition of the state and its need for support from society. The gentry-merchants and intellectuals themselves were in a stage of transformation and growth, and they could not play the roles they envisioned. Economically as well as politically, the private sector and civil society could not fully evolve in early twentieth-century China.

In short, theoretically, Chinese intellectuals' search for civil society and the models and ideals they advanced in discourse carry significance that goes far beyond academic discussions. Today, the term "civil society" has been widely adopted in discussions of China's political reforms, and the ideals of civil society have become the goals of many NGOs. As later chapters will demonstrate, Chinese intellectuals, among them Chinese scholars of civil society and NGOs, have played a crucial role in promoting NGO development. Following their analyses, a Chinese civil society model addresses "constructive interactions between the state and civil society" as well as the important roles of economic activities and civic associations in the economic realm. As China rapidly enters the global community, Chinese scholars have reasons to believe in the applicability of civil society and NGOs in China.

Historically, for a short period in the late Qing and early Republic, chambers of commerce and intellectual associations indeed facilitated the emergence of civil society in some regions, and the lessons and traditions left behind are valuable to Chinese reformers and NGO activists today. After several decades of interruption, history has given the intellectuals and entrepreneurs another chance to continue what their predecessors did not complete. Some traditional situations persist, as the closely tied yet potentially conflicting relationship between the newly founded NGOs and the government reminds us. Most of all, China is still not a country that upholds the rule of law. China's party state is strong and is largely in control of society. Nevertheless, the broad context of state–society relations has profoundly changed. For its political future, the government is determined to carry on a state-led reform that has given and will continue to allot society more space and autonomy. In addition, the Chinese people are more knowledgeable than ever of the outside world and of their own rights and power, and they are even more determined to control their own lives and to make China better for their children. As the following chapters will demonstrate, self-organization and citizen participation are instrumental to this purpose.

2 "Small government, big society"
The Chinese government's NGO policy and its dilemma

Despite twenty-five years of reform and increasing openness in China, the party-state continues to dominate Chinese society, and the policies it formulates towards non-governmental organizations (NGOs) necessarily serve as the greatest determinant of their status and health. In general, two major influences have shaped the government's NGO policy. First, in response to economic, social, and political crises, the government has turned to non-governmental institutions to shoulder responsibilities on numerous fronts, including social welfare, economic development, and disaster relief. The government believes that the resources, development programs, and services brought in or provided by the non-governmental sector, domestic or international, will help the CCP restore its legitimacy, reduce public pressure on the government, and bring social stability. On the other hand, the CCP's top leaders remain keenly aware of the political risks of associational actions, a lesson they learned in the late 1980s from the Tiananmen students and workers' democratic movement, as well as Poland's Solidarity Movement.

An examination of the official NGO policy reveals the CCP-state's unmistakable determination to legalize and promote non-governmental organizations and entrust them with responsibilities previously controlled by the government. The flexibility and adaptability of the party and government in adjusting their policies to new situations is evidenced in their reformulation of traditional institutions such as trade and professional associations and the new campaigns launched for societalization of social welfare (*shehui fuli shehuihua*) and community construction. At the same time, the increasingly strict and comprehensive NGO regulatory system that has been in place since the late 1980s indicates that the CCP and government intend to use all available means to control the potentially radical growth of the non-governmental sector. Thus, government policy wields a powerful influence over the growth of the NGO sector.

The party-state's contradicting policy vacillation between promoting and restraining NGOs derives from its fundamental understanding of non-governmental organizations. For the CCP and the government, NGOs should not be the fruit of people exercising their rights of association. Rather, they are subject to official approval and regulation, and are desirable only in so far as they deliver what the party-state needs. This study concludes that by and large the party's NGO policy has had a positive impact on NGO development, and yet it is responsible for the NGOs' unbalanced and unhealthy condition. This chapter analyzes the motivations behind the government's promotion of NGOs and explains the major features of official policies towards NGOs. It also considers the dilemma the CCP faces as it struggles to decide how much restraint to impose and how much freedom to allow NGOs.

The government's motives for promoting NGOs

By the end of the Cultural Revolution, the CCP was in grave danger of losing its legitimacy and thus its hold on power. "By 1976, when Mao died, the Party was widely unpopular" (Nathan 1997: 40). When Deng Xiaoping came to power in 1978, he made it clear that economic development was essential for political as well as economic reasons. The economic reforms undertaken since 1978 are a strategic response by the CCP to its political crisis. Faced with enormous pressure for change, the party and the government realized that only reform and development would endow their authority with trust and legitimacy. This perception has become the major motivation behind the reforms that followed the Cultural Revolution, and this conviction has shaped official policy towards the activities of non-governmental organizations as well.

Kang Xiaoguang, a Chinese political scientist, argues that there are occasions when the state and society share basic interests, and that when a government has the means to control society it tends to respond to reform pressures on its own initiative by resorting to a strategy of development in order to survive. He, like other Chinese scholars, argues that China's economic and political reforms are an instance of "the government-led reform model" (Kang 1999: 145–7). Even though conflicts between state and society have in many ways intensified since the reforms began, CCP officials remain convinced that they can continue to control the situation, and that the reforms introduced since 1978 will continue to work in their best interest. This attitude largely explains why the government has vigorously promoted certain types of NGOs despite the knowledge of political risks.

Looking back at the CCP's history and its political foundation, one can understand why the party feels confident that it can rely on certain NGOs to further its aims. During the period of revolution, mass organizations such as workers' unions, peasants' associations, and women's organizations were the CCP's most reliable allies. The current official policy towards NGOs illustrates that the CCP continues to hold to the notion that mass and social organizations (SOs) serve as bridges for the party and government to reach out to the people, as adjuncts to assist the party's cause, and as a complementary force able to take over responsibilities that the government no longer wishes to carry.

Today, the official release of NGOs is not unconditional and across-the-board. While the government has given a green light to certain types of non-governmental institutions at various times in line with current reform agendas and strategy, it has suppressed political, religious, and advocacy organizations. Consequently, the NGO development in China is unbalanced in many ways. Organizations engaged in economic and social development, have especially won the government's favor. Consider, for example, the types of organizations the government selected to vigorously promote during 2004: social welfare organizations, trade associations, farmers' technology groups, and community-based NGOs.[1] The following section will discuss why and how at certain times the government endorses particular types of organizations to meet the social and economic challenges and achieve the goals of reform.

From "mobilizing all social forces for education" to "societalization of social welfare": the state is no longer the sole bearer of social responsibilities

Nick Young, the chief editor of *China Development Brief*, a Beijing-based and US-registered newspaper focusing on Chinese NGOs, frankly pointed out the profound social problems created by the economic and social changes in the past twenty years:

> prostitution; crime; drug use; trafficking in women and children; the structural problems of a large rural–urban migrant population without full urban residency rights or access to basic services; a growth in numbers of street children, vagrants, and beggars; an increase in single parent families; and, arguably, an increase in people suffering from depression or other kinds of mental illness as a result of societal stress . . . Finally, as Chinese cities become larger, more anonymous, and more dominated by concrete and cars, and as rural environments become more degraded, there is very likely to be a surge in demand for improved environmental amenities and quality of life.
>
> (Young 2002a: 35)

Young was pessimistic about the willingness of China's leaders to confront these challenges: "the Party and government face a daunting combination of existing service gaps, expanding demand for services, and severe fiscal constraints, but show little appetite for the task" (35).

In fact, since the 1980s, the government has withdrawn, by design or by default, from many social responsibilities and has passed them along to society, or, in China's modern political vocabulary, to the social forces. This is clearly evident in education, economic development, disaster relief and social welfare services, where non-governmental institutions have played an increasingly important role. The first area opened by the government to society and the private sector was education. Ten years of Cultural Revolution dealt a devastating blow to education, scientific research, and all kinds of cultural domains, and tens of millions of students lost educational opportunities. Even in 1987, after 10 years of reform, 25.1 percent of the Chinese population remained illiterate or semi-literate, and only 1.4 percent of China's total work force had a college education (Guan 1989: 1).

Intellectuals as a group suffered manifold ordeals in the waves of political movements since the CCP took national power in 1949, and all their associations were eventually controlled, if not eliminated, by the government. Right after the Cultural Revolution, however, the government saw the desperate need for rejuvenating education and science, and thus strongly encouraged scholarly associations. As a consequence, scholarly associations made the fastest growth among all types of NGOs in the late 1970s and 1980s (Ma 1999: 310–12). They played an active and important role in restoring social status to intellectuals, promoting academic conferences and research, and, ultimately, fostering the development of higher education.

The education crisis continued through the 1980s and 1990s, especially in the impoverished rural regions. One reason was the depressingly low investment in education by the government. From 1949 to the late 1980s, the state investment in education hovered around 2 percent. By comparison, according to studies by the UN and the International Monetary Fund, countries at a similar level of development and with $300 GNP per capita invested 3.3 percent (Min and Li 1995: 142–3). When the state did not have the resources or refused to put its resources into education, the state monopoly of education was bound to break. Until the eve of the establishment of the CCP regime in 1949, private higher education was a crucial part of China's modernization, and private universities accounted for over 40 percent of all universities in China. In 1952, over 1,400 private middle and high schools remained nationwide. However, during the 1950s all universities were nationalized and placed under tight state control. By 1965, the state and state-owned institutions ran almost all urban secondary schools, yet left education in rural areas to society (Zou 1989: 52, 58). When the government finally restarted higher education in 1977 after ten years of suppression, there were not enough universities to enroll the students who had graduated from high school during the Cultural Revolution.

Under enormous pressure from society, in the early 1980s the government began to call for "mobilizing all societal resources for education," thus opening education to the private sector. When the People's Congress revised the Constitution in 1982, it added the following sentence: "The state encourages enterprises of collective ownership, state enterprises and non-commercial institutions, and other social forces to run all kinds of educational institutions according to the law." Since the 1980s, more and more educational, academic, and cultural institutions have emerged outside of the state system. By the early 1990s, in Beijing alone, more than eleven hundred non-state owned schools and colleges attracted thousands of students, including 21,500 students at the college level (Chen Jixia 1993: 19–20). A 1996 count showed 21,800 private secondary schools established nationwide (Wong et al. 1996: 263).

As the proportion of the government fiscal income in the GDP was shrinking, especially during the first two decades of reform (Wang 2003: 31–3), the government turned increasingly to private resources for social welfare and disaster relief. In comparison to the rapid economic growth, the government's expenditures on social welfare lagged far behind. From 1978 to 1998, the GNP increased 21.53 times, and GDP per capita increased 16.88 times. Meanwhile, the increase in governmental social welfare and relief funds only rose by 7.64 times (DCSNBS 1999: 3, 17). Against this background, the government organized an impressive number of foundations to generate domestic and international donations for disaster relief, economic development, and social services. The China Teenagers' and Children Foundation (CTCF), headed by a former vice-premier, was the first of its kind in the PRC, and by 1996 the government had organized 73 national foundations (DNFI 1996). By 2003, the total number of foundations nationwide had climbed to 1,268 (NBS 2003: 159). Foundations have become important mechanisms for attracting private money, and, to a great extent, the government has monopolized such channels. Prior to the 2004 Regulations of Foundations, the government did not allow private enterprises or individuals to establish private foundations.[2] Even in the 2004 Regulations, private foundations are categorized as non-public fundraising institutions (*fei gongmuxing jijinhui*) and are not allowed to raise funds in public (CSC 2004).

These foundations, especially those directly devoted to economic and social development, have greatly helped the government. For example, when the China Foundation for Poverty Alleviation (CFPA) was founded in 1989, the government gave it 100,000 Renmin Bi (RMB) (equivalent US$ 25,000 based on the 1980s exchange rate) as an opening endowment. From 1993 to 1996, the CFPA attracted 94 million RMB (equivalent US$11.8 million based on the 1990s exchange rate) of monetary and material donations, and its total capital in 1996 reached 126 million RMB (Yang 1996: 22). The government's contribution to poverty alleviation was 4 billion RMB in 1989 and 15 billion RMB in 1996. By comparison, from 1993 to 2000 NGOs poured at least 30 billion RMB into the same cause (*People's Daily*, June 11, 2001). Another study suggests that NGOs raised 18 to 28 percent of the total funds spent on poverty alleviation in the second half of the 1990s (Saich 2003). The CTCF raised 200 million RMB in 2002, the largest amount in that year among all foundations (CDB 2003, no. 14: 2). By 2002, 83 national foundations had been established with 3 billion RMB in hand, and 2 billion went to all kinds of programs, governmental or NGOs, for public goods (CYDF 2004).

Also to lend support to the government, fundraising institutions such as charity federations have been founded around the nation since the 1990s. Yan Mingfu, the former minister of the Ministry of Civil Affairs and after his retirement, the first president of the China Charity Federation (CCF), expressed the government view on guiding NGOs to boost social welfare. Yan said, "Under a market economy, government service provision monopolies of this type begin to disappear. The task of the government is to determine policy, but the actual implementation of policy should become the responsibility of non-government organizations." According to Yan, CCF's primary task is to carry out work handed over by MOCA, such as disaster relief and poverty alleviation. In the flood relief operation of 1998, for example, CCF raised $43.4 million in cash donations and over $82.5 million in donations in kind (CDB 1999a: 21). From its birth to 2002, CCF has received donations of more than 1.3 billion RMB and has used the money mainly to address natural disasters and poverty (*Beijing Youth Daily*, November 17, 2003). In 1999, the ratio of state to domestic/overseas private donations for disaster relief was 1: 0.37 (Liao 2000: 19). In addition, the first public donation law was passed in 1999 to further facilitate the flow of private funds (LD 1999).

In the late 1990s, facing the enormous social problems brought about by high unemployment, an aging society, and the lack of a comprehensive system of social and health insurance, the government further de-monopolized social welfare by launching a vigorous campaign entitled "societalizing social welfare". The government asked society and the private sector, for profit or non-profit, to share in the effort to provide all kinds of social services, thereby again expanding the scope of NGO activities. In 1998, MOCA selected thirteen large and mid-sized cities, including Shanghai, Guanzhou, and Wenzhou, for an experiment in welfare reform. In 2000, 11 state ministries announced a joint effort: a five-year plan to establish a social welfare system comprising of state-, privately- and community-owned service institutions (*People's Daily*, April 13, 2000: 4, 10).

One major problem, among others, is the vast elderly population and the lack of sufficient social welfare. By 2000, the population of Chinese people over 60 years old had reached 132 million, and this number increases at a yearly rate of 3.2 percent (*People's Daily*, March 18, 2002: 4). The growth in the elderly population has produced strong pressure for better health care, improved living standards, and more nursing home facilities. The new policy has resulted in a rapid increase in the numbers of private nursing homes and hospitals, both for profit and non-profit. According to official statistics, in 2000, among 41,489 social welfare institutions nationwide, only 2,561 were run by the government (NBS 2000: 762). In 2003, 90 percent of 36,000 nursing homes nationwide were non-state-owned (Cai 2003: 21). In some provinces, the non-state investments in social welfare have exceeded the provincial governments' (Li Xiaoji 2000: 10).

No statistics show what percentage of the non-state-run social services is non-profit; moreover, in the social service arena the line between for profit and non-profit is blurred. The government's foremost concern is to let society share the burden. Interestingly, to the NGOs, the most significant policy change is that the state is no longer the sole player in education, social

"Small government, big society"   53

welfare and relief. The price the CCP government pays by passing responsibility to NGOs is to lessen its power over society.

From departmental management to macro-management: trade associations as intermediaries between the state and enterprises

As Chapter 5 will elaborate, trade associations are among the most numerous and rapidly growing NGOs since the 1990s, a direct result of economic reforms and governmental support. In fact, the development of trade associations was a key step in China's economic structural and managerial reforms. The core reform was to transform the state's total control of industrial and trade management, which most Chinese economists called "departmental management (*bumen guanli*)," into a model where the state macro-manages with trade associations serving as intermediaries between the state and enterprises (Rong 1996).

Briefly, in the 1950s and 1960s the Chinese state eventually nationalized all industries and trades. On the eve of Deng Xiaoping's economic reforms in 1978, China's non-state-controlled economy represented only 1 percent of the GNP. In the state-planned economy, the state's complete control was accomplished via a multi-tier, top-down managerial structure that directed all resources, production, and distribution. Under the State Council, a few dozen national industrial departments stood at the top, while local industrial bureaus at the county and township levels occupied the lowest rungs. The incurable problem with this type of management was that the strict top-down control of every step of industrial production and product distribution left enterprises with very limited authority over their business. "Management by official orders, vertical top-down control, and the separation of trades from each other were the major characteristics of this type of management" (Rong: 49). State control extended beyond the domain of production: personnel and employee wages and benefits were also subject to governmental regulation. In Shanghai, the biggest industrial and trade center in China, for example, "before the reforms, every factory in the city needed the approval of one official in the Shanghai Bureau of Labor if they wanted to hire a new worker."[3]

The state's tight control over industry and trade seriously hampered the ability of enterprises to survive in a market economy. By 1996, twenty years after the first move towards openness, the state-owned enterprises still had not won the most arduous reform battle: their separation from the state and adjustment to the market. These enterprises were deeply in debt, and in 1995 the capital debt rate among state-owned national enterprises was 80 percent, and the rate reached 100 percent among some small- to medium-sized local enterprises (Liu *et al.* 1996: 36, 42). One major drawback of state-owned businesses was an unsuccessful effort to reform departmental management. Despite years of government promises, the allocation of managerial power to enterprises was far from complete. Indeed, industrial bureaus from the top echelon to the local level still had the ability to reclaim power given to the enterprises. A research report in 1996 on national development concluded that, "the lagging administrative reform and the persistent unity of the state and enterprises have become the biggest obstacles in enterprise reform. It has prevented enterprises from becoming autonomous corporate entities and the mainstay of the market" (Wong et al. 1996: 151).

Another serious problem of the old managerial system was its rigid separation of business management by category. Numerous managerial departments and bureaus were set up to direct enterprises according to their business type, ownership (state-owned or collective-owned), and locality (national, provincial, county, or district) (Chen and Xu 1999: 2). This system divided industries into *"tiaotiao"* (lines along business categories or ownership) and *"kuaikuai"* (localities). Often, the same industry or trade was managed by different bureaus because of their different *tiaotiao* or *kuaikuai*, and one enterprise might have more than one "mother-in-law." Repeated and inconsistent regulations and administrative directives made state-owned businesses the least ready for a market economy.

Since the 1980s, however, the rapid growth of all types of non-state-owned enterprises has become the most vibrant sector of China's economy. By 1992, the output value of the non-state-owned economy exceeded that of the state-owned (Cheng 2000: 67). Tables 2.1 and 2.2 indicate the changes in the overall proportions of state-owned and non-state-owned businesses in China since the reforms.[4] By 1996, the latter employed over 40 percent of the total urban working population (Liu 1999: 13). The increasing diversity and multiplication of businesses and trades have completely erased the boundaries of the official classifications on business type, ownership, or location; the

Table 2.1 The industrial GNP (%) divided by ownership

Year	State	Collective	Individual	Others
1985	64.9	32.1	1.8	1.2
1990	54.6	35.6	5.4	4.4
1997	26.5	40.5	15.9	17.0

Source: NBS 1998b: 318

Table 2.2 The development of individually owned businesses

Year	Households (thousand)	Number of people (thousand)	Business value (billion RMB)
1993	17,669.9	29,393	330.92
1994	21,866	33,759	421.14
1995	25,285	46,139	897.25
1996	27,037	50,171	1,155.42

Source: Liu 1999: 13

new enterprises have literally disabled the foundation of departmental management. As the old managerial bureaus did not cover private businesses, the latter therefore operated with scant supervision. For example, in 1995, only 21.9 percent of the textile factories in Shanghai were under the management of the Shanghai Textile Bureau, and only 1 percent in the plastics business (Chen and Xu 1999: 8).

The fast-growing privatization of the economy has created an enormous and urgent need for marketing, technical information, and professional assistance, as well as for regulatory and arbitration mechanisms. On the one hand, traditional departmental management was not able to reach out to these non-state-owned businesses, nor could it provide them with services or supervise their operations. On the other hand, under the state-planned economy, no alternative non-governmental intermediate institutions were available to assist the market in acting as an "invisible hand" to readjust the economy. As the state gradually withdrew its control of the economy and as private businesses grew beyond state control, the insufficiency of macro-management and the absence of intermediate managerial mechanisms resulted in chaotic conditions. China's leading official newspaper, *People's Daily*, states,

> In recent years, the un-planned and repetitive constructions have caused serious overproductions in many industries, and productions in market much exceed the purchasing ability. Consequently, enterprises are increasing their competitiveness by cutting prices; adverse competition often leads to high debt, cripples the efficiency of businesses, and interrupts orderly market competition. This poses a severe problem for the economy to operate normally.
> (*People's Daily*, September 11, 1998: 2)

Lü Dong, a former high official and then the director of the Chinese Industrial and Economic Association, castigated departmental management and strongly advocated a trade management based on a non-governmental intermediary – trade associations. Lü explained the stubborn complexity of the problem:

> After several institutional reforms ... our current industrial managerial system still has not been able to break the departmental management model. The functions of the government and enterprises are misallocated; the government has not done a good job in things it should administer, but interferes and controls matters that should belong to enterprises ... Manmade departments are separating objective connections of social production, and thus resources cannot circulate rationally; remaining capital flows with difficulty across distances and departments. The structural readjustment of production has become awfully hard because of the respective interests involved. Since the management of each

department can only cover a narrow proportion of enterprises within the system ... the macro-plan of trade development has become almost impossible. Incredible amounts of repetitive production, construction, and imports have reoccurred after being prohibited many times. The lack of trade associational management has caused disorderly and suicidal competition, while forgery and poor quality products have run wild.

(Lü 1999: 18–25)

Lü's speech was later circulated among and approved by the top leaders in the State Council. After a seesaw of many managerial institutional reforms, the Chinese government finally adopted a trade-oriented management. This policy made the trade associations, chambers of commerce, and other economic intermediary institutions separated from the state and beholden to serve both their constituents and the government. Historically, private economic organizations prior to the establishment of the People's Republic in 1949, as Chapter 1 discussed, were numerous and influential. Even in the early 1950s, many trade associations were still active. When private organizations were largely eliminated or replaced by governmentally controlled federations in the mid-1950s, trade associations, both the name and the concept, persisted under the CCP's regime (ACFIC 1996). Therefore, it is understandable that when China's economy headed to privatization and marketization, the government turned to chambers of commerce and trade associations to mediate industrial and trade management. It was within this broad context that all types of trade associations flourished in the 1990s (Chapter 5).

Downsizing the government, expanding the social organizations

Parallel with and related to the transformation of departmental management, another reason behind the promotion of trade associations as well as other SOs has been the urgent and mounting pressure to downsize the administrative apparatus. During the Cultural Revolution, the State Council was reduced to 32 ministries and departments, but by 1981, this number had rebounded to over a hundred. From 1979 to 1989, the government cadres doubled from 2,791,200 to 5,435,000 (Zhang, G. 1999: 226–9). Before the economic reforms, government expenditures totaled 48 billion RMB in 1978. By 1990, this figure had increased to 225 billion RMB and by 1998 to 948 billion RMB (DCSNBS 1999: 6). In 1995, the party and the government's cadres represented 32 percent of total employees on the state payroll at a cost of 470 billion RMB in salaries and benefits (Zhang Zuye 1999: 67). These numbers include only officials in urban areas; if the salaries of cadres in rural areas are added, then 20 percent of the gross national product went to support the government (Zhang, Z.: 67). It must be noted that these numbers do not reflect the remarkable amounts of gray incomes, embezzlement, and bribery that commonly occur (He, Q. 1997: 9, 151–5). As cited earlier, the government's revenue as a portion of total GDP decreased during the first two decades of reforms, and thus the huge expenditure on the administrative body imposed an unbearable burden.

In addition to consuming a disproportionate share of government income, the unwieldy and oversized administration cannot function efficiently and effectively. In fact, the immense bureaucracy and its institutions, riddled with all kinds of corruption among officials, had, to use Deng Xiaoping's words, "reached the situation that one can no longer tolerate" (Deng 1993: 287). And since Deng Xiaoping's time the bureaucracy has become even more maddening and corrupt, epitomized in the extreme case of a construction project in a medium-sized city that struggled for over three years to obtain approval and had to acquire 130 official stamps in the process (Zhang, G. 1999: 227). When the government's role in the economy shifted from total control to macro-regulation, eventually a large proportion of the managerial body would have to be cut.

Downsizing the administration, however, has proved to be a complicated and tricky matter, with the most difficult part being how to place the party cadres and governmental employees and redistribute political and personal interests. The reform of the government apparatus has not been well planned, with uneven and sometimes contradictory changes that see some departments expand while others cut employees and budgets. The whole process has involved a reallocation of political and economic interests between the national and local governments, as well as between different departments. In most cases, the redistribution is governed less by logic than by the personal interests of officials and governmental employees and their relations to powerful figures. Under China's current political culture, the status of office holder means not only a decent income, benefits, and political privilege, but also power, fame, and the opportunity to receive a sometimes stunning amount of gray or even illegal income. Consequently, the downsizing has become extremely complicated, and attempts at reform have resulted in oscillations between streamlining and expansion.

Beginning in the early 1980s, the government initiated four major institutional reforms (1982, 1988, 1993 and 1998) in an attempt to downsize the administrative body. For example, in the round of administrative reforms in 1991–93, the ministries and bureaus within the State Council were trimmed from over 100 to 59, and the number of staff members fell by 20 percent (Pu 1993: 417). Among the casualties were the Ministries of Textile Industry and Light Industry that were transformed into federations. During this downsizing, the number of employees in the Federation of Textile Industries was cut by 50 percent. Officials within the two federations complained that their former ministries were too weak to stand up against the State Council's decisions on reforms.[5] The largest downsizing took place in 1998, when Zhu Rongji was the premier, as two million governmental employees nationwide left their positions. For purposes of political stability, these people were promised their usual salaries and benefits (Lin 1998: 45–9). Yet, the most difficult problem was where to relocate them.

Since downsizing focused mainly on economic managerial departments, as Chapter 5 discusses, the transfer of an entire tier of industrial bureaus, or at least a large number of them, to non-governmental intermediaries would certainly help the government cope with the relocation of the dismissed employees. Thus, from the very beginning, the promotion of trade associations has been entangled with administrative reforms; the government aimed to create a market-oriented non-governmental intermediary while simultaneously reducing the administrative body. At the same time, other types of SOs, especially GONGOs, also shared the burden of "hiring" those who lost their official positions during the downsizing. For example, the China Social Workers' Association (CSWA) is under the supervision of the Ministry of Civil Affairs (MOCA). From its establishment in 1991 to 2001, MOCA has appointed the CSWA's executive committee three times, and all of these appointments were to relocate MOCA's retired officials or those who lost their positions during the downsizing (He 2002: 54–5). A study of the relation between downsizing of government apparatus and growth of social organizations concludes that the decrease in numbers of governmental officials paralleled the increase of SOs (Wang et al. 2001: 83).

Community construction: for social services and social control

In general, community-based grassroots organizations are the most vibrant and dynamic component in civil society. Chinese did not have a word for "community"; the current social meaning of community was imported from the United States in the late 1980s.[6] The concept *"shequ"* (community) first appeared in official vocabulary in 1986 when MOCA advocated a community service campaign.[7] In 1991, Cui Naifu, then the minister of MOCA, was the first Chinese official to campaign for "community construction", but not until the mid-1990s did the government start to realize the importance of community development to China's social progress and stability. In 1996, Jiang Zemin called for vigorously strengthening community construction, and two years later community construction was formally listed in the State Council's agenda of institutional reform. A new governmental bureau, the Bureau of Local Government and Community Construction, was established to carry out the campaign (Xu and Chen 2002: 11–15).

Several economic, social, and political factors have influenced the government's commitment to community development. To begin, the decline and transformation of the PRC's "work unit" (*danwei*) has had a profound effect on China's urban social welfare system. Originating in the economic, social, and cultural institutions that served the Red Army bases during the CCP's revolution (Lu 1989: 71–2), the *danwei* persisted after the establishment of the PRC as "an enclosed, multifunctional and self-sufficient entity ... the most basic collective unit in the Chinese political and social order" (Dittmer and Lü: 2000: 185). Before the reforms, all state-owned enterprises (SOEs)

"Small government, big society" 59

belonged to such a system. A *danwei*, such as a factory, a store, or a school, was so much more than an economic entity; rather, it constituted a small society in urban China. The complexity of the work unit "derived from the fact that the *danwei* was the unit for the delivery of a variety of services and also for the exercise of political control" (Naughton 1997: 181). On the one hand, the CCP's multi-tiered organizations penetrated to the smallest work groups, and weekly meetings to study the party's and government's documents were mandatory. On the other hand, the employees received all their benefits and services from the *danwei*, from housing, health care, and retirement pensions to movie tickets, shower house tickets, and coupons to buy scarce but necessary items such as furniture and bicycles. All important social occasions, from childbirth to marriage to funeral, fell under the aegis of the *danwei*.

Thus, while the party-state tightly controlled the working people in the SOEs via *danwei*, it also redistributed resources through *danwei*. Under such a political–economic–social system, the traditional Chinese social networks and along organizations the lines of clan, trade, profession, religion, and region entirely disappeared. The ethics of charity and mutual help also withered, and a wealth of social capital was lost as the old groups faded. As a consequence, the social functions removed from their old contexts and taken over by *danwei* became a tremendous burden for the SOEs. A study shows that China's SOE managers had to spend 26 percent of their time on personnel and welfare, while only 4 percent of their time was put toward supply and marketing (Naughton 1997).

The economic reforms that commenced in 1978 are causing dramatic changes in the *danwei* system. For instance, in order to survive competition in a market economy, the SOEs have had to cast off the "cradle-to-grave welfare provision." When the SOEs no longer run kindergartens, schools, clinics, or dining halls, and when they no longer see as their responsibility the tasks of caring for retirees and injured workers, who or what institutions are going to take over? The need to continue these kinds of social service is one of the most urgent reasons behind the government's promotion of community construction. An increasing proportion of welfare provision is now passing from SOEs and the government to the community-based service providers. The rapid upsurge of non-governmental service providers in communities, both for profit or non-profit, has created a new landscape in China's urban life (Chapter 3).

It is true that *danwei* survived the reforms, and they continue to have an important role in China (Naughton: 169). However, the growth of the open market and the shifting responsibility for housing, health care, and social security concerns have in many ways altered the urban social structure and greatly undermined the government's control over *danweiren* (people in *danwei*), who are, in fact, becoming *shehuiren* (society people). Now, workers in SOEs face a more fluid situation and can be outspoken because the factors that tied them to the *danwei*, such as job security, housing, and health care, are not so pressing.

Other even more urgent and serious social issues challenge, such as the number of rural workers who continue to migrate to the cities, the existing system of social welfare and social control. According to a 1998 statistic, this number reached 44.2 million, equal to 9.5 percent of the rural labor population (CML 1999: 128). The migration phenomenon has created extreme demands on municipal governments to furnish new arrivals with some kind of housing, health care, and education, and to protect these people's basic rights. Yet, in the past two decades, the rural migrants have received very limited services and benefits from the government. For instance, rural people have a difficult time getting their children accepted by schools that only admit students in their districts with urban *hukou* (a special city residential ID issued by the government). In another example, Zhengjiang village, a byword for the streets in Beijing home to migrants from Zhengjiang, has become notorious as a dangerous and disorderly place, where residents survive in poverty and filth (Xiang 2000: 5). In general, these people have no protection for their rights (Hu 2002: 77).

In addition to the floating population of rural migrants, the government also faces a dangerously high unemployment rate. Between 1996 and 2001, SOE employment fell by 27.9 percent, or 31.4 million jobs, and employment in enterprises of urban collective ownership fell by 50.2 percent, or 15 million jobs. Even with the numerous new jobs created by private businesses and foreign investments, in 1999 the urban unemployment rate was 8.2 percent. A large proportion of the 15.1 million unemployed is attributable to the economic structural reforms (Hu: 45–6). Unemployment has caused serious social instability, in addition to its direct economic consequences. One effect has been an increase in all kinds of litigation; labor disputes alone shot up to 120,000 (NBS 2000: 750–1). The 1999 statistics also show that criminal cases reached a historical high in that year, and among 2.25 million recorded cases, 64 percent were for robbery (Hu: 60).

In the past, besides the *danwei* system, the government relied on residents' committees (RCs), the governmental agencies at the lowest level, to control people outside of SOEs. Under the new conditions, with a large mobile population, high unemployment, and *danweiren* becoming *shehuiren*, the old RC system can no longer exercise its social control function. In 2000, MOCA issued a detailed document on community construction that laid out the goals, guidelines, and contents of reform, aiming at transforming the RC system to community self-governance. To further encourage community-based service providers and grassroots organizations to grow, MOCA exceptionally reduced the registration requirements for those organizations. For example, the operating fund for establishing a local NGO is 30,000 RMB, reduced to 5,000 for community-based organizations. The supervision institutions should be, according to general policy, governmental institutions in the respective professions. However, because it is almost impossible for community organizations to find such mothers-in-law, MOCA allows the RCs to supervise these organizations.[8]

As new communities develop, the party-state is hoping that they will eventually provide a wide range of vital services: health care, child and elderly care, community security, job training and relocation, and environmental protection as well as all cultural and entertainment activities. Meanwhile, these services will no doubt create many jobs for the community residents. According to an investigation by the Ministry of Social Security, community services in large or medium cities nationwide may provide 15 million jobs, giving the government reason to feel optimistic (Ren and Chen 1995). While the government has appropriated funds from the social welfare budget for community construction, the bulk of anticipated services and jobs actually fall on the shoulders of private institutions and community committees. Consequently, community construction has opened vast opportunities for the grassroots NGOs.

Thus, community development, together with the societalization of welfare services and administrative/managerial reforms, constitutes the Chinese government's strategy of "small government, big society." To implement all of these reform steps, the government has given space, power, and responsibility to society and the private sector.

Major features of China's registration-regulation of NGOs since the late 1970s

The official management of NGOs in China is in fact a registration-regulation; in other words, the government regulates NGOs mainly through a registration process. This section discusses the major features of this registration-regulation chronologically. The establishment of the People's Republic of China in 1949 crowned the Chinese Communist Party's successful seizure of national power. From that date, the CCP government's policy towards non-governmental organizations can be roughly divided into three major periods: (1) nationalization of private institutions and founding of governmentally controlled "non-governmental" organizations, from 1949 to 1966; (2) the Cultural Revolution period from 1966 to 1976 when all formally established "non-governmental" organizations ceased operation; (3) the reform period during which a comprehensive regulatory system over NGOs became established. This section focuses mainly on the third period.

As discussed in the last chapter, associations and organizations that engaged in political, social, or cultural activities outside of state control had deep roots prior to the PRC, and gentry-merchants' and intellectual associations, among others, were the most dynamic local political reform forces. Soon after 1949, China's party-state harshly suppressed most independent organizations, including political organizations and religious groups. In 1950 the government issued its first regulation on SOs, and accordingly all private organizations had to register with the Minister of

Internal Affairs or its provincial branches (CSC 1950). Only dozens of national organizations, mostly academic associations, survived the registration process; and some high-profile political organizations survived by being categorized by the government as "democratic parties." Eventually, these organizations and parties lost their independence and no longer functioned autonomously in their respective fields.

From 1956, when the Ministry of Internal Affairs was reorganized, there was no single governmental ministry in charge of registration of SOs, and, instead, newly established organizations were under the management of respective governmental departments according to their professional missions. This situation lasted until 1989 when the Division of Social Organizations (DSO) under the Ministry of Civil Affairs (MOCA) was established to register SOs. Above all, the SOs of all kinds were under the strict control of the CCP government and literally became a part of the government apparatus. The leaders of SOs were often governmental officials, and their staff were on the government payroll. From the organizations' political status to their decision-making and governance, these "non-governmental organizations" operated similarly to any governmental institution.

Then, the Cultural Revolution stirred social turmoil and overturned the institutional order. During that decade (1966–76), countless "revolutionary mass organizations", such as the Red Guards swept the country. These groups could not at all be considered as NGOs in the terms used in this study; they functioned as political tools of Mao Zedong's revolution. Meanwhile, formally established SOs were all either paralyzed or disbanded, and no new SOs were formed.

Two years after the end of the Cultural Revolution, Deng Xiaoping initiated a period of economic reform; political control relaxed and NGOs rapidly increased. From then to the present, official policy regarding NGOs has gone through two distinct stages. From 1978 to the eve of the 1989 students' democratic movement, the government started to allow associative activities outside of the state system. The MOCA was not assigned to take charge of SOs until 1989. The unprecedented flourishing of student associations during the 1980s provided the real dynamic behind the 1989 democratic movement (Gold 1990a: 18–31). This all occurred so fast that Chinese officials not only fell in with this social change but also failed to comprehend the profound challenges the new associations could pose, as evidenced in the absence of both a regulatory policy and an official bureau responsible for registering SOs. During this period, the founding of SOs was almost unregulated. Any government bureau or organization, or even a social organization, could approve new organizations and place them under supervision. The "offspring" of SOs sometimes multiplied to the fifth generation. Later, the government referred regretfully to this time as "a chaotic period when there was no rule to follow and no person in charge" (Chen 1997: 25, 39).

"Small government, big society" 63

At the national level

The State Council ─────────────┐

↓

The Ministry of Civil Affairs (MOCA)

↓

The Bureau of Management of NGOs[2]

At the local level

Provincial and Municipal People's government

↓

The Bureau of Civil Affairs (BOCA)[1]

↓

The Division of Social Organizations

↓

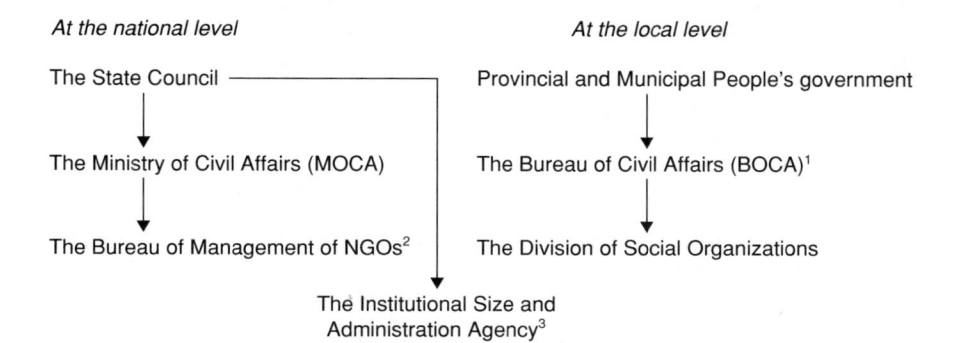

The Institutional Size and Administration Agency[3]

Figure 2.1 The official administrative structure over the NGOs.
Notes
1 The lowest level bureau of civil society is at the county level.
2 The original name of this agency is Division of Social Organizations, and it was not just renamed; the rank of new agency was also elevated from a division (*chu*) to bureau (*ju*).
3 This agency is in charge of the organizational size and management of those organizations that are exempted from registration with MOCA, such as the people's organizations.

The dramatic burst of political energy from organizations of students, workers, and city residents during the 1989 democratic movement demonstrated the enormous potential of organized groups in China's political life, and this event forced the CCP government to rethink its NGO policy. During the very heat of the 1989 movement, the Division of Social Organizations (DSO) was formed within MOCA to oversee NGO activities, and it launched the official regulatory system over the NGOs (Figure 2.1). From 1988 on, many official documents were issued that addressed NGO management; and based on these, a regulatory system of NGOs gradually became established (Table 2.3). The development of the NGO policy points to a stricter and more comprehensive regulatory system.

In 1996, facing the rapid growth of SOs and the political consequences of this new development, Jiang Zemin, then the chairman of the CCP, convened a special meeting of the Standing Committee of the CCP's Politburo to discuss strengthening NGO management, the first such meeting in CCP history devoted to NGOs.[9] This meeting resulted in a new series of comprehensive official regulatory documents more detailed and confining than the 1989 system. Since the early 2000s, the government has continued to revise the existing regulations. The State Council passed a new Regulations of Foundations in 2004, and a revised regulation of SOs is expected soon.[10] Yet, as will be discussed, the 2004 Regulations of Foundations was a bitter disappointment to the NGOs, Chinese or international, that had been pushing the government to provide a better environment for NGO growth. The following discussion will focus on certain distinctive and controversial issues concerning China's current official NGO policy.

64　*"Small government, big society"*

Table 2.3 Relevant official documents on NGOs in the People's Republic of China

Year	English name	Chinese name	Status
1950	Temporary Regulations of Social Organizations Registration	shehui tuanti dengji zanxing banfa	annulled
1950	PRC Law of Trade Unions	zhonghua renmin gongheguo gonghui fa	annulled
1988	Regulations for Foundations	jijinhui guanli banfa	annulled
1989	Temporary Regulations on Foreign Chambers of Commerce	waiguo shanghui guanli zanxing guiding	In effect
1989	Regulations for Registration and Management of SOs	shehui tuanti dengji guanli tiaoli	annulled
1992	PRC Law of Trade Unions	zhonghua renmin gongheguo gonghui fa	in effect
1998	Regulations for Registration and Management of SOs	shehui tuanti dengji guanli tiaoli	in effect
1998	Temporary Regulations for Registration and Management of NGNCEs	minban fei qiye danwei dengji guanli zanxing tiaoli	in effect
2004	Regulations on the Management of Foundations	Jijinhui guanli tiaoli	In effect

The most contested NGO regulation in China is the dual registration, summarized as "registration by professions, dual responsibility and multi-tier management." Such a practice can be traced back to the 1950 regulation that required the approval of a supervisory institution prior to an organization's registration.[11] Under current policy, NGOs are obligated to register with the Ministry of Civil Affairs or local bureaus of civil affairs; yet to do so a social organization or non-governmental and non-profit enterprise must have the approval of its professional supervisory agency (*yewu zhuguan danwei*), usually a governmental institution or GONGO. NGO leaders refer to these supervisory agencies in vivid language as "mothers-in-law" because they exercise day-to-day oversight. Strict rules determine what types of organizations or governmental departments can be "mothers-in-law"; they have to be in a similar professional field and at the same administrative level as the organization seeking a sponsor. For example, a national social organization engaging in women's affairs should have the All-China Women's Federation as its mother-in-law, whereas an environmental organization in Yunnan Province would likely have the Yunnan Provincial Environmental Bureau as its supervising institution. Many GONGOs in fact have two mothers-in-law: besides "*yewu zhuguan danwei*," they also have a "*guakao danwei*" that provides them with operating budgets and staff benefits.

From the government's point of view, the mother-in-law agencies help the government to control NGOs politically and legally, because the MOCA and the local bureaus do not have the capacity to oversee NGO operations.

"Small government, big society" 65

One official study argues that under China's unique historical context, the mothers-in-law help SOs raise their social status and gain public trust. Thus, the supervisory institutions are necessary because China's legal system is not sufficient to regulate and discipline private organizations that lack self-disciplinary mechanisms. The dual registration restrains the overly rapid growth of NGOs and fosters communication between the government and NGOs (Chen 2003: 289–92).[12] During the revision of the Regulations of Foundations, some foundations and NGO leaders were invited to exchange their opinions with MOCA officials. The NGO people had pushed hard to abolish the mother-in-law practice, and to a point they thought that they had succeeded.[13] Nonetheless, the 2004 Regulations of Foundations continued dual registration. Moreover, a high official in the Bureau of Management of NGOs clearly informed me that dual registration would continue into the future.[14] Some Chinese officials also emphasized that China is not the only country to use dual registration, and thus China's policy appears reasonable.[15]

The dual registration system and the "mother-in-law" practice, however, are problematic in many ways. Legally, the question is whether a mother-in-law can be held accountable for its NGO's actions. According to the most recent registration document (1998), all registered SOs must be corporate entities (*faren tuanti*); thus they are legally accountable for all their actions. The mothers-in-law, on the other hand, are beholden to the government should any political problem occur in a social organization. This has become the most obvious reason why so many organizations cannot find a mother-in-law for themselves: no governmental agencies want to take on such a political liability. Not uncommonly, small independent NGOs register as *for-profit* business firms because they cannot find a "mother-in-law." Ge Yunsong, a Chinese legal expert, criticizes the absence of a legal basis for such a practice. He argues that since the government requires NGOs to obtain a supervisory agency, legally the latter is obliged to take on responsibility. However, in practice, not only has the matter depended completely on the will of the governmental agencies, but the mothers-in-law also have the power to end supervisory duty at any time (Ge 2003: 253–5).

The 2004 Regulations of Foundations allows foreign foundations, for the first time in the history of PRC, to register in China for a representative office (CSC 2004). However, like their Chinese counterparts, foreign foundations are also required to have a Chinese mother-in-law. When the Ford Foundation opened its office in Beijing in 1988, the China Academy of Social Science became the host institution (*jiedai danwei*) to which the Foundation reports each year. Yet, that was a special arrangement approved by top CCP leaders.[16] How easy is it for foreign foundations generally, and eventually other types of international NGOs, to locate a Chinese mother-in-law? This is a tricky matter. While Chinese governmental organizations are definitely aware of the political risks involved in supervising a foreign organization, benefits such as overhead charges and grants from the foreign foundations can be very attractive.[17] The Chinese government is also willing to help foreign organizations should any hurdle occur during their registration process.[18]

In practice, however, are the governmental agencies really able to guide or supervise their supervisees? In actuality, governmental institutions that choose to play the mother-in-law role vary greatly in how effectively they exercise their supervision. Most mothers-in-law give a free hand to their supervised organizations, as long as they do not make political trouble. For example, the Ministry of Culture and the State Committee of Education have over a hundred non-governmental entities under their supervision, and the offices in charge of the matter do not have enough staff to carry out the work. By contrast, some governmental agencies that supervise only a handful of NGOs do not even have an office allocated to NGO affairs. In either case, the supervision is rather limited.[19]

In the past ten years, aware of the limitation of its actual control over NGOs, the government has resorted to reregistration as a major means to tighten its leash on the NGOs. During each reregistration, many organizations are rejected by MOCA. In the nationwide reregistration of 1991–92, 118,691 organizations applied, but only 89,969 registrations were approved (Zhang 1996: 99). The most recent round started in 1998, and by 2000 the total number of SOs registered nationwide had dropped from 186,956 to 136,841 (NBS 1998a, 2001: 274, 114). The justification of reregistration is that it allows for the elimination of NGOs that are either badly managed or involved in illegal actions.[20] However, according to the 1998 regulations of SOs and non-government and non-commercial enterprises (NGNCEs), MOCA and local Bureaus of Civil Affairs (BOCAs) have the authority to shut down those entities only after problems have occurred. Furthermore, it is the responsibility of judicial institutions to punish illegal activities.[21] There are no legal grounds for the periodic reregistration.

Besides dual registration, another major obstacle for private organizations wishing to register is the high bar set for establishing an NGO. According to the 1998 Regulations of Registration of Social Organizations, for example, SOs must be corporate entities, and they must have over 50 members (or 30 institutional members) as well as 100,000 RMB in operating funds for establishing national organizations (or 30,000 RMB for local organizations). Offices and regular staffs are also required to register. As for foundations, the required founding endowment increased from 100,000 RMB in the 1988 regulations to 8,000,000 (for national foundations) in the 2004 regulations. The required endowment is steep even for private foundations: 2,000,000 RMB (CSC 1988, 1998a, 1998b, 2004). These conditions are not at all encouraging to private and small organizations. In fact, many of them are therefore not able to legally exist as NGOs. It is clear that the most significant feature of China's official NGO policy is the use of registration to control the development of NGOs, especially grassroots NGOs.

The dual registration is not the only controversial issue. In contrast to the strict regulations governing registration, current policy leaves ample room for the government to interpret the policy according to the Chinese Communist Party's current agenda or political situation. In other words, the current system is in many ways misleading, and at times official actions rest on incomplete legal authority. For example, current NGO policy is based entirely on executive documents, which do not have approval from the People's Congress. Many rules governing NGOs derive from the speeches of high officials, or from unpublished speeches and documents of which NGO leaders may not be aware. Some experts on Chinese law have pointed out that asking NGOs to follow regulations they do not know about is an unlawful practice (Su *et al.* 1999: 43). On February 26, 1998, the CCP's Central Bureau and the MOCA issued a joint document requiring every NGO with three or more CCP members to establish a party branch to supervise its political behavior. What authority do these party branches have over NGO operations? Unlimited? No legal explanation has ever been offered. Official policy on NGOs varies from time to time, from place to place, and from one type of organization to another. This situation has put the NGOs in a vulnerable position. If the government should suddenly decide to act against the NGOs, nothing can stop it.

Another major feature of the official NGO policy is the "anti-competition" rule. This important revision of the regulations since 1989 prohibits the establishment of any new organization if an organization already exists in the same administrative field and in the same region, which usually is the case. This rule was directed primarily against the 1989 democratic movement when many students and workers formed their own organizations. The government subsequently declared the new organizations illegal based on the prior existence of the All-China Federation of Trade Unions (ACFTU) and All-China Students' Federation. Shocked by the political impact of the Solidarity Trade Union in Poland, the Chinese government was determined to prevent similar events from occurring in China.[22] In 1992, the new Union Law clearly stated that China may establish only one united federation of trade unions (LD 1992). This regulation reveals the crucial nature of the government's control over SOs. While in many respects the government does give these organizations some free rein, politically or ideologically related matters remain in the firm grip of the government.

In a similar example, the 1998 Regulations of Social Organizations bar national organizations from having regional branches. However, a handful of government-controlled people's organizations and mass organizations such as the ACFTU, the Chinese Communist Youth League (CCYL), and the All-China Women's Federation (ACWF) are allowed to do so. For organizations that previously had provincial and local branches, such as the National Writers' Association, MOCA required all branches to become independent organizations and register with their corresponding bureaus of civil affairs. National and local organizations with similar missions and/or in the same fields can only engage in cooperation or exchange, not directional and organizational relations. An explanation for this is that national organizations cannot always be aware of the local branches' actions. Thus, to avoid a confusion of legal responsibilities, national and local organizations should be separately managed. While this may be a reasonable justification, a concern over the potential power of national organizations is no doubt another motive.

Under the new policy, SOs and NGNCEs are entitled to similar NGO status; nevertheless, the state's control over SOs is tighter. Even though the 1998 Regulations stipulate, in their 40 detailed items, very strict principles in registering SOs, many other CCP and MOCA circulars institute additional regulations. For example, a MOCA document requires all SOs' charters to follow a standard model that contains 48 articles. These articles include the nature of the organization, its mission, type, members' responsibilities, managerial structures, governing principles, and financial policy. In addition, organizations need to declare clearly their willingness to follow laws, government policy, social moral standards, and their mother-in-law's supervision as well. In contrast, there is no suggestion in the official registration documents for NGNCEs that these enterprises must adhere to political or moral principles, nor is there any regulation dictating their managerial structures and governance. The NGNCEs are professional institutions or service providers, and not only are they small, but they are also scattered in various professions. At present, their political influence is very limited. Thus, it is not difficult to understand why the government's main concern now is the growth of SOs (DLSC 1999).

Having described problematic aspects of the current official NGO regulations, however, this study does not conclude that government policy is only detrimental to the organizations covered by the regulations. In general, the government has taken a positive view of the entire NGO matter, believing that the state can obtain assistance from societal resources. Reforms have led the state to withdraw from many aspects of China's society, with a consequent change in the political power structure. The above examples indicate clearly that to the government, social organizations and private institutions have become an indispensable part of its attempt to transfer major responsibilities to society. When the reforms are pushing China towards a country rule of law, there is no doubt that it is progress that the government has legalized most of the NGOs and improved their legal environment.

Furthermore, by creating the status of NGNCEs for private non-profit service providers, and by placing both SOs and NGNCEs in a unified regulatory system under the supervision of MOCA, the government has greatly enlarged the scope of entities considered to be NGOs, while simultaneously strengthening its supervision over them. Before 1998, no consistent policy addressed private professional service providers, and they had to register with and accept supervision from a host of administrative departments with various policies. Many even had to register as for-profit entities with the Bureau of Industry and Trade.[23] The 1998 system registered them, for the first time, under a unified status. By doing so, the new policy has created a sense of a united NGO sector with a common legal and political ground. Recently, SOs and NGNCEs have attended the same conferences to discuss policies and issues that concern them all. In 1999, Beijing hosted two international conferences on Chinese NGOs, and the issues discussed proved pertinent to both SOs and NGNCEs.[24] Although the Chinese NGOs are still far from an integrated and independent sector, the new managerial system offers them the opportunity to grow together.

Many NGO activists, Chinese and international, have criticized the 1998 regulations as being too harsh towards the NGOs. It is also true that reregistration does not have a legal foundation. Nevertheless, the new regulations and reregistration have helped the NGOs in certain ways to become healthier. From the outset, quite a number of organizations used their non-profit status to attract private funds but then put the money to personal ends rather than the public good. I was told by a Chinese NGO scholar of a person deeply in debt with his company who, three years later, by operating an NGO not only made a bundle of money but also paid off all his debt.[25] As an official explained, the government aims to prevent the kind of illegal or inappropriate behavior by SOs that has harmed the reputations of NGOs badly since the 1980s.[26] Indeed, the reregistration did eliminate many organizations of this kind. In fact, some NGO leaders I interviewed welcomed the new policy and recognized the necessity to consolidate the NGO sector by strengthening official regulation, even though they knew this would further restrain the autonomy of the NGOs. They were concerned primarily about the long-term development of NGOs and believed that Chinese NGOs had yet to acquire the means for effective self-governance. Thus, ironically, the NGO leaders rationalized the government's intervention in the desire to improve their organizations.

Contradictions in the government's NGO policy

The Chinese government summarizes its official NGO policy as one of "nourishment, development, supervision, regulation" (*peiyu, fazhan, jiandu, guanli*). The officials in charge of NGOs at MOCA believe that the government has been successful in balancing the two sides of the policy, to encourage growth while controlling it.[27] As explained above, the government indeed has many reasons to promote NGOs and let them become self-sufficient. As one MOCA official readily admits, "now it is impossible not to develop NGOs."[28] A review of the official management of NGOs, especially since the late 1980s, however, reveals an increasingly restrictive regulatory system. The inconsistencies and even contradictions in the party-state's attitude towards NGOs in the past two decades have stunted the healthy development of NGOs. Ultimately, the failure of NGOs to grow as much as they might have will impair the government's efforts in social and economic development.

70 *"Small government, big society"*

The most serious inconsistency in the NGO policy is that not all NGOs enjoy the same legal status and corresponding rights (Chapter 3). Moreover, the government continues its political repression of dissident groups and unauthorized religious practice. After the 1989 students' democratic movement, self-organized student clubs or associations on campuses came under strict scrutiny, and faculty members who expressed liberal opinions lost their positions.[29] The party was even more concerned with workers' organizations, however. In the 1990s, when a great number of workers lost their jobs, the CCP leaders worried that the discontent would lead to organized opposition. As described by Marc Blecher, an expert on China's labor condition, the party feared

> the specter that inchoate social protest was showing signs of becoming organized. Unofficial trade unions were forming and, shrewdly, began to engage in legal activities such as running employment services and petitioning the National People's Congress. Even more unsettling to the leadership, intellectuals began working with these organizations, a partnership that resembled the alliance at the heart of Polish Solidarity.
> (Blecher 2000: 35)

Therefore, as mentioned above, China recognizes only authorized trade unions, and official regulations allow only one trade union, usually government-controlled, to be organized in a given industry.

Religious organizations are also subject to government control, whether they are promoting traditional activities of worship and prayer or offering charitable and social services. After the Cultural Revolution, churches and temples reopened, and in the last two decades China's Christian population has grown remarkably. Some studies estimate that currently 13 million Protestants belong to registered churches and another 50 million to house-churches[30] (Marshall 2002: 6). The figure for the Roman Catholic Church is 12 million (Aikman 2002: 8). Faith-based organizations engaged in religious work do not have the legal status of social organizations, however, despite their non-governmental and non-profit nature. They have to register with the State Bureau of Religious Affairs and local agencies, and in early 1996 the government required that all places of worship must register (Blecher: 35). The rapid rise in the numbers of followers of various faiths has caused concern among party leaders. In a meeting of top leaders in the CCP and State Council, Jiang Zemin, then president of the PRC and secretary general of the CCP, made it clear that "religion was so important that the officials both of the State structure and the Party itself should focus very much on working to control it . . . (Aikman: 9)."

The clearest and most notorious instance of religious persecution by the government occurred with the sudden crackdown on the Falun Gong movement in 1998. The sit-in demonstration by Falun Gong members in front of *Zhongnanhai*, the CCP and government leadership compound, shocked the CCP leaders, who immediately denounced the Falun Gong as a cult organization. Interestingly, the CCP was especially "alarmed by the cult's tight, secret society-type organization, which bears some resemblance to that of the underground CCP in the 1930s and 40s" (Zheng 2004: 141). Yet, according to Nick Young, it is Falun Gong's "wide reach among the general population, including Communist Party members, that has alarmed the Party leadership." He argues that the whole Falun Gong affair has thrown the government bureaucracy concerned with non-governmental activities into a state of semi-paralysis (Young, N. 2001: 15). The public displays of dissent by Falun Gong prompted the vigorous suppression of all unauthorized religious groups, and a large number of Falun Gong members were arrested. Since late 1999, the government has destroyed 1,200 churches in one eastern province alone. In 2002, 33 Catholic bishops and priests were known to be imprisoned, under house arrest, or to have disappeared (Young: 8, 10).

Distinct from churches or temples, faith-based non-profit organizations such as the YMCA, YWCA, and Amity Foundation are registered with the civil affairs bureaus as SOs. This type of organization provides social services outside the religious sector. Although the government welcomes their services, these organizations often find themselves restricted in various ways. For example, faith-based organizations such as the YMCA are usually barred from engaging in educational programs for young people, even though educating the young is a cornerstone of their founding mission. Ironically, the Shanghai YMCA, the largest in China, has devoted itself to the elderly. The Luoshan Community Center, operated jointly by the Shanghai YMCA and the local community, has become a great success among non-governmental nursing homes for the elderly; yet, aware of the political sensitivity surrounding Christianity, the YMCA tries not to draw attention to their work.[31]

In comparison with its repression of independent political and religious organizations, however, the government continues to lend full support to government-controlled political organizations, especially the people's organizations and mass organizations. While the next chapter will further discuss the political origins and terminology of these organizations, it is important to indicate here the strikingly different treatment accorded the various types of NGOs. Under the current NGO policy, the people's or mass organizations, such as ACFTU, CCYL, and ACWF, are classified as SOs. However, unlike all other SOs, these two categories of organizations do not register with MOCA, one political privilege among many others. Some of these organizations were the CCP's closest political allies in the early days of the revolution, and they have kept close ties with the party ever since (Chapter 3). Today, these few yet influential organizations continue to deliver CCP policy, and their prestigious status represents the reach of the party into society.

Official policy towards people's and mass organizations has changed little over the years, although the conditions of non-governmental organizations have altered tremendously since the 1980s. In its effort to trim a bloated bureaucracy, in recent years the government has pushed previously government-funded organizations to become self-sufficient.[32] However, the government still furnishes full financial and personnel support to its favored organizations (COSC 1996). Most importantly, the leaders of these organizations continue to be high-ranking officials in the party and the state structure. For example, the rank of president of ACFTU, CCYL, or ACWF is equivalent to vice-premier, and sometimes these leaders are members of the Standing Committee of the CCP Politburo. Since 1949, almost all presidents of the ACFTU have been members of the CCP Politburo. Both Hu Yaobang, CCP's secretary general during the 1980s and Hu Jintao, the current President of the PRC and CCP secretary general, were heads of CCYL. The people's and mass organizations are simply too important to the CCP's political power to grant them independence.

The political hierarchy of social organizations in China has created a vexing dilemma for the government in its effort to apply a uniform regulatory and managerial policy to all non-governmental organizations. The political status of organizations also accounts for the reluctance to formulate a clear social organization law.[33] Whether repressing dissidents' organizations, restraining autonomous NGOs, or manipulating large mass organizations, the CCP's policy reveals the party's basic understanding of the non-governmental sector. As the party-state continues to dominate Chinese society, the CCP leaders do not view NGOs as associations representing the people's interests, nor do they agree that people have the right to associate without the approval of the party. In this regard, one sees no substantial change in the party leaders' mentality. The party-state continues to muffle independent voices it considers a possible threat to its power. At the same time, the party relies increasingly on mass organizations with top-down institutional systems to penetrate and control society.

Another serious problem in official NGO policy is the deficiency of government funding, especially to autonomous NGOs. Chinese NGOs are now dealing with problems whose scale, range and complexity are way beyond their capacity. They undoubtedly need the government's support. One of the Western theories on the uprising of NGOs is "government failure," which is based on the conviction that the private sector can do a better job than the government in many matters concerning social control and development. Therefore, when the government refrains from taking on many responsibilities, it entrusts them to the non-profit sector along with funding and power. In contrast, the Chinese government has put many tasks on the shoulders of NGOs, but without giving them money or sufficient authority. On the one hand, the government refuses to let NGOs become autonomous because, in a MOCA official's words, they are undergoing a "weaning period," meaning that the NGOs are not yet strong enough to become independent.[34] On the other hand, it has been pushing NGOs to pursue financial self-sufficiency since the mid-1990s, and, in fact, the official policy of NGO autonomy means no governmental funding.[35] Understandably, this policy reflects government efforts to reduce its size and deal with fiscal constraints. Yet while its revenue as a percentage of GDP has climbed since 1996, the government has not increased its funding to the non-profit sector (Wang, S. 2003: 32).

It is common practice for the government's assistance to the non-profit sector to take the form of a tax break. China passed its first Public Welfare Donation Law in 1999, which made a general commitment to tax relief for charitable donations. However, the law does not stipulate the level of relief, nor does it make clear which organizations can receive donations. "In the absence of specific guidelines, it appears that donors, recipients and tax authorities will be left to negotiate the exact levels of tax relief" (CDB 1999b: 24). In reality, SOEs usually count their charitable donations as production costs, but private companies must deal with tax officers if they want to receive a tax break for their donations.[36] Furthermore, according to this law individuals receive tax breaks for their donations, but in practice this policy has not been implemented. Huang Haoming, the Executive Director of the China Association for NGO Cooperation (CANGO), complains, "China has a Public Welfare Donation Law, but it's a complete mess. In practical terms, even if you provide evidence of an individual donation, the tax authorities won't recognize it" (Liang 2003). For independent and grassroots organizations that lack government funding and have to rely on private donations, the effects of the official tax policy are disappointing.

NGOs and GONGOs in China often run for-profit businesses to support their non-profit programs and cover administrative expenses. The government allows this practice, considering how it enables a cut in funds to GONGOs. Operating funds, profits, and service charges provided either by the businesses or NGOs themselves are all subject to taxation, however. Interest earned by the endowment of a foundation or organization is also taxable. Currently, only three types of NGO income are tax exempt: governmental funding, membership fees, and donations from private resources.[37] For years, NGO activists have pushed the government to give NGOs tax relief; nevertheless, as recently as early 2004, a MOCA official stated clearly that changing the current tax policy for NGOs was impossible because the policy was determined by the current state of China's economy.[38] The tax policy is in fact a compromise between the Ministry of Civil Affairs and Ministry of Finance. It took two years for the Public Welfare Donation Law to be passed, and during that time the concept of tax relief met strong resistance from the Ministry of Finance as it struggled to standardize and maximize revenue collection (CDB 1999b). The MOCA's efforts to win tax breaks for NGO income also ran into resistance from the same ministry.[39]

These examples highlight the conflicts of interest among different governmental departments. It is not surprising that governmental departments or regional governments have divergent and competing interests. China, however, is in the midst of a most remarkable transformation during which a continual redistribution of power has created a stunningly complicated political structure. Consequently, a unified official stand towards NGOs has not emerged, and NGO matters are handled in ways that best suit the interests of respective regions or institutions. When the Ministry of Civil Affairs encourages international organizations to invest in China, for instance, the Bureau of National Security brings a very different attitude to bear on the matter.[40] Some mothers-in-law find their supervised NGOs beneficial and thus do not want them to become independent, while others consider supervision of NGOs as politically risky and try to avoid the role of mother-in-law. The inconsistencies and contradictions in official policy grow out of the brew of competing interests, and thus the practices of individual institutions do not necessarily follow the dictates of state policy.

Entangled with this interest-driven practice is a core rule of China's political game: do not make political mistakes. As mentioned earlier, positions in the party and state structure bring many privileges and material benefits, and thus the office holder's top priority is to hold on to his or her position. In other words, most office holders, if not all, think first about avoiding mistakes rather than trying to accomplish something. This explains why the officials in charge of NGOs are usually conservative, averse to change, and why the government's entire regulatory system is based on registration. The registration process is designed, above all, to eliminate organizations the CCP sees as potential threats to its power. The fundamental principle underlying the CCP's NGO policy is not to protect people's associational rights as asserted in China's Constitution, but to defend its own interests.

A major contestable official review of NGOs' functions is that social organizations, especially mass organizations and trade/professional associations, should serve both the government and their constituency. According to the government's expectation, SOs are transmitting belts sending the CCP's and government's policy down to members of these organizations and members' information up to the party and government. At the same time, they also need to deliver all kinds of services to their members. This dual role is based on a CCP's assumption that the party-state and society/individuals have the same interests, and indeed puts NGOs in a dilemma. Unfortunately, when conflicts between the two occur, which is common, the NGOs often have to compromise their members' interests to avoid more serious ramifications.

What does the overall picture mean for NGOs? Both NGO people and scholars think that current official policy is heavy on regulation and supervision and rather light on nourishment and support.[41] As the next chapter will discuss, under current policy, the great majority of SOs, small and autonomous ones in particular, tend to avoid political issues; they strive to stay "apolitical." At the same time, the only existing political organizations seek to identify themselves with the party. As the grassroots NGOs struggle with the problems of legal status and operating funds, for practical reasons the GONGOs try to prolong their ties with the government. To a great extent, the party-state's NGO policy has created an unbalanced and unhealthy climate for Chinese NGOs. Thus, government action contradicts the claim that government policy is determined by the desire to nourish NGOs in an effort to further China's economic and social development.

In short, the most significant change in China's official policy of NGOs is the government's recognition of non-governmental efforts as an indispensable part of China's reforms and transformation. In the past decade, the Chinese government has taken measures to complete and improve its management of NGOs, and the most recent official classification and unification of various types of NGOs in 1998 reflected its effort. The current policy provides, to an impressive extent, the political and legal environments necessary for NGOs to grow, and Chinese NGOs have responded positively. In alternating between policies of promotion and restraint, however, the government has shown its contradictory feelings about the role of NGOs. The new regulatory system gives enormous leeway to a government that has never hesitated to use its initiatives and resources to influence and repress NGOs. No doubt, the official governance of NGOs will continue to be the most effective and even decisive factor in the development of a third sector in China in the future.

3 NGO landscape in China
Classification, scope, and autonomy

The Chinese non-governmental and non-profit organizations (NGOs, or NPOs) have made unprecedented progress in number, size, type and functions as a direct outcome of the state's encouragement and society's response to the new challenges brought on by the reforms begun in 1978. Surging from different backgrounds, today these new entities engage in a wide array of operations, and carry out diverse missions. Despite the increasing interest in China's state–society relations among students of modern China, the face of the NGO sector remains unclear. Not until 1998 did the government finally establish a legal structure for China's NGO sector by issuing regulations for both social organizations (SOs) and non-governmental and non-commercial enterprises (NGNCEs). Yet, at the same time, many different terms are used to describe NGOs without having any official or legal interpretations. Furthermore, the strong official influence on non-governmental matters and the close relations between the government and many NGOs have raised serious questions as to whether Chinese NGOs are real NGOs and whether they play independent roles that differ from the party-state. The NGOs' autonomous nature and their relations with the government have become such major issues in this field of study that they merit further discussion before proceeding to an analysis of NGO roles.

This chapter focuses on basic organizational facts about these NGOs as the first step to understanding the NGO sector in China. Using field data, limited official statistics and case studies, it intends to answer the following questions. What are Chinese NGOs? How many of them are there and what are their missions? How does the government define and classify them, and what are the major features of China's legal NGO structure? What is China's NGO terminology and why it is important to this study? What has been the growing pattern of Chinese NGOs, and what are the geographical and professional distributions of these organizations? How do we interpret Chinese NGOs' continuing close relations with the government, and how significant are these relations in terms of affecting NGO behavior? The first section of the chapter illustrates the overall structure of the NGO sector and explains the historical origin and political meanings of the terminology;

the second one maps the NGO landscape; and the last examines their autonomous conditions.

In terms of legal status, typology, geographical and professional distribution, and autonomous condition, the NGO landscape in China presents a richly colorful, intensely unbalanced, and hazy picture. This study reveals that the Chinese NGO sector is highly diverse, rapidly growing, generally underdeveloped, and as yet not independent. The NGO sector's structure, based on the official policy, presents a hierarchical system, and the confusing NGO terms in fact reflect the unequal and inconsistent treatment that officially controlled GONGOs and grassroots civil organizations receive. The data analysis of NGO development indicates an uneven, yet impressive growth of various types of NGOs that rises and falls in accordance with changes in official NGO policy. A close look at the controversial NGO–governmental relations shows a strong trend of NGOs, including GONGOs, moving away from the party-state's control and generating government resources for their growth.

This chapter argues that the current state of Chinese NGOs is shaped by the present political culture, the party-state's continuing intervention in the private sector, and the mixed influence of Western ideas and traditional Chinese thoughts. The complicated identities, unstable growth, and ambiguous autonomy of NGOs are very much a part of their emergence from a society that is still under the control of a party-state and that historically lacks a strong civil society tradition. This study concludes that evaluation of Chinese NGOs' autonomy in popular Western terms must be set in the context of China's broad political and socio-economic conditions, and that autonomy is neither the only nor the most important criterion by which to interpret the conditions of these organizations' operations and decision-making. On the whole, NGOs are very new to China and are gradually becoming an independent sector that is distinctive from the state and businesses, and they are non-governmental in their unique roles and organizational operations.

Defining NGOs in China: classification and terminology

The term "NGO" is widely used to refer to various types of organizations outside of state systems, including advocacy organizations, non-profit service-providing institutions, religious groups and social welfare organizations. Lester Salamon and Helmut Anheier list the key features of international NGO sectors as follows: formal, private, non-profit-distributing, self-governing, and voluntary (Salamon and Anheier 1992: 134). This set of characteristics includes the most important and generally recognized features that distinguish the private non-profit sector from the governmental and for-profit private sectors. Within different cultures and political systems, the meaning of the term varies. In his discussion of NGO evolution in the United States, Akira Iriye summarizes NGOs as "voluntary and open

78 NGO landscape in China

(non-secret) associations of individuals outside of the formal state apparatus (central and local governments, police and armed forces, legislative and judicial bodies, and so on) that are neither for profit nor engage in political activities as their primary objective" (Iriye 1999: 417). In Western Europe, "NGO" often refers to a non-profit advocacy or service organization that is active internationally. In East European countries and republics of the former Soviet Union, "NGO" tends to designate all charitable and non-profit organizations (Fisher 1998: 5).

This section first illustrates the structure of China's NGO sector based on the official definition and classification, and then turns to the six popular NGO terms adopted by the CCP and by SOs themselves. It emphasizes the Western influence on the Chinese definition of NGOs and the hierarchical and incomplete state of the Chinese NGO sector. It clarifies the confusions in existing NGO classification and terminology and reveals the complicated historical origin and political implication of these definitions.

To begin, the process of legally defining NGOs has taken two decades, and it is not yet complete, for even today a large part of NGOs, such as religious groups, human rights organizations and policy advocacy associations, are excluded from the legal NGO category. In terms of establishing a Chinese definition of NGOs, the fourth World Conference for Women (WCW) held in Beijing, 1995, and the visits of international NGO (INGO) experts to China afterwards have had an immense impact on both the Chinese government and on scholars. The Ministry of Civil Affairs' (MOCA) officials and Chinese legal experts had no real substantial knowledge of the definition of NGOs when they were making NGO regulations in 1989, nor did they understand the meaning of "non-profit".[1] Thus, the regulations left the term "social organization" unexplained, and also sidestepped the issues of non-profit and voluntary participation.[2] *The Encyclopedia of Chinese Social Organizations*, collectively written by many scholars and supervised by MOCA, is a further testament to the confusion officials and scholars felt at the time (Fan 1995). The encyclopedia's definition of social organizations was both unclear and against widely adopted international notions of NGOs. According to this book, "Social organization is a general term for those organizations engaged in economic or social public affairs for certain interests ... Its primary features are: formal organization; a constitution and office(s); and registration (sometimes waived)." It goes on to state that they can also be either for-profit or non-profit (Fan 1995: 55–6). This explanation limited private organizations' activities to only public affairs and ignored their most important features: independence from the state, non-profit status, and voluntary nature. Even in 1996, some top officials of the Division of Social Organizations thought non-profit meant not engaging in any activities that produced profit.[3]

Today, ten years after the fourth WCW, the basic features of NGOs articulated by Salamon, Anheier, and Iriye are widely accepted by Chinese NGO leaders and scholars. To an impressive extent, these Western concepts have influenced official definitions of NGOs, as reflected in official definitions of social and non-profit organizations. The latest Chinese government regulatory documents, issued in 1998 and 2004 (see Table 2.3 in Chapter 2), provide by far the clearest legal explanation of the non-governmental sector in PRC history, and serve as the key documents by which to analyze the Chinese definition of NGOs. According to these documents, the term "NGO" in China includes all organizations and institutions that are outside of the state system and operate as non-profits, and the entire NGO body includes two general categories: social organizations and non-governmental and non-commercial enterprises (CSC 1998a, b).

In 1998 regulations, the government defined SOs for the first time, and it states that "Social organizations are non-profit organizations that are voluntarily founded by Chinese citizens for their common will and operated according to their charters." The regulation further stipulates that such organizations "cannot engage in for-profit activities" (CSC 1998a: 3). That year, the government also created the legal status "non-governmental and non-commercial enterprises" for those income-making institutions that did not produce products, but rather provided social or professional services. The 1998 regulations defines NGNCEs as "social entities that are organized by enterprises, non-commercial institutions, and other social forces with non-state funds that engage in not-for-profit social services" (CSC 1998b: 3). A 1999 official clarification of the term "non-profit" indicates a certain new comprehension of the international interpretation: "Members of NGOs do not share the profit from NGOs' assets or income, nor split the assets if the organization ceases to exist" (DLSC 1999: 19). These changes in official interpretation of NGO definition no doubt reflect the influence of international NGO theory.

The governmental regulations further divide all SOs and NGNCEs into corporate organizations and non-corporate organizations. Corporate status indicates an organization's formalness, establishment and legal responsibility. Currently, there are four officially recognized corporate statuses: governmental corporate; business corporate; non-commercial corporate; and social organization corporate.[4] The 1998 SO regulations require that all registering SOs possess corporate conditions, though, without explanation, the current policy does not require NGNCEs to be corporate entities. The question of whether NGOs in general and SOs in particular should hold corporate status is a controversial issue. Some scholars argue that this requirement denies many small or semi-formal organizations their right to register as SOs simply because they do not possess corporate conditions. The government, however, is convinced that such status is important as it encourages NGOs to take legal responsibility for their actions and improves NGOs' social image.[5]

The official legal classification of SOs divides them into different and unequal statuses: people's organizations and organizations under the Institutional Division of the State Council that are corporations and exempt from registration; registered SOs with corporate status; and non-registered

80 *NGO landscape in China*

```
                         ┌── People's/prestigious organizations:
                         │      Official data: over 30 national, 200 nationwide (2003)
                         │      Legal status: SO corporate
                         │      Registration requirement: exempt
                         │
                         │   Corporate organizations:
                         │      Official data: 1,712 national, 133,340 nationwide (2003)
                         │      Legal status: SO corporate
                ┌── SOs ─┤      Registration requirement: with MOCA/BOCA
                │        │
                │        │   Organizations within government, state-owned enterprises or
                │        │      non-profit entities:
                │        │      Official data: none
                │        │      Legal status: non-corporate
                │        │      Registration requirement: exempt
  Chinese       │        │
  NGOs ─────────┤        └── Grassroots organizations at villages/community level:
                │               Unofficial estimation: several millions
                │               Legal status: non-corporate
                │               Registration requirement: most do not register
                │
                ├── NGNCEs:     8 national, 111,212 nationwide have registered (2003)
                │               Official estimate: 700,000.
                │               Legal status: non-corporate entities
                │               Registration requirement: with MOCA and BOCA
                │
                └── SOs or NGNCEs that are registered with the Bureaus of Industry and Trade
                    as for-profit entities
```

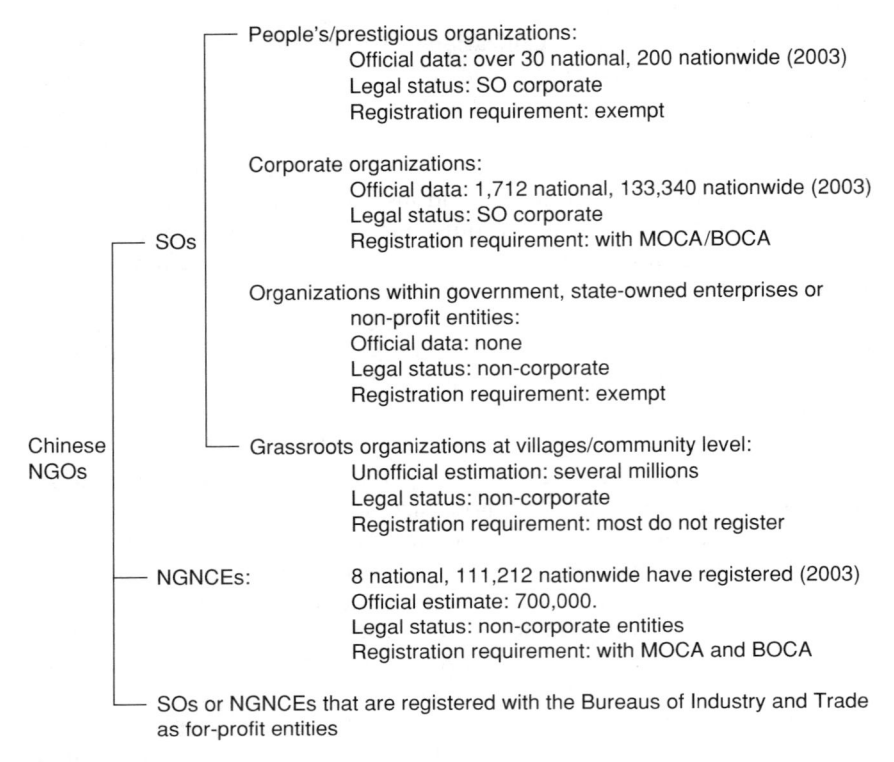

Figure 3.1 Hierarchy of Chinese NGOs.
Source: NBS 2003, Shang 2002, and interview with Li Yong, 2001

SOs without corporate status but supervised by governmental institutions (CSC 1998a). Outside of these are numerous loosely organized groups that are neither registered nor supervised. The government does not say whether these are legal or not; however, these organizations are not entitled to legal status and protection. Such grassroots organizations are treated differently from formally established corporate SOs; they cannot, for instance, open a bank account. Thus, China's official definitions have created a hierarchy of people's and prestigious organizations at the very top with grassroots organizations at the bottom. Based on official documentation, Figure 3.1 illustrates the legal conditions and prevalence of each type of non-governmental entity.

In comparison to NGNCEs, SOs have a much longer history and a more complex and diverse body. The many terms used to refer to these membership organizations reflect their political status, historical background, as well as relationship with the government. As a result of the CCP's confusing policies towards NGOs, some of the terms do not have clear legal standing or consistent defining criteria. At different times, various terms have been

Table 3.1 Six equivalents of social organizations

English term	Chinese term	Organizations (examples)
Social organization	Shehui tuanti	General term for NGOs or NPOs
People's organization	Renmin tuanti	"The eight big organizations," such as All-China Federation of Trade Unions; All-China Women's Federation; Chinese Communist Youth League; All-China Federation of Industry and Commerce (All-China Chambers of Commerce)
Mass organization	Qunzhong zuzhi	All-China Federation of Workers Unions; Chinese Communist Youth League; All-China Women's Federation
Folk organization	Minjian tuanti	All-China Chambers of Commerce; Western Returned Scholars' Association; Chinese International Chambers of Commerce
Non-governmental organization	Fei zhengfu zuzhi	Usually this refers to foreign NGOs, but Chinese organizations are increasingly using this term.
Non-profit organization	Fei yingli zuzhi	Most Chinese social organizations use this term alternately with social organizations

adopted to define the same group of organizations, or one term has been used for multiple types of NGOs. In order to understand the complexity of Chinese NGOs and the dilemma of official efforts to unify the classifications, a clarification of these terms with brief explanations of their historical origin and political implication is required.

At present, at least six terms are used for organizations within the SO category (Table 3.1).[6] The government distinguishes among them, yet has never issued an official explanation of all of them, nor a complete set of regulations that apply to different classes of organizations. Nevertheless, the historical origins of the classifications and the political lexicon of the Chinese government and the CCP belie the implications behind the terminology.

Social organization

Shehui tuanti or *shetuan* (social organization) is the most commonly adopted term for membership organizations. In Chinese language, both *she* and *hui* mean association, and together *shehui* means "society." The term SO predates the PRC, and some scholars believe that the earliest forms of Chinese SOs can be traced back to the Spring–Autumn period (770–476 B.C.) (Fan 1995: 1). From the late Qing on, SOs refer primarily to new private associations that first appeared at the beginning of the twentieth century and then blossomed in the first half of the century. Since 1949, the PRC government has continued to use this term, and three of its regulatory documents on this subject (1950, 1989 and 1998) all use the term "social organizations" for civic organizations.

People's organizations and mass organizations

Whereas social organization is adopted by the government as a general term for all organizations outside of the state, the remaining five terms are used more specifically. From a historical perspective, the terms people's and mass organizations clearly inform upon the CCP's notions of non-party organizations and how it employs SOs as political tools. The term "people's organization" implies a mission for the united front, and the term "mass organization" indicates a close but subordinate relationship with the party.[7] Only a small number of prominent organizations have ever been classified as either "people's organizations" or "mass organizations." The so-called "eight big organizations" (*ba da tuanti*), for example, are all people's organizations, and some of them are also mass organizations.[8] The two terms are not mutually exclusive, and the CCP uses them according to its political agenda. For example, the All-China Federation of Trade Unions (ACFTU), the Chinese Communist Youth League (CCYL), and the All-China Women's Federation (ACWF) all claim that they are mass organizations in their charters, but they are also referred to as people's organizations to indicate their prestigious status (COSC 1996). These two types of organizations are not under MOCA's supervision, but rather fall under the CCP or the State Council.

First, the term *renmin tuanti* (people's organization) was created by the Guomindang (Nationalist Party) government in the 1920s and is still used in Taiwan. After 1949, the PRC government accepted the term, but altered its meaning. In the early period of the PRC, the term referred to organizations that participated in the First Chinese People's Political Consultative Conference (CPPCC) in September 1949, a month before the establishment of the PRC (CSC 1950). The CCP was directly involved in founding these non-CCP organizations to unify various political forces joining the upcoming new CCP government. Such organizations have been China's most prestigious SOs ever since, and serve as the backbone of the united front as represented by the CPPCC. Legally, the term appeared in the 1954 and 1982 PRC Constitutions and other government documents.

In Chinese political vocabulary, the word "people" is presented in opposition to the "enemy" or "CCP's enemy." Its meaning changes from one political period to another, depending on the targets of the revolution. For instance, during the anti-Japanese War (1937–45), the landlord class was included in the category of "people," while during the land reform movement (late 1940s to early 1950s), this class became the "enemy." In 1949, shortly before the establishment of the PRC, Mao Zedong published an important article, "On the People's Democratic Dictatorship." He asked,

Who are the "people"? At the present stage in China, they are the working class, the peasant class, the petty bourgeoisie, and national bourgeoisie. Under the leadership of the working class and the Communist Party, these classes united together to form their own state and elect their own government [so as to] carry out a dictatorship over the lackeys of imperialism – the landlord class, the bureaucratic capitalist class, and the Kuomintang reactionaries... The democratic system is to be carried out within the ranks of the people, giving them freedom of speech, assembly, and association.

(Mao 1968: 1364)

Consequently, all Chinese people are divided into the leading classes, the united front (the classes with whom the CCP can ally at the present time), and the enemy.

The CCP wanted to enlist "people's organizations" so that they would join the fight against the Guomindang and convince the nation that the CCP truly represented the people. As a reward and to ensure future support, the CCP offered many political privileges to these organizations, including exemption from registration with the government.[9] This term carries substantial political weight; very few organizations have obtained the title since 1949. When organizations do use this title, their missions are usually related to the united front. For instance, during the early 1950s, the former chambers of commerce and other merchant and entrepreneurial associations were reorganized as the All-China Federation of Industry & Commerce (ACFIC). The ACFIC received the status of "people's organization," and its charter's stated purpose is to strengthen the united front.

Qunzhong zuzhi (mass organizations) also carries significant political implications. While it has never been used in any legal or official regulatory documents of NGOs, this term has been used officially on many occasions. In Chinese, "*qunzhong*" means groups of individuals or the majority, but the CCP applies new meanings. First, the term is used to distinguish people as either non-CCP members (*qunzhong*) or CCP members (*dangyuan*). This standing directly affects people's political status and their daily lives, and influences access to academic study or job opportunities, as well as political and social treatment. Second, according to CCP ideology, the masses and the party are two essential elements in a unity of contradiction. The CCP recognizes the masses as the foundation of its rule and the object of its service; it defines its own actions as the "cause of the masses," "masses' movement," and "mass struggle." At the same time, the party requires the masses to follow its lead as the head of the revolutionary cause.

Accordingly, political value of "mass organization" is twofold. On the one hand, the CCP defines itself as "the vanguard of the working class" and "the core force of the mass movement," with mass organizations on the periphery around the party. Since the party represents the people's interests, these organizations must follow CCP's leadership and cannot challenge its authority. The political struggle between the ACFTU leaders and the CCP during the 1950s over the independence of trade unions sent a clear signal to other mass organizations about their subordinate position to the party. In a study on trade unions in China, Jude Howell opines:

> Under the leadership of the Party the ACFTU has over the past four decades played a crucial role in incorporating the labor force into the planned economy and weaving the fabric of a new socialist society... However, it would be unfair and incorrect to ignore the past efforts of particular trade union leaders... who tried to push for a more autonomous role for the ACFTU from the Party and thus to prioritize the representation of workers' rather than Party interests.
>
> (Howell 1998: 158–9)

Briefly, by 1949, Chinese industrial workers had experienced thirty years of autonomous unions, so Chinese workers in major cities understood the meaning of solidarity and unionization. This tradition was the first casualty of the CCP's policy towards mass organizations (Liu 1996: 91). Union leaders and the party debated the issues of workers' interest, the unions' independent role and their relationship with the state (Wang 1992: 342–57). During his presidency of ACFTU (1950–51), Li Lisan insisted that the unions' unique function was to represent workers' interests independently from the party. His successor Lai Ruoyu (1951–58) argued that bureaucracy would not only infringe workers' interests, but that state and workers' interests could also conflict. Mao Zedong opposed these views and answered decisively that an overemphasis on workers' interests was harmful to state interests. Union leaders who fought for union independence were criticized as "anti-party" and "anti-people," and many were punished severely by the party (Wang: 342–57).

On the other hand, the CCP relies on mass organizations to reach out to different groups as they provide a bridge between the CCP and the people; this was true during the revolutionary period and remains the case today. Before 1949, many mass organizations were grassroots organizations fighting directly for their members' interests. After 1949, the CCP became the ruling party, and trade unions, women's federations and youth leagues became governmental organizations entirely dependent upon and closely controlled by the party and government. The interests of their members came to be ignored, or, to use the CCP's words, individual interests follow state and party interests. The duties of mass organizations shifted to propagating Communist ideology, assisting the party, and recruiting CCP supporters. The government entrusted them with important administrative functions, and endowed them with the privileged status of government agencies.

Folk organizations

The term *minjian zuzhi* (folk organization) is deeply rooted in Chinese culture and history. In Chinese, the word *minjian* conveys the non-official nature of matters. *Minjian zuzhi* indicates groups organized by people in their space, and serves as an antonym of "governmental organization" (*guanban* or *zhengfu zuzhi*). Some scholars even argue that the word *minjian* implies opposition to the government (Chapter 1). Understandably, soon after the CCP seized national power in 1949, they identified and banned nine religious *minjian zuzhi* and their nationwide branches as "anti-revolutionary secret societies" (Ma 1997: 62). As a conspicuous political event, the dismissal of the *minjian zuzhi* sounded a clear signal, and eventually these organizations vanished from China.

From then until the 1980s, this term was only used to refer to foreign NGOs such as the Japanese *minjian zuzhi* that functioned as important communication channels for the Chinese government to the outside world. The CCP revived and legalized the term in 1995 when Jiang Zemin called the ACFIT a *"minjian* chamber of commerce" (ACFTU pamphlet 1996). In 1999, the government renamed the MOCA agency in charge of all national NGOs as *Minjian Zuzhi Guanliju* (literally, Bureau of Management of *Minjian* Organizations), though its official English name is the Bureau of Management of NGOs (the English name later changed to Bureau of Management of NPOs). Some NGOs prefer this term today, because of its Chinese roots and the emphasis on "by the people."

NGOs and NPOs

The term *fei zhengfu zuzhi* (NGOs) is not authentic to the Chinese language and is a literal translation from the English "non-governmental organization". When China hosted the fourth WCW, the Non-Governmental Forum made this term well known to the Chinese. Since then, *fei zhengfu zuzhi* and, later, *fei yingli zuzhi* (non-profit organizations, NPO) have become formal terms in China's political lexicon. However, while the term is used to refer to foreign organizations, Chinese social organizations are reluctant to call themselves by this name. In Chinese, the word *"fei"* not only means "non-" or not, it also connotes "wrong," "censure" or even "anti-." For example, the Chinese name for "Federation of Anti-Christianity," and the "Great Federation of Anti-Religion Movement" during the May 4 Movement (1919) used *fei* for "anti."[10] Instead of choosing *fei zhengfu* to indicate their nature, many new Chinese NGOs today prefer to use NPO.

The confusion and inconsistency in the classification of social organizations reflect the uncertainty of the government's policy towards SOs as a whole and reveal problems more profound than clarification or categorization. As discussed in Chapter 2, the government has undertaken substantial measures

86 *NGO landscape in China*

to improve the legal and political environment for the growth of NGOs and has promulgated a series of regulatory documents. Indeed, since 1998, the government has more clearly and consistently classified most organizations outside of the state system than during any previous period of the CCP regime. However, these efforts are not without obstacles and costs. To well-established GONGOs like people's or mass organizations, the change in status quo stands to cost them privilege and security. Government also faces the political risk of losing control if they let organizations become autonomous in financial and managerial matters. Without a comprehensive and long-term policy, the government simply cannot provide a unified definition to all SOs, change the status quo of people's and mass organizations, or offer Chinese SOs the rights that INGOs enjoy.

Analyses of Chinese NGO growth

A major challenge facing students of Chinese NGOs is the absence of sufficient and available information. The statistics furnished by the *Civil Affairs Statistical Yearbooks* are by far the most reliable data.[11] They are accurate in terms of how many organizations register, repeal and persist each year, because all formally established NGOs must register with the respective civil affairs agencies. However, some of the most crucial information about NGOs, such as founding date, location, mission, size, income resource, supervisory institution, and leadership, is not available to the public.[12] In addition, MOCA's collections on SOs started in 1990 and on NGNCEs in 2000; thus, the earlier histories of both types of NGOs remain unknown.[13] In a way, the *Encyclopedia of Chinese Social Organizations* (1995) is a complementary source as it includes a large proportion of organizations founded prior to the PRC, and from 1949 to 1993. While incomplete, the *Encyclopedia* does provide some organizational information such as founding date, mission, and location.

In order to cope with this challenge, Chinese and international scholars have in recent years introduced and conducted some questionnaire surveys popular in Western sociology and political science.[14] The major drawback of these surveys, however, is the low return rate. For example, a 1999 survey of NGOs in Beijing areas sent out 1500 questionnaires, and only 10.8 percent responded (Wang 2000: 25). Most Chinese NGOs are not yet used to responding to non-governmental surveys; those who do respond are usually well-established groups. Thus, representativeness of the data is questionable. Adding to the difficulty is that Chinese organizations, both governmental and non-governmental, lack transparency; rarely do they publish or open organizational records to the public.

This study draws upon the available official statistics, limited though they may be, as they provide a more reliable source than small-scale questionnaires. So far, while official sources, such as the *Civil Affairs Statistical Yearbooks* and the *Encyclopedia of Social Organizations*, have been largely ignored by studies on Chinese NGOs, this study finds them helpful in accomplishing two things. First, they illustrate the scope of China's NGO sector by time, region, category, and growth and decline; second, they provide empirical evidence to support major arguments of this study. Unfortunately, there is no statistical data on the large number of informal and grassroots groups at the community or village levels or operating within the governmental agencies or enterprises, because official regulations do not require them to register. Thus, only registered organizations are considered here despite the importance of unregistered, grassroots organizations.

First, the statistics show the growth pattern of China's NGOs and reveal the impressive progress they have made in the past quarter of a century. According to the *Encyclopedia*, from 1950 to 1966, the government organized a total of 72 new SOs at the national level, the majority of which were academic and cultural (Table 3.2). On the eve of the Cultural Revolution, including those organizations founded prior to the PRC, China only had 98 national and 6,000 local SOs (Wu and Chen 1996: 4–7). Immediately after the open policy, the political control loosened and SOs blossomed. As Table 3.2 shows, the national SOs established between 1977 and 1980 exceeded the total number of SOs founded in the PRC's first sixteen years; the 1980s witnessed another wave of new SOs. The increase of local organizations was even more remarkable. In Shanghai, the total number of SOs mushroomed from 628 in 1981 to 2,627 in 1984 (Chen 1997: 4). By the mid- to late 1990s, both national SOs and the total number of SOs nationwide reached their peaks (Figures 3.2 and 3.3). These figures, together with a significant multitude of unregistered grassroots NGOs, represent a substantial change in China's power structure and state–society relationship.

The statistics in Figures 3.2–3.4 also reveal that the ups and downs of SOs at both the national and local levels coincide with the swing between release and restriction in official NGO policy. 1996 was a crucial year for NGO policies. That October, Jiang Zemin called for the strengthening of control over NGOs in a CCP Politburo meeting (Chapter 2). His speech was followed by the immediate tightening of NGOs in 1997, the promulgation of strict regulations in 1998, and the reregistration process of 1998–99. The official data confirms that the reregistration process reduced SO numbers significantly, and the strict registration rules have effectively controlled the growth of SOs since then. Before 1996, SOs made steady progress; registered SOs reached their peak in 1996 at about 200,000 total groups, over 1,800 of which were national. From 1996 to 2002, the total number of the SOs dropped by over one-third, and growth of SOs since 2002 has been quite slow.

In some cases, provincial declines were devastating. For example, from 1997 to 2003, the total number of registered SOs in Shandong declined by over 50 percent and almost 50 percent in Heilongjiang. From 1995 to 2002, Tibet was the only region where numbers did not drop, but the number of SOs was very low to begin with (Tables 3.5 and 3.6). Although national

Table 3.2 Formation of national SOs (1950–94)

	Academic associations	Professional associations	Trade associations	Cultural organizations	Religious organizations	Foundations	Federation	Total
Before 1950*	24	4	2	1			3	34
1950s	10	15	1	11	5			42
1960–66	15	15		2				32
1977–80	65	4	1	3			1	74
1980–90	228	86	89	26	3	12	8	452
1990–94	69	61	63	8		8	8	217
Total	411	185	156	51	8	20	20	851
% of total	48.30	21.74	18.33	5.99	0.94	2.35	2.35	100

* These organizations were established before 1949 and continued to exist in the PRC.

Note: All SOs were shut down during the Cultural Revolution (1966–76).

Source: Fan 1995

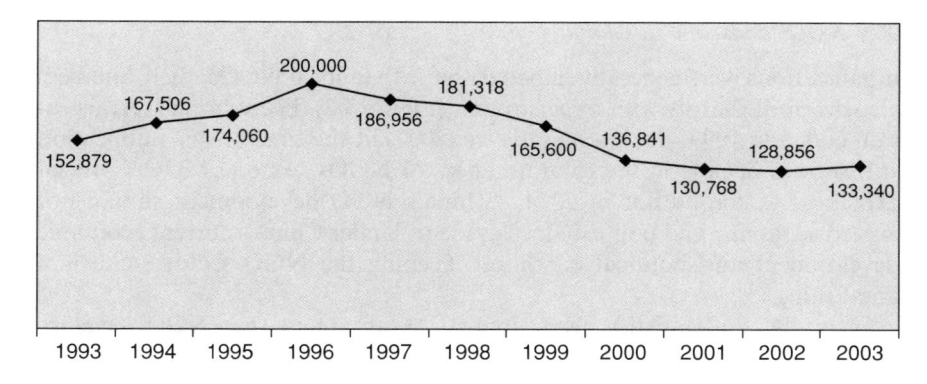

Figure 3.2 SOs nationwide (1993–2003).
Sources: Fan 1995; NBS 1995: 144, 1998: 274, 1999: 192, 2000: 132, 2001: 114, 2002: 102, 2003: 156; Interview with the director of DSOs, 1996 (for the total number of SOs in 1996)

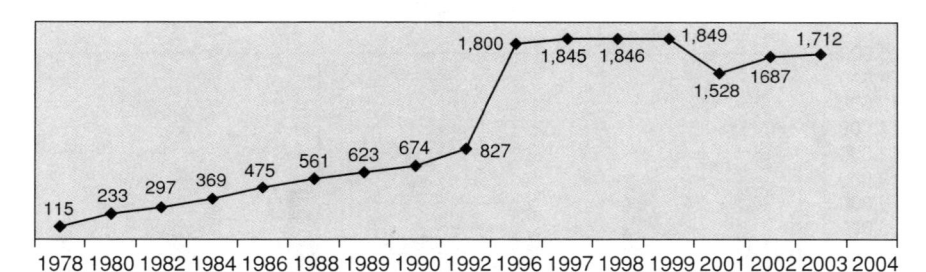

Figure 3.3 National SOs (1978–2003).
Sources: Fan 1995; NBS 1995: 144, 1998: 274, 1999: 192, 2000: 132, 2001: 114, 2002: 102, 2003: 156; Interview with the director of DSOs, 1996 (for the total number of SOs in 1996)

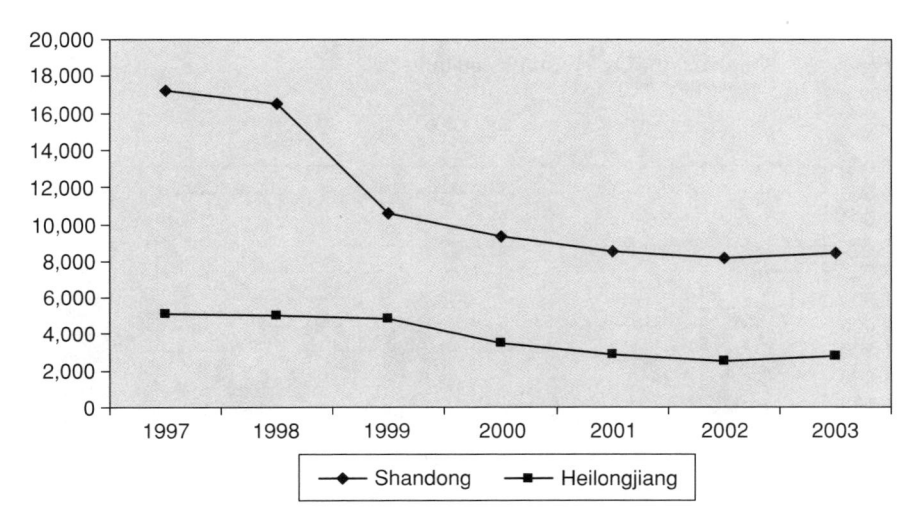

Figure 3.4 Decline of SOs in provinces since 1996.
Sources: Fan 1995; NBS 1995: 144, 1998: 274, 1999: 192, 2000: 132, 2001: 114, 2002: 102, 2003: 156; Interview with the director of DSOs, 1996 (for the total number of SOs in 1996)

90 *NGO landscape in China*

organizations were generally in better shape than local NGOs, their numbers also dropped sharply with reregistration (Figure 3.3). Even though reregistration ended in 1999, the latest statistics (2003) at the time of this publication still show a decline in the total numbers of NGOs. As one MOCA official explained to the author in 2004, "China's NGO development should not exceed economic and political development. Under China's current economic development and political condition, keeping the NGO sector small is a good thing."[15]

Secondly, the statistics also support the argument that NGO development has been unbalanced (Figures 3.5–3.6, Tables 3.2–3.3). Geographically, coastal areas are more prosperous than inland provinces, and the statistics show that the private sectors in the coastal provinces, both for profit and non-profit, are also more numerous. In Figure 3.5, the left shows three

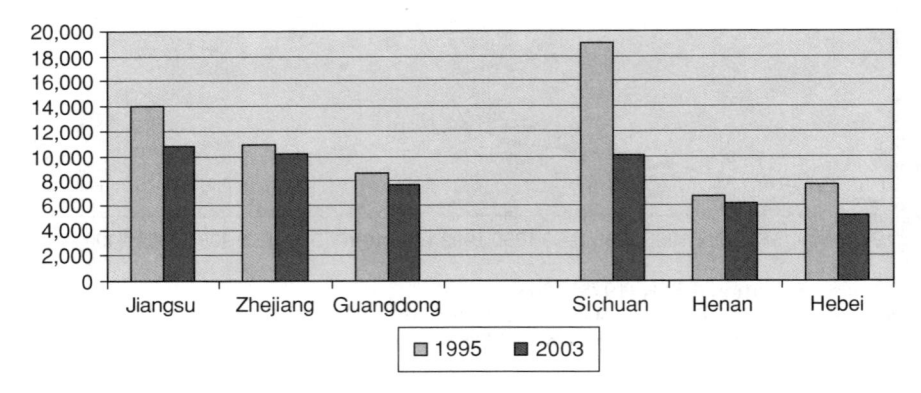

Figure 3.5 Numbers of SOs: coastal vs inland.
Sources: NBS 1995: 144, 2003: 156

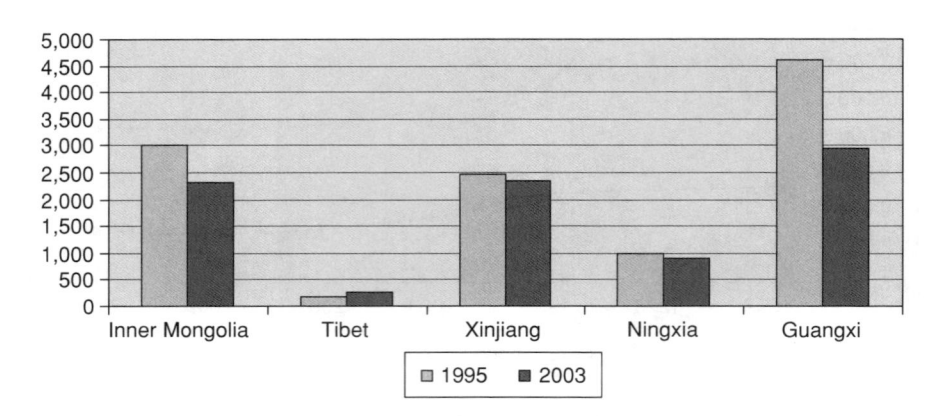

Figure 3.6 SOs in minority autonomous regions.
Sources: NBS 1995: 144, 2003: 156

Table 3.3 Comparison of provincial SOs by population (2003)

Province	Number of SOs	Population	People/1 SO
Coastal provinces			
Shandong	8,408	88,380,000	10,513
Jiangsu	10,780	71,820,000	6,662
Guangdong	7,636	71,430,000	9,354
Zhejiang	10,173	44,560,000	4,380
Fujian	5,725	32,990,000	5,762
Inland provinces			
Henan	6,143	93,510,000	15,164
Sichuan	10,087	84,930,000	8,420
Hebei	5,200	65,690,000	12,632
Shaanxi	3,494	35,960,000	10,286
Gansu	2,791	25,190,000	9,025

Source: Population: DCSNBS 1999: 112; Number of SOs: NBS 2003: 156–7

Table 3.4 SOs and population ratio in minority autonomous regions

Minority regions	Number of SOs	Population	People/SO
Inner Morgolia	2,307	23,450,000	10,165
Tibet	266	2,520,000	9,474
Xinjiang Uygur	2,363	17,470,000	7,393
Ningxia Huizu	879	5,380,000	6,120
Guangxi Zhuangzu	2,965	46,750,000	15,767

Source: Population: DCSNBS 1999: 112; Number of SOs: NBS 2003: 156–7

Table 3.5 SOs and population ratio in China's four largest cities

	Total SOs	Population	People/SO
Beijing	2,256	12,460,000	5,523
Tianjin	1,680	9,570,000	5,696
Shanghai	2,650	14,640,000	5,525
Chongqing	2,636	30,600,000	11,608

Source: Population: DCSNBS 1999: 112; Number of SOs: NBS 2003: 156–7

coastal provinces (Jiangsu, Zhejiang, and Guangdong) that are known for their active NGO sectors, and the right shows three of the most populated inland provinces (Sichuan, Henan, and Hebei).[16] At the same time, development has been uneven within inland and coastal regions. The disparity becomes even more obvious when viewed under the lens of population. For example, in the coastal province of Zhejiang, which is known for its vibrant private sector, one SO serves 4,380 people, while in Shandong and

Guangdong one SO serves 10,513 and 9,354 people respectively. Among the inland provinces, Sichuan has a much higher ratio of SOs to population (one SO serves 8,420 people), while in Henan, the most populated province in China, one SO serves over 15,000 people, and in Guangxi Zhuangzu Autonomous Region, the most populated minority region, the ratio is one SO per 16,000 people. In general, whether in coastal or inland regions, NGO development is still incipient when contrasted with population.

These figures highlight the fact that across the board, cities and provinces with larger populations have lower ratios of NGOs per capita. This may be partly explained by the fact that government rules permit only one SO per trade or profession in a given region, no matter what the population of that region. These ratios confuse some common assumptions about NGO development and indicate that the complete picture of the NGO development in China cannot be captured without accounting for grassroots organizations. For example, while the statistics by and large confirm the prevalence of SOs in large cities or economically developed regions, the data do not support this conclusion consistently or strongly. Guangdong is one of the richest provinces and with an active NGO sector; yet, it has fewer NGOs per capita than Gansu, one of the poorest regions in China (Tables 3.3 and 3.5). Nor do the statistics suggest that the number of registered NGOs per capita in minority regions is lower than in Han nationality provinces (Table 3.4). Tibet, for instance, has been under strong CCP political repression and had only 74 organizations in 1999 and 266 in 2003; yet, because of its small population, it seemingly has more SOs than Guangdong or Sichuan per capita.

In addition to the quantitative data, the official statistics also provide typological data. According to MOCA's typology, SOs are categorized as academic (*xueshuxing*), professional (*zhuanyexing*), trade (*hangyexing*), federations (*lianhexing*) and foundations.[17] Each year, the MOCA yearbook collects data on the number of organizations in each category; unfortunately, this information does not state their activities. Still, the data confirm the argument made in the last chapter that the official attitude towards different types of organizations greatly affects their growth rates. For example, when the government strongly encouraged education and science research in the late 1970s and 1980s after the Cultural Revolution, academic associations saw their most impressive growth (Table 3.2, Figures 3.7 and 3.8). Then, as industrial management reform shifted into high gear in the latter part of the 1990s, government promotion resulted in the fast growth of trade associations and professional organizations (Figures 3.7 and 3.8). As Chapter 5 discusses in detail, while other types of SOs declined during the late 1990s, trade associations continued to grow.

The ups and downs of foundations also support the argument on government's impact on NGOs' growth. No foundation existed before the open policy and the first five foundations appeared in the early 1980s. As stated in the last chapter, the sudden emergence of a large number of foundations in the late 1980s and early 1990s was a direct result of the

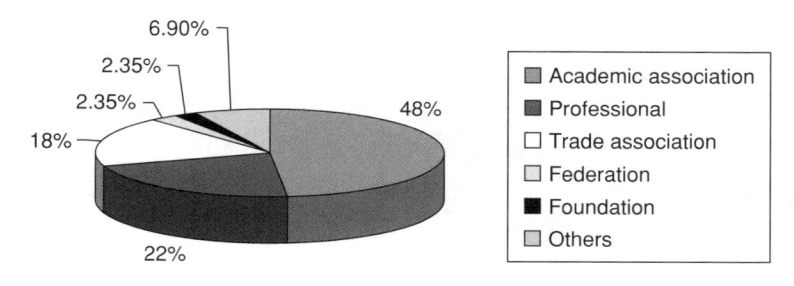

Figure 3.7 SOs by type (1994).
Source: Fan 1995

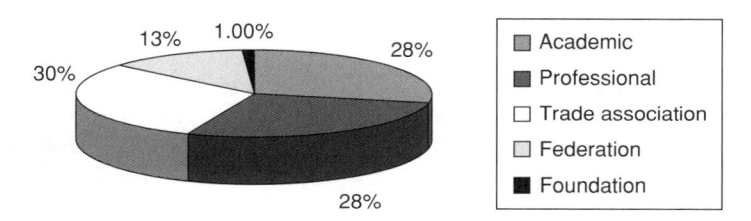

Figure 3.8 SOs by type (2003).
Source: NBS 2003: 156–7

government's efforts to attract private resources. A 1996 study showed that, of 69 national foundations, 33 were founded during 1985–90, and 33 during 1991–95 (DNFI 1996). By then, over 1,800 foundations nationwide had been established. However, after the reregistration process, only 1,268 foundations remained in 2003 (NBS 2003). This setback came about as a result of the government's scrutiny of NGO performance, and indicates the incompetence of many GONGOs in a competitive NGO environment in China.

Only a few foundations continued to receive government financial support after their establishment. Among these, The Soong Ching Ling Foundation was established in 1982 to honor the memory of China's Honorary President and former wife of Sun Yat Sen, the founder of the Republic of China; the China Foundation for the Handicapped was founded by a son of Deng Xiaoping. Rather, the great majority of foundations received a one-time governmental endowment of 100,000 RMB or more, after which they were expected to raise their own money. Given China's circumstances, the obstacles for these organizations are many. To use national foundations as an example, around half began with an endowment of 100,000–500,000 RMB, either from the government or private donations, much of which was used for renting offices and hiring staff.[18] With low interest rates, the total interest gained from endowments of most national foundations was under one million RMB and less than 100,000 RMB for most.[19]

94 *NGO landscape in China*

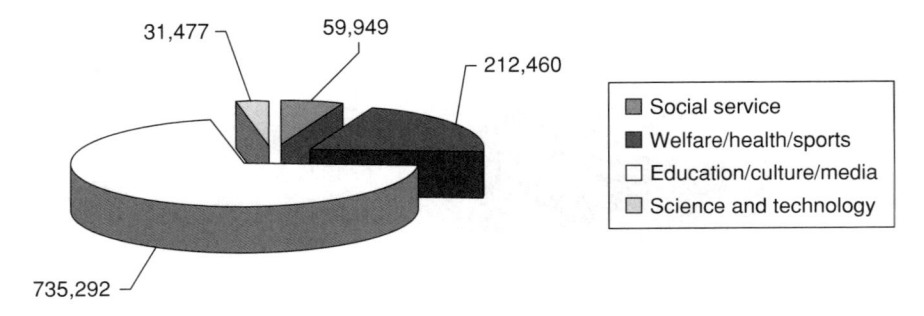

```
31,477    59,949
             212,460

■ Social service
■ Welfare/health/sports
□ Education/culture/media
□ Science and technology

735,292
```

Figure 3.9 NGNCEs by type (2000).
Source: Yang, T. 2000: 381. Yang's article does not provide the source of these numbers, nor is the total number of NGNCEs in Yang's article (1,039,170) close to the MOCA's estimated total number of 700,000 NGNCEs nationwide. Interview with Li Yong, 2004

Understandably, no foundation can play an active role on such a small budget, and almost all foundations depend heavily on their flagship projects to raise funds for such expenses as daily operation. Some of the best-known projects of this nature include the Hope project of the Youth Development Foundation, the poverty alleviation projects of the China Foundation for Poverty Alleviation, and the Happiness Project of the Population Welfare Foundation. Thus, unlike their international peers that function exclusively as grant-giving institutions that rely solely upon their large endowments, Chinese foundations are more akin to program-operating organizations. Under such unique circumstances, only those foundations that have clear missions and strong leadership survive and thrive. Foundations that failed to design solid projects could not generate public support, and subsequently became inactive and were rejected in reregistration.

Juxtaposed alongside social organizations are the non-governmental and noncommercial enterprises (NGNCEs), which include non-state-run schools, hospitals, research institutions, and various social service providers. As experiences in many other countries indicate, these public service-oriented institutions hold much potential in terms of their social, economic and political influence. In the United States, for example, the total number of public service institutions exceeds the number of membership organizations by a factor of three (Salamon 2001a: 24). Chinese officials and scholars estimate that the total number of NGNCEs is between 700,000 and one million (Figures 3.1 and 3.9). The government divides the NGNCEs into ten general types: education, health care, cultural, science/technology, sports, social welfare, intermediary services, employment service, legal service and other (MOCA 2000b: 35–6). Unfortunately, there is not enough statistical data to evaluate at the time of writing, because the MOCA only started to register NGNCEs in 2000. Beyond the estimated numbers in Figure 3.9, based on the work of Yang Tuan, a Chinese sociologist, no further information about the number, location, size and financial condition is available.

NGO–government relations in China: how much autonomy?

According to Goran Hyden, autonomy is the first criterion that Western civil society scholars consider in understanding which associations qualify as part of civil society. Hyden explains autonomy as follows: "A civil society association should be independent of the state in terms of decisional competence, recruitment of leaders, and control of important economic and managerial resources" (Hyden 1997: 16). Yet, what should people or organizations do when the associational space is limited and civil society is underdeveloped? Hyden points out that the most common answer has been that "it is better to move slowly and try to enlarge available space without invoking the rage of those in power." Other scholars, however, argue that entering into a relation that allows the state to influence associational priorities may undercut an association's autonomy (Hyden: 13–14). This is the predicament that faces Chinese NGOs, and the great majority of them, perhaps all, have done exactly what Hyden stipulated.

According to the Chinese government, NGO autonomy signifies self-operation, self-hiring or self-selection of leaders, and self-sufficiency (the "three-selves policy"). In a 1996 official estimation, about 50 percent of SOs achieved this standard, which included large numbers of unregistered grassroots groups.[20] Although the number of financially self-reliant SOs has increased since 1996, it is still safe to say that a large proportion of registered SOs continue to rely on state resources. These include people's and mass organizations with their numerous local branches, academic or professional associations within state-owned institutions and enterprises, many trade associations that were formerly managerial bureaus of industries, and foundations organized and principally endowed by the government.

It is true that Chinese NGOs, both GONGOs and "true" NGOs, do not enjoy the degree of autonomy that characterizes NGOs in most other countries. But the issue of autonomy must be understood in the content of China's circumstances. Currently, some general conditions restrict the independence of Chinese NGOs. In China, all institutions must conform to the CCP's ideological principles, and all NGOs need the government's political approval as the precondition to registration. Due to the scarcity of private funds, a large proportion of registered SOs continue to depend on, to varying degrees, funds or other forms of assistance from the government or state-owned institutions for their daily operating costs. Many staff members working for GONGOs continue to receive such government benefits as housing, health care, and pensions. The most serious threat to all NGOs' independence is the party-state's power over their legal existence. This reality has greatly affected the attitude of NGOs, GONGOs in particular, towards the government. For them, survival and persistence are tough challenges.

This account suggests that instead of addressing how Chinese NGOs may be illegitimate because of their lack of autonomy, scholars should examine the progress they have made, the directions they are heading toward, and the distinct roles they have played in China's ongoing reforms. From mission to operation, NGOs increasingly differ from government organizations, and their emergence has changed China's state–society relationship. Baogang He in his study of China's civic organizations argues that, "The question of autonomy is only a matter of degree" (He, B. 1997: 9). The vast array of Chinese non-governmental institutions encompasses a high diversity of missions, governance styles, financial conditions, independence, and influence on society and government. Thus, individual organizations should be examined according to their specific situations and according to the changes in their relations with the party or government since the reforms.

In the past two decades, Chinese NGOs have made impressive progress in their organizational autonomy despite their seemingly close relations with the government. In general, the imperative of non-governmental action, the government's inability to implement its control over all NGO activities, and the impact of global civil society all contributed to the expansion of NGO independence in China. In particular, two major efforts initiated by NGOs themselves are changing the nature of China's NGO–government relationship. The first is the reinvention of non-governmental identity by all GONGOs to adjust to a market environment. This section will use a case study of the All-China Women's Federation (ACWF) to demonstrate that even the most tightly controlled GONGOs are trying to become more independent. Secondly, contrary to the general assumption that close relations with the government signifies governmental control, Chinese NGOs have intentionally maintained or initiated good relations with the government to aid their own organizational growth. The case study of the China Youth Development Foundation (CYDF) indicates how this organization successfully created China's best-known non-governmental program and did so by using the national network of the Chinese Communist Youth League, the CYDF's supervisory institution.

Currently, the SOs have shown a strong centrifugal tendency away from the government. A fundamental difference between NGOs, including most of the GONGOs, and governmental organizations is that the interests of the former are independent from those of the state. Since the government's downsizing reforms in the late 1980s, it has seriously trimmed its funding to some GONGOs while pushing others to become entirely self-sufficient. For example, the government funding to big GONGOs such as mass or people's organizations has not caught up with the rapid inflation since the reforms, and the appropriations to those trade associations that were transformed from industrial agencies is going to stop within the foreseeable future.[21] This policy has widened the gap in interests between the government and GONGOs and intensified the latter's insecurity. By moving out of the state system, these organizations face a market economy and intense competition among NGOs for limited private resources. This financial insecurity has motivated GONGOs to reach for outside resources and streamline governance. Official restraints and supervision thus become obstacles in their advances towards competitiveness. Meanwhile, more and more SOs are dependent upon membership fees and service charges, and all NGNCE income comes from their services or programs. This has caused them to shift attention from their relations with the government to focus on their constituents and society. Experiences of NGOs in the past two decades have shown that the success and future of these organizations ultimately rely on the support of their members and service recipients. Independence has thus become essential to survival.

Since the late 1990s, Chinese NGOs have undergone a substantial transformation towards greater autonomy. The growth of NGOs in number and activities over the past two decades has gained them more autonomy and authority. Again, the rate of transformation and degree of autonomy vary greatly. Success stories among GONGOs have seen them become more independent, indicator of their ability to launch effective programs and deliver services. In contrast, other GONGOs cling to the status quo, afraid of losing their privileges. Some organizations, such as mass organizations, are simply too important to the party for it to relinquish control. Nevertheless, the trend towards autonomy is inevitable. One former MOCA minister who later headed a national SO in retirement acknowledged the necessity for change. He admitted, "Now when we work for NGOs, we must think as NGOs. We cannot think as government officials any more, because the interests have changed. If an NGO wants to be sustainable, it has to do what it's supposed to do."[22]

Ironically, NGOs have tried to become more independent by holding on to their relations with the government while pursuing their own ends. The government–NGO relationship in China is a two-way street and both sides benefit. As NGOs still do not have great impact on government organizations or state-owned enterprises, and are largely unknown to the public, they often have to rely on the government's authority to increase the size and influence of their programs. Under China's political culture, close relations with the government, governmental organizations, or office holders bring NGOs such crucial benefits as approval of registration, green lights on activities, political protection, free or low-rent office space, and program funding. These relationships are what the Chinese call "intangible capitals" (*wuxing zechan*) and, since the exchange of favors is accepted political behavior in China, it is a key survival strategy for NGOs. In order to curry favor, NGOs resort to a number of strategies: they invite high officials to serve as honorary presidents or ask retired officials to head their organizations; attribute achievements to their mother-in-law institutions; cooperate on programs with government organizations; and offer moonlighting opportunities to researchers in the state institutions. For example, the great majority of Chinese NGOs depend on the income from their activities, one of the most popular of which is training workshops. To increase enrollment necessitates cooperation with government. The trainees, mostly from state enterprises or institutions, simply do not think that NGOs have the authority to ask them to attend (He 2002: 47).

Many Chinese NGOs interviewed in this study gave a similar justification for their ties to the government. The common opinion runs along the lines of, "There are so many things that need to be done and which we can do, and if a close relationship with the government is helpful, then we do not see what is wrong with it." This practical and pragmatic attitude parallels Deng Xiaoping's philosophy, "It does not matter whether the cat is black or white, so long as it catches mice." The NGOs' major concern is to accomplish their goals in a manner that conforms to the best interests of the general public and their own ethics. As the next chapter shows, in the past two decades, Chinese NGOs have undertaken many tasks that government organizations disregarded or did not do well. All this suggests that, in the short run, close relations with the government have not necessarily hindered the growth of the NGO sector. Nevertheless, the situation is complicated and controversial. The following case studies show that the continuing intimacy between NGOs and government results in long-term damage because it prevents NGOs from gaining the public's trust and heightening public understanding of the importance of civil society.

A case study of the All-China Women's Federation (ACWF)

The ACWF, a people's organization and a mass organization, is one of the most prestigious SOs in China, and it has been a loyal ally of the CCP since its establishment in 1949. Yet, the past two decades have witnessed the ACWF's strong efforts to reinvent itself as a true and effective NGO for women. Its experience reveals the domestic and international impacts on the GONGOs' transformation towards being more autonomous and competitive. To a large degree, the limited progress towards the ACWF's independence also indicates the dilemma facing all GONGOs.

On the eve of the establishment of the CCP's national power, the women's organizations in CCP's five major liberation bases organized the ACWF, with direction from Mao Zedong (ACWF 1991: 1–4). In its Second National Assembly (1953), the ACWF clearly stated that it was led by the CCP; later, its role was announced as "to bridge the CCP and China's female population." Even though the ACWF always claimed to represent the interests of Chinese women, its primary work up until the 1980s was the generation of women's participation in the CCP's socialist construction and political struggles. However, the profound socio-economic transformation following 1978 forced the ACWF to adapt. The turning point came at its sixth National Assembly (1988), when the ACWF, for the first time, set its principal task as the safeguarding of the rights of women and children, a significant shift from its traditional role. The ACWF then established centers for the protection of women's rights nationwide. Today, the Federation and its local agencies serve as an important voice in advocating women's interests and rights (Xu 2003: 36–42).

The ACWF also made substantial organizational changes, which in turn affected its vision. Before the reforms, it had a vertical hierarchy from the national to the provincial, municipal, and township levels. At each tier of administration, a women's federation essentially served as a government department in women's affairs. After the reforms, its network stretched out horizontally. First, the ACWF organized over 200,000 female workers' committees within unions and women's friendship associations so that they became organizational members at ACWF or local federations. These organizations similarly established many women's committees and delegations at the village and community level (Liu 2000: 111–12). These extended networks made women's problems and difficulties tangible to the ACWF and its local federations. Since the 1990s, many grassroots women's organizations also have joined the ACWF system as organizational members, most of them as service providers and research centers (Chapter 4). On the whole, this fresh blood brought to the ACWF a new mission, program, method, structure, and overall dynamic.

Another strong push for ACWF reform came from the Fourth World Conference for Women. To prepare the conference, delegations of the ACWF joined in a series of international meetings. As some participants later recalled, it was at this time that they came to realize the unique and influential role of NGOs in contemporary world politics. The ACWF cadres were impressed by the fact that NGOs in many countries hold much clout over issues that governments were reluctant to face. The ACWF also organized 47 Chinese NGO workshops for the NGO Forum, in which participants learned about the fundamentals of a non-governmental organization. Training workshops instructed how to select priorities, present papers and answer questions, and they provided a history of NGOs and women's movements in other countries.[23] The fourth WCW led to an upwelling of grassroots women's NGOs in China as well as government-organized "non-governmental" women's organizations prior to the conference (Liu 2000, also Chapter 4).

In order to host the conference, in 1994 the Chinese government in its state report on China's implementation of the UN Nairobi Strategy announced that the ACWF is "China's largest non-governmental organization (*feizhengfu zuzhi*) to elevate women's status" (*People's Daily*, February 5, 1994). In a brochure disseminated to the fourth WCW delegations, the ACWF also describes itself as "China's largest NGO to represent and safeguard the rights and interests of women" (Howell 2000: 137). This was the first time that the Chinese government had used "NGO" to define any Chinese SOs, and it was a big step in ACWF's reinvention of itself. Though ACWF is far from holding all the characteristics of a true NGO, this title grants it legal grounds to claim more autonomy.

A further source of change came from pervasive economic and social dislocation, as the reforms after the Mao era struck disadvantaged groups the hardest. Many women and children's problems, from high unemployment rates, family violence to child labor, have intensified. As China's most recognized organization for women and children, the ACWF felt increasing pressure to fight these problems and provide both protection and services to their constituency. Effective implementation of this mission directly affected the organization's future and relations with the government. The ACWF still depends heavily upon government funding for staff salaries, daily operation and many programs; however, funding has been severely cut. Most of the support is for programs rather than organizational expenditures; thus, to continue receiving funds, the ACWF's programs must receive the government's approval.[24] Yet, a significant change in ACWF's revenues has taken place, and now a large proportion of its income comes from the enterprises they run, as some of the local federations are doing impressively well financially. The growth of financial independence has complicated the ACWF's attitude towards the government, since it can run programs on its own budget.[25] Lastly, since the mid-1990s, staff members of all mass organizations no longer enjoy civil servant status, which is now reserved for government employees only. This policy has caused serious insecurity among ACWF cadres who foresee major changes and believe the ACWF's future now rests upon its relations with women.[26]

Since the mid-1980s, and especially around the mid-1990s, a large number of grassroots women's organizations have emerged in China that actively advocate women's rights and the necessity of bottom-up organizations. These grassroots NGOs present a potential challenge to the authority of the ACWF, as evidenced in the 1993 Manila Asian and Pacific NGO Forum and again in the fourth WCW when INGOs questioned the NGO nature of the ACWF and asked whether the ACWF or grassroots organizations represented Chinese women (Liu 2000: 110; Howell 2000: 126; Xu 2003: 46). The relations between these two spheres are particularly interesting in the context of the ACWF's ambiguous quasi-governmental and quasi-NGO nature. The government entrusts the ACWF, along with the All-China Federation of Trade Unions and Chinese Communist Youth League, with the authority of supervising SOs, which in actuality is a government responsibility. That is why many Chinese grassroots women's organizations have become organizational members of local federations of the ACWF. When they do so, these grassroots organizations "automatically" obtain NGO status because of the ACWF's NGO status (Liu 2000: 111). Ironically, their membership in the ACWF also brings them trust from both the government and society because of the ACWF's well-established political status. At the same time, cooperation between the two has benefited the women's federations greatly because of the NGO image of grassroots organizations.

Over the years, the ACWF's leadership has also changed. Before the reforms, most ACWF leaders and staff were the wives of CCP leaders; many of them were revolutionaries. They continued to see the ACWF's role as assisting the party, just as women's organizations did during the CCP's revolution. However, since the 1980s, a large number of young cadres have entered the ACWF, and they understand the role of the ACWF quite differently. More of them possess higher education than the older cadres, and the new generation of leaders, especially at the lower rank or local levels, often act with a more independent mindset.[27]

Since the fourth WCW, the ACWF has called itself an NGO in all international activities. Nevertheless, the CCP does not grant the ACWF full autonomy, as the latter continues to be an indispensable part of its political system. The ACWF's multi-tier system has been a major channel through which the party-state collects information and enforces its policies upon women. For example, the ACWF and local federations are the most effective mechanisms of implementing birth control policy and repressing the Falun Gong. Thus, the party and government continue to entrust ACWF with quasi-governmental functions. Its continuing prestigious status and its new responsibilities have increased the ACWF's authority and monopoly, because the NGO regulations do not allow other independent women's federations to exist. At the same time, the close relationship with the government restrains its autonomy. The ACWF's experience points to the dilemma facing GONGOs: even as their autonomy is confined to the extent that the party-state can tolerate, they must become more autonomous to adapt to the new socio-economic environment.

A case study of the China Youth Development Foundation[28]

The growing experience of the China Youth Development Foundation (CYDF) provides a convincing case to show why the autonomy of Chinese NGOs is a complicated and even controversial matter, and how a close relationship with the government can be beneficial for NGO development. The CYDF was founded in 1989 as a registered, non-governmental foundation under the supervision of the Chinese Communist Youth League (CCYL), at the initiative of Xu Yongguang, former director of the CCYL Organization Division. Deeply disturbed by the fact that hundreds of thousands of children in destitute areas had lost their schooling, Xu and several of his colleagues decided to design CYDF's first program to help these students return to school.[29] Thus began the now famous Hope Project.

Xu and his colleagues were aware of the risks and possible political consequences of their actions. Launching a nationwide campaign for these children, they first had to reveal the devastating reality of China's rural education. For example, in the 1980s, Chinese governmental appropriations to education were not only lower than the average level in the world, but also lower than the average among developing countries. In 1985, the average proportion of investment in education with respect to GNP was: world 5.7 percent, developed countries 6.1 percent, developing countries 4.0 percent, and China 2.94–3.12 percent (Xia 1996: 4–9). Publicizing these facts would definitely provoke the government and impinge upon the state territory, as it is a government responsibility to provide nine years of mandatory and free education for all children. When the CYDF campaign for the Hope Project announced that China had two hundred million illiterates and two million school-age children who were too poor to go to school, this acute situation was quite an embarrassment to the State Education Council.[30]

The resultant tension between the Council and the CYDF during its early years caused the Foundation to hesitate to advertise the Hope Project in newspapers.

Today, the Hope Project is the Foundation's best-known program and has built 8,355 elementary schools and helped more than two million children from poor families to return to school (CYDF 2000: 47). It is by far China's largest NGO education project, and from 1989 to 2003, the CYDF received almost a billion RMB in domestic and international donations, while similar projects at all levels nationwide collected almost two billion RMB in private donations by 2000. The Hope Project has become a byword for "assisting needy students" or even "charitable behavior" in China, and the CYDF serves as a model for many other charities and public interest groups that imitate its fundraising strategies and program design.

One of the key factors behind the CYDF's success is its autonomous condition: its ability to make decisions and act independently, allowing it to adjust to new situations and seize opportunities quickly. The CYDF was founded in January 1989, and by October that same year, its first aid reached a village elementary school in Hebei province and 13 needy students. It would be unthinkable for a government organization to act this efficiently and promptly. The Hope Project has been driven by a series of street-wide promotion campaigns in major cities, multi-media publicity on the education crises in impoverished rural areas and the urgent need for popular action, performances and exhibitions for fundraising, and one-on-one sponsorship of four years of elementary education. The CYDF staff members are motivated by the cause and are creative in making the project work effectively and efficiently, in contrast with officeholders who are typically more concerned with not making mistakes and following party rules. A CYDF slogan promoting the Hope Project was "One + One Does Not Equal Two", meaning that in CYDF programs, two RMB in donations should produce a bigger result than just two RMB, highlighting the well-organized operation and magnification of social efficacy.

There are many reasons, however, to consider CYDF a GONGO and, in fact, many people, from NGO scholars and activists to ordinary Chinese, do consider it so. To begin, the establishment of CYDF involved four governmental organizations, including the CCYL, and it received an opening endowment of 100,000 RMB from the CCYL. During these years, the Foundation has maintained a close relationship with the CCYL, and the chairmanship of its council of executive directors, an honorary position, has always been an official appointed by and from the CCYL. After its early success, the Hope Project started to receive strong government support; most if not all government departments, governmental organizations and top CCP officials, including Deng Xiaoping, donated money. After Deng Xiaoping's donation was publicized by the media, China's major official newspapers, such as the *People's Daily*, *Chinese Youth Daily* and *Guangming Daily*, and TV stations have become the most powerful advertising channels for the Hope Project. The CYDF has certainly benefited from such support and publicity, yet the government has gained more from society by setting the Hope Project and CYDF as an example. In fact, the Youth League also benefited greatly from its involvement in the Hope Project, because after the Cultural Revolution its traditional image as the CCP's loyal assistant was losing its attraction to the young.

One successful yet controversial method the Foundation undertook was to utilize the Youth League's nationwide networks to generate funds for the Hope Project and then to deliver Hope scholarships through the same system to village children and schools. The Foundation started with four or five people and eventually extended into a mid-size organization with a staff of 50–60. Considering the size of the donations it raised since its commencement and the large numbers of Hope Elementary Schools built, it would be inconceivable that the Foundation not resort to external institutional mechanisms to carry out these tasks. The Youth League is one of the few mass organizations with a top-down organizational system from the central committee in Beijing reaching down to every village and urban community. With the Foundation's agreement and the CCYL's promotion, Hope Project funds have been established in almost all provinces with impoverished counties, and these funds are managed directly by the CCYL local branches (Kang 1997a: 123–31). Eventually, under the Foundation's leadership a nationwide youth development network was established. Certainly, without the Youth League's system the Hope Project would not have achieved its current scale and impact. Moreover, the relationship between the two is mutually beneficial. The direct involvement of the CCYL in the Hope Project has given this highly governmentally controlled mass organization a new look and new vitality. Especially for the CCYL's local branches, the Hope Project has become a major part of their work.[31]

However, the CYDF's relationship with the CCYL is a double-edged sword. Not only have problems in the local Youth League's management of Hope funds become the CYDF's fault, the CCYL's significant role in the Hope Project and the Foundation's other programs have blurred the CYDF's NGO image. Even as one of the bright stars in China's NGO sector, the CYDF cannot evade the shadow of GONGO. My interviews with Xu Yongguang and Gu Xiaojin, the current secretary general of the CYDF, revealed that they apparently were very much aware of the ambiguity of the CYDF's NGO status. They insisted that the CYDF's NGO nature was based on its independent decision-making, financial self-sufficiency, and the organization's roles distinct from the governmental organizations. The controversial issue of the CYDF's autonomy seemed not to trouble them. The CYDF's governmental affiliation in general helps the Foundation gain the trust of the Chinese public, whereas in its overseas fundraising campaigns, the CYDF highlights its NGO markings. Still at an early stage of development, Chinese NGOs, as represented by the CYDF, need all the help they can get. For Xu Yongguang and his colleagues, the CYDF provides opportunity and institutional space for fulfilling their ideas and ambition. As long as they do not cross the CCP's lines and legal regulations, the CYDF is quite autonomous under China's political conditions.

In short, within a quarter of a century, the NGO landscape in China has rejuvenated from a desert into a luxuriant green field, as evidenced in the establishment of legal NGO status, impressive increases in numbers, and the improvement of autonomous conditions. The organizations outside of the state system are rapidly changing China's state–society power structure, and they are forming a more independent sector. Yet, this picture is far from perfect. NGOs are subject to party-state intervention, and they still have to fight for the rights and space that they are entitled to legally. To the international NGO community and scholars, organizational autonomy is a crucial element in the independent role and healthy development of NGOs. Given China's conditions, however, the major concern of Chinese NGO activists is to carry out their operations without alerting the state. To them, openly confronting the state for their independence is not a practical move; thus, ironically, they resort to maintaining relations with the government in order to obtain autonomy quietly. The bottom line is that even though the autonomous nature of these organizations remains ambiguous, this form of NGO has furnished the Chinese people with new institutional options to meet the challenge of urgent economic and social problems.

4 Social capital

The significance and dynamics of grassroots NGOs and social networks

The 1980s Chinese student democratic movements marked the peak of the upsurge of political organizations in the PRC. Ironically, this movement, along with the East European revolutions and Poland's Solidarity movement, greatly alarmed the CCP about the potentials of civil society organizations. Since the Tiananmen incident in 1989, the state's coercive policy towards independent workers' unions, intellectual dissidents' organizations, and religious activities, as discussed in Chapter 2, has silenced society's political voices. In striking contrast to the frailty of political associations, the past twenty-odd years after Mao's regime have witnessed the resuscitation of all types of "apolitical" associations. On the one hand, semi-governmental membership organizations such as the All-China Federation of Workers' Unions, Chinese Communist Youth League, and All-China Women's Federation are expanding and transforming themselves into more autonomous and substantial associations in social and political realms (Chapter 3). On the other hand, grassroots civic associations and non-profit institutions are rapidly growing. At one end of the continuum are formally established and registered NGOs, while at the other are vast numbers of unregistered, informal, and loosely associated networks from hobby clubs, morning exercise gatherings, and performance groups to community voluntary groups and college environmental organizations. While it is virtually impossible to know how many of these informal networks exist and what they engage in, Chinese officials at the Ministry of Civil Affairs believe that they are more numerous than registered organizations.[1]

Furthermore, the IT revolution has considerably changed the way people communicate and associate. According to the "Thirteenth Semiannual Survey Reports on the Internet in China" released by the China Internet Network Information Center, the number of Internet users in China reached 79.5 million by January 2004 (Wang and He 2004). The estimate of the number of Internet bulletin board systems (BBS) in China is 100,000; these boards provide both open and closed forums through which members discuss political issues, such as constitutionalism and democracy. This virtual associational life then easily transfers into formal or informal associations in the real world; get-togethers of "net-mates" are now quite common for the BBS users (Wang and He).

106 *Social capital*

Some Chinese scholars are convinced that a sizable group of Internet intellectuals has emerged in this "Internet age", and thus has broken "the iron board" of China's political environment (Ya 2004). Chen Kuide, the chief editor of *Observation*, an Internet magazine outside of China, concludes that the Internet has promoted the upsurge of human rights movements in society and changed the state–society relationship. According to Chen, independent Internet intellectuals and the evolution of civil society together have created a forceful pressure group in society, and the most recent cases of official handling of intellectual dissidents indicate a "silent bargaining" between the state and non-governmental sector (Ya). To explain this new phenomenon, the terms "e-NGOs" and "e-civil society" have now appeared in China.

This chapter focuses on Chinese people's participation in civic associations, formal or informal, for personal or public interest, and it addresses especially the significance of grassroots and informal social networks that have long been ignored by studies of Chinese associational behavior. Theoretically, it adopts the concept of social capital to examine how individuals utilize their economic, social and cultural resources to establish social links as well as to determine the primary features and functions of those social networks. Thus the first section of the chapter deals with interpretation and application of social capital under China's specific circumstances. The chapter then, discusses grassroots civic organizations from two angles. First, it uses case studies of different types of social networks to analyze why and how people associate and what effect people's engagement in civic associations has with respect to the evolution of Chinese civil society. Second, it studies the dynamics and leadership of Chinese grassroots NGOs by examining intellectual NGO activists' role in China's associational revolution. This chapter gives special attention to small, grassroots, voluntary and often unregistered organizations and networks that are not discussed in other chapters in this book.

The following sections intend to answer a key question of this book: what is the significance of non-governmental and grassroots organizations and do they facilitate civil society in China? By highlighting the outcomes of civic engagement, it argues that civil society and democracy can only be achieved in China with the increase of public access to information, knowledge, and opportunities to participate in associational activities and decision-making. It shows that for millions of Chinese, self-organization is an empowerment process and an opportunity to exercise their rights. Even associations that are informal and for personal gain carry on activities that nourish the spirit of volunteerism, humanitarianism, trust and civic duty, all of which are important elements of a democratic society. Grassroots organizations champion interests that had hitherto been ignored or lacked cohesiveness, and their associative influence on public policy is slowly yet undoubtedly increasing. The development of environmental NGOs (see the case study in the second section) presents powerful evidence for this trend. Although the Chinese have yet to obtain the freedom to express their political opinions or organize political parties, these grassroots NGOs and informal networks present the clear political message that people are starting to take control of their own lives and exercise their own rights. Thus, these organizations are indeed facilitating the emergence of a civil society in China.

The concept of social capital and its application in China

In recent years, the concept of social capital has been widely used in NGO studies. Although scholars continue to debate the definition and application of this concept, they generally agree that high levels of social capital stock and active civil society are indispensable to a functioning democratic system. What is social capital? According to Pierre Bourdieu, a French sociologist who first systematically analyzed this concept in modern terms, social capital is "the aggregate of the actual or potential resources which are linked to possession of a durable network of more or less institutionalized relationship of mutual acquaintance and recognition . . ." (Bourdieu 1997: 51). Following Bourdieu, American sociologist James Coleman furthered the concept by addressing its function and the importance of trust:

> Like other forms of capital, social capital is productive, making possible the achievement of certain ends that would not be attainable in its absence . . . For example, a group whose members manifest trustworthiness and place extensive trust in one another will be able to accomplish much more than a comparable group lacking that trustworthiness and trust.
> (Coleman 1990: 302)

Robert Putnam's renowned works on regional governments and civic associations in Northern Italy and the decline of citizen participation in civic associations in the United States have attracted much attention to this concept's political significance and its impact on civil society (Putnam 1993, 1995). Putnam defines social capital as those "features of social organization, such as trust, norms, and networks, that can improve the efficiency of society by facilitating coordinate actions" (Putnam 1993: 167). Based on Putnam's definition, Kenneth Newton highlights three important facets of this concept. First, he argues that with reciprocity and trust, social capital can turn individuals "with little social conscience and little sense of social obligation into members of a community with shared interests, shared assumptions about social relations and a sense of common good." Thus, it becomes the social cement that binds society together (Newton 1999: 4). Second, the main features of social capital can be found in formal or informal networks, "which link friends, family, community, work, and both public and private life" (Newton: 6). Last, the function of social capital is productive and can be defined in terms of "collective goods, facilities, and services which are produced in the voluntary sector, as opposed to being produced by families, markets, or government" (Newton: 7). As the later sections will demonstrate, in China's recent associational revolution, these features all become rather clear.

It is true that many associations are motivated by self-interest, and yet, as some scholars point out, they bring positive influence to society. Nan Lin, an American political scientist, argues that "institutionalized social relations with embedded resources are expected to benefit both the collective and the individuals in the collective" (N. Lin 2001: 26). According to Putnam, "One special feature of social capital, like trust, norms, and networks, is that it is ordinarily a public good . . ." He points out that though often a byproduct of other social activities, social capital helps to overcome dilemmas of collective action by inducing reciprocity and social networks, thereby creating opportunities for new action (Putnam 1993: 167, 170). Accordingly, associational life breeds trust, cooperation and self-discipline; in turn, civic engagement stimulates political involvement, citizenship and general interest in the public good. Sidney Verba, Kay Schlozman and Henry Brady in their study of American civil volunteerism argue, "Both the motivation and the capacity to take part in politics have their roots in the fundamental non-political institutions" (Verba et al. 1995: 3). Coming full circle, Putnam connects social capital stock and democracy when he concludes that "social capital, as embodied in horizontal networks of civic engagement, bolsters the performance of the polity and the economy, rather than the reverse: strong society, strong economy; strong society, strong state" (Putnam 1993: 176).

Even though the theoretical framework of social capital discussed above is a Western paradigm, its features are clearly evident in the recent development of social networks in China. In contrast to the concept of civil society, which focuses on demarcating the roles of the state, business, and non-profit sectors and underscores the political impacts of formal, autonomous and voluntary NGOs, the social capital approach discusses people's engagement in civic associations and addresses the positive subsequent economic, social and political effects on individuals and society. Shaoguang Wang and Jianyu He, Chinese political scientists, in their study of Chinese NGOs, argue that, since associations that generate social capital do not have to be formal, voluntary, or fully autonomous from state control, the fullest possible array of associations can be included in any research thereof (Wang and He 2004). Thus far, studies of Chinese NGOs and the non-governmental sector have largely focused on the concept of civil society and ignored the significance of informal social networks. While it is beyond the capacity of this study to engage in the theoretical discourse of social capital, this chapter considers the social capital approach to be pertinent in explaining the profound change in China's associational life, especially in depicting informal and non-political social networks or grassroots groups.

Nevertheless, this study argues that social capital in China takes its own forms as it becomes shaped by contemporary social and cultural circumstances.

For instance, the strong social function of a relationship, *guanxi*, is a form of social capital that is uniquely Chinese and has greatly affected Chinese people's associational behavior. *Guanxi* is essentially about establishing relations with people with the power, resources, and ability to achieve outcomes that would otherwise not occur. Although every culture uses relationships for all kinds of purposes, the pervasiveness and notorious "magic" of *guanxi* in post-reform China have become a serious political problem. This term has a clearly negative connotation in Chinese, as *guanxi* generally indicates bribery, corruption and inappropriate or illegal activities.

Yet, to a great extent, the practice of relationships has become a cultural norm that compels people's social behavior. By Bourdieu's classic definition, *guanxi* is a form of social capital in China because people utilize their relationships to get things done and to exchange with other types, such as cultural, monetary and political capital. With regards to associational life, people with *guanxi* bring social capital to their organizations, while others join for the express purpose of building their own network. As some of the following case studies show, networks and associations use their *guanxi* to obtain access to resources or political protection that help their operations. Practicing *guanxi* in associational actions is undoubtedly a controversial exercise in ethics; nevertheless, it has benefited the growth of democratic and grassroots civic associations.

The social capital approach helps us see clearly the importance and major features of grassroots and informal organizations. Both Putnam and Newton recognize that these informal groups may be as important as formal ones for social capital research; in some respects, they may be even more important (Newton 1999: 11–13). In Putnam's words, these informal associations alter people's associational behavior, for "Taking part in a choral society or a bird-watching club can teach self-discipline and an appreciation for the joys of successful collaboration" (Putnam 1993: 90). One of the most noticeable changes in daily life brought on by the pluralistic economy and culture that infiltrated China's urban society after the 1990s was the level of engagement in civic associations. While there are no reliable statistics on their quantity, a 2004 study estimates that there are 41,000 philately associations and 70,000 elderly associations (Wang and He 2004). These organizations are highly informal, small, and lack sufficient means to operate large-scale activities; nevertheless, they are voluntary, autonomous, and greatly influence their members.

It is no exaggeration to say that the upsurge of this enormous number of informal networks in China has a great social and political potential in China's associational revolution. The mushrooming of all kinds of networks in China since the reform and open policy indicates the resurfacing of people's urgent need for social connection, information, friendship, exchange, humanitarianism, or civic duty that had been long denied or existed in different forms. After over twenty years of reforms, participation in civic associations, traditional or modern, formal or informal, for public purposes or personal interests, has entered China's mainstream culture and become an indispensable part of ordinary people's daily lives.

As the following examples show, the significance of engagement of civic associations is multi-fold. First, grassroots networks at the informal, community level have embraced a broad and diverse array of interest groups with people who may not be members of well-established and formally registered organizations. For example, bird-watching and environmental groups aim to attract youths from elementary school level upwards, while caroling and folk dancing groups in parks are mostly made up of retirees. Unlike formal organizations that are often organized around the workplace or professions, grassroots networks attract people with common interests across career or geographic boundaries. Their sustained participation points to the important space that associations fill in popular life.

Second, while some scholars address the value of the social capital approach for its inclusiveness of involuntary organizations in studies of China's NGO landscapes (Wang and He 2004), this study addresses the significance of the voluntary nature of grassroots and informal networks. Chinese people have been under political pressure for the past half-century to join officially controlled associations such as the All-China Federation of Workers' Unions, Chinese Communist Youth League, and All-China Women's Federation and the CCP, or to participate in so-called "voluntary activities."[2] In contrast, grassroots associations are truly voluntary, in terms of membership and level of dedication, and allow ordinary Chinese people to try out the freedoms of association and self-expression.

Third, the following cases demonstrate that the resuscitation of networks entangles traditional Chinese values and associative customs with new Western ideas, such as volunteerism and civil society.[3] This cultural amalgamation has expanded the variety of ideas and the forms of association that enact those ideas. Accordingly, even while traditional associations like extended family, kinship or village fellows have blossomed in recent years, particularly in the rural areas, the new forms of grassroots organizations for public interest, such as environmental groups and social services for marginalized populations, have extended far beyond the boundaries of self-interests and locality.

Last, the grassroots associations are nourishing and reawakening the trust, reciprocity, spirit of cooperation and collective actions initiated by people that were destroyed by the CCP's coercive government prior to the reforms. Putnam argues that "trust is an essential component of social capital" (Putnam 1993: 170). In this chapter, trust means that joiners trust others in the association to work collectively to pursue the objectives of the association. Trust is an especially important feature in China's associational life because the Cultural Revolution completely dissolved people's trust in institutions and other individuals. Thus, networks, particularly informal ones, often begin within circles of friends, acquaintances, or people with similar backgrounds, where people are predisposed to trust others. In cyclical fashion, trust leads to reciprocity and cooperation, which in turn nourish cooperation and expand associational engagement to new levels. As we can see in the cases of the Beidahuang 58th Regiment Friendship Association and Peking Opera Fan Clubs below, many people initially joined networks for their own interests, and yet they eventually launched activities aimed at helping others and society in general.

The significance of grassroots organizations

This section considers grassroots networks with diverse age groups, cultural backgrounds, structures, sizes, values, missions and governance styles. Despite these variations, they were all initiated and operated by the members themselves and enjoy a substantial amount of autonomy. These case studies examine what motivates ordinary people to participate in civic associations and the impact of their participation on individuals and the evolving civil society.

The rejuvenation of traditional associational values

The upsurge of associations in China has always been marked by China's tradition and culture. China has a deep-rooted, family-centered culture; traditionally, extended family and kinship networks dominated relationships and were the main source of support, knowledge, and personal development. These networks then radiated out to those of similar backgrounds, such as classmates, alumni, fellow villagers, colleagues, followers of the same master, or comrades. In the Chinese language, words for these groups all start with the character "tong," connoting people with something in common (Yang, X. 2000: 39). In the late Qing Dynasty and early Republic, new forms of networks among intellectuals and gentry-merchants emerged, and the most numerous were professional associations and chambers of commerce. These new organizations then became the driving force behind the emerging of civil society in contemporary China (Chapter 1).

However, during the first thirty years of the CCP's regime (1949–78), the private organizations ceased to function, and *danwei* (work units) in cities and communes in agricultural areas replaced traditional social structures such as kinship networks, neighborhoods, clan systems, religious and cultural groups, and people's social lives became subject to political control. For example, folk religious groups long embedded in rural society were banned when the commune movement started in the mid-1950s and totally vanished during the Cultural Revolution (Gao 2000: 101).[4] The so-called class struggle reached its peak in the Cultural Revolution, and set family members, friends, fellow workers, and villagers against each other. Under the total control of a coercive state, trust, civic engagement and associations became fragmented.

112 *Social capital*

When associational life rejuvenated, various traditional social networks re-emerged. In the countryside, kinship and clan networks rapidly revived, recovering genealogical trees, rebuilding ancestral halls, organizing festival activities, and resuming charitable works such as helping widows, orphans, and the disabled, and giving scholarships for promising students (Gao 1999: 28–66; Jiang 2002: 5–6). Folk culture revived in the form of temple associations, folk religious groups, and traditional seasonal and holiday entertaining groups, especially in rural areas. For example, by the late 1990s, there were over a hundred folk cultural groups (*huahui*) in Beijing alone, and, at the annual temple festival held by the Dragon Tablet Association of a village in Northern China, over 100,000 participants came from villages in the vicinity (Gao 2000, 100–5). Piggy-backing on these festivals are the lively temporary markets that promote inter-regional trade. None of those groups are registered, and a large proportion of them are seasonal and exist irregularly. The official attitude towards them is one of ambivalence. While wary of the potential risk of trespass of the government's religious taboos, the local governments nevertheless depend on the same dispersed organizations for cultural activities and market opportunities (Gao 2000, 1999: 28–35). In addition, traditional organizations like chambers of commerce and trade associations are registering and reassuming important functions in the economic realm at an impressive rate (Chapter 5). Other urban associations such as those of hometown fellow and alumni are also increasing.

The Ningbo Fellows' Association (*Ningbo tongxiang hui*, NFA), located in Ningbo, Zhejiang Province, demonstrates the revival of the traditional valuation of social capital.[5] The origin of NFA can be traced back to 1797 when Ningbo businessmen working in Shanghai founded the "Siming Public House" (*Siming gongsuo*). Its purpose was to help the population of workers in Shanghai from Ningbo locate housing, funeral services, and healthcare. During the late Qing and early Republic, when Ningbo businessmen became the main source of Shanghai's industry and trade, the NFA's functions extended to economic, social, and political spheres. The organization opened a hospital, elementary schools, a vocation training school and other charitable programs not only to Ningbo fellows but also to the Shanghai public. Within the Shanghai General Chamber of Commerce, Ningbo networks became the most vocal representatives of the national bourgeoisies' interests, key among them the battles against foreign invaders and businesses in Shanghai.

The CCP's policy towards the national bourgeoisie forced NFA to close in 1954 and lie dormant for a quarter of a century. In the 1980s, when Deng Xiaoping launched the economic reforms, he recognized the tradition of Chinese people valuing their hometowns. To encourage overseas Chinese to contribute to China's economic development, Deng used the Ningbo businessmen's network as an example. In the late 1980s, Deng instructed the Ningbo government to "generate gangs of Ningbo (*ningbo bang*) around the world to help Ningbo's development." Interestingly, Deng dismissed the normally negative connotations around networks (*bang*) in order to revive what was now pragmatically useful. Responding to his call, the Ningbo Fellows' Friendship Association in Shanghai opened in 1989; it aimed to attract fellows abroad and in Shanghai, where now over two million Ningbo people lived, to help their hometown's economic and social development. The plan succeeded. The head of NFA concludes, "It was China's traditional conception and value of hometown as well as Ningbo businessmen's financial success that had kept the Ningbo networks active for almost two hundred years before the PRC; and it was these same factors that guaranteed NFA's success today."[6]

Social networks for personal interests: providing needs and fostering trust and reciprocity

The rapid economic development has led some to seek cultural and spiritual enrichment in their lives, while the economic and social dislocation of others has created enormous needs; in both cases, the government is no longer capable at any level of fulfilling all people's needs, as it once attempted to do. An impressive number of professional, non-profit service providers have been filling the gaps between the needs and the governmental means, and at the same time, informal social networks are increasingly active in helping people cope with difficulties and fulfill their personal needs.

The Beidahuang 58th Regiment Friendship Association is one such organization.[7] Beidahuang (the great northern wilderness) is a vast and remote region along the China–Russia border in Heilongjiang province. Hundreds of thousands of young students were sent there by the government in the 1960s and 1970s and organized into military regiments to cultivate the wild lands. After the Cultural Revolution, the great majority of these students returned to their homes, mostly in Beijing and Shanghai, but most had lost the opportunity for higher education and a good career. In the face of serious readjustment difficulties, members of the 58th regiment turned to each other and organized a friendship association in the mid-1990s. Hundreds joined and together they published newsletters and established networks to circulate employment, financial, and business information that each member collected from his or her own work unit and social network. Annual and bi-monthly gatherings allowed members not only to exchange information, but also to receive much needed moral and emotional support. The key to this association was the trust established in the course of their common ordeals in Beidahuang. In the late 1990s the association was preparing to invite all twelve regiments to join them in building a much larger friendship network.

Peking Opera fan clubs present another example of how civic networks foster social capital. As of 2004, Beijing had over 200 Peking opera fan clubs, all non-registered groups whose members were mostly middle-aged or elderly. It was an old tradition that Peking Opera fans called themselves "ticket friends" (*piaoyou*) and were not only patrons but also amateur players themselves. After 1949, the *piaoyou* tradition slowly vanished and, during the ten years of the Cultural Revolution, the party barred all traditional operas and replaced them with eight revolutionary operas. However, since the 1990s, the *piaoyou* tradition has gradually revived, and fans are organizing clubs to develop their personal interests and enrich their lives.

In 2004, I visited one *piaoyou* club during its rehearsal. The club had about 15–20 regular members who met every weekend and was one of the best performance groups. Unlike most other hobby groups, *piaoyou* clubs need larger budgets in order to put on quality shows. As *piaoyou* shows are traditionally free to the public, clubs must find their own financial support. Thus, members learn how to fundraise, borrow or buy costumes, rent theater and rehearsal space, and pay their professional band players. At the club I visited, the income derived mainly from one member who was a successful businessman and a great Peking Opera fan.

I later interviewed a singer at the club, whose story, I was told, was typical of the experiences of many participants at such associations. She had loved singing since she was young, but the Cultural Revolution took away her chance to sing professionally. Forced to retire early due to her work unit's rundown conditions, she felt very much unfulfilled with her life. "Joining the club and singing changed my life. I have never felt so proud of myself as when my family and friends came to watch my performance for my 50th birthday celebration. Now I am healthier, more confident, and I have realized my dream." Since she joined the club, she learned not just to sing operas, but also to work with the band and other singers to handle all matters relating to the shows. "You have to learn everything," she said, "and this is the exciting part."

In contrast, Sina Drivers' Friendship Club (SDFC) is an Internet network mainly for young people. Sina is China's largest Internet company, and the SDFC is one of many e-social groups formed under Sina's online bulletin board system.[8] The SDFC has several sub-clubs on the makes of cars, such as Fukong, Jieda or Songtana. Within each sub-club, members organize special interest groups, including badminton, billiards, or travel, among others. Each group usually has several dozen members and one volunteer in charge of organizing activities and creating and maintaining the web page. The members become virtual friends first and then go on real-life outings, which are often attended by over a hundred participants. Since there is no membership fee, all activities are run by volunteers, and participants share the cost of these trips.

Who are these people and why do they join? "Just for fun and to make friends," a former member told me. Members of the SDFC range in age from 20 to 40, belong to China's new middle class, earn monthly incomes around 5,000–6,000 RMB (US$ 625–750) and usually have their own apartments. Their common ground lies in the ownership of a China-made car – a symbol of *xiaokang* (a decent financial condition) under China's current economic situation. Yet, despite their relative economic well-being, they felt that they needed more than comfortable living conditions. Most of them are the only child in the family, some have difficulty dating or making friends, and some are even alienated by their new lifestyles. Chatting online gives them a new way to make friends. In fact, members put stickers on their cars so that they can recognize their fellow members on the road and chat via car phones. In a way, as interviewees explained to me, the network has given them a relatively stable circle of friends who discuss where to find good deals on car parts, the government's latest set of traffic rules, and anything else under the sun.

Community-based associations are also emerging rapidly. In the six communities in Beijing, Shanghai, and Shenyang I visited in the early 2000s, associations of various kinds are becoming a part of community development. Focusing on social service, voluntary assistance, and cultural activities, a sense of community is growing among residents. In newly opened commercial apartment compounds, for example, new neighbors find their common interests in issues relating to safety, apartment management and service, and surrounding environmental conditions. Should the community build a fence? What summer programs are there for kids? These seem like minor decisions, but the mechanisms for people to express their opinions are forming, and this is the most important element for civil society.

Common concerns become reasons for associating, and the number of apartment owners' associations, both virtual and in communities, is rising. One resident in a northern suburb of Beijing told me that she and some retired women in the neighborhood were discussing the pollution caused by a nearby factory, and were considering founding an organization to have a stronger voice in this matter. The ongoing experimental direct election of neighborhood community committees has given hope to residents that their associations may play important roles in both electing and cooperating with the committees. In many communities, a new form of mutual-assistance networks is growing. Residents are not only learning to self-govern, but they are also providing each other with services and assistance.

The networks discussed above are not registered organizations, and yet they are among the most pervasive and grassroots of all the NGOs in China, so much so that they represent ordinary people's associational life. People participate in networks for all different purposes, but in each case, their involvement increases their trust and sociability, provides them with useful information and knowledge, and helps them fulfill their personal interests and, as my interviewees indicated, elevates their self-esteem. Although most informal networks were initially formed on behalf of personal interests, the outcomes of these associations have stretched far beyond personal gain. When Beidahuang returnees organized a friendship association to help each other, they also developed a desire to help those who still live in Beidahuang. The association organizes trips to revisit Beidahuang and members donate money to local elementary schools and clinics. They also established the Beidahuang Fund and programs to promote trade of Beidahuang's agricultural products in Beijing. The Peking opera fans are pushing the government to lend more support for preserving and reviving this traditional performing art. The club I visited played for the public during China's 2004 Spring Festival at the district government's invitation. A member observed that the true significance of their performance lay not in government recognition of their existence, but in this evidence of their usefulness to society. It is true that at this stage these social groups do not have direct influence on government policy-making; nevertheless, the political consequence of people's exercising of their associational rights and self-expression will be profound and significant.

Raising social conscience and advocating for public interest: the case of environmental NGOs

In contrast to associations that focus on personal interests, the upsurge of voluntary, grassroots NGOs devoted to the public good represents the rapid increase of a social conscience and citizen participation in China. Although Chinese social organizations emerged soon after the reforms in the 1980s, the phenomenal growth of grassroots NGOs for public causes came after the fourth WCW in 1995. This conference essentially delivered the concept and practice of NGOs to China's general public; ever since then, grassroots NGOs have become a new institutional field in China. The grassroots NGOs have acted in a broad spectrum of societal issues, from environmental protection, education, poverty alleviation, and the rights of women, children, and sex workers, to combating AIDS and drug abuse. For many of these social injustices, grassroots NGOs are the first and sometimes only resort in China. For instance, hotlines for abused women, sexually transmitted diseases, family consultation, AIDS education, assistance for sex workers, drug abuse rehabilitation, and education centers for autistic children, among many others, were first launched and sometimes still solely run by grassroots NGOs.[9]

Of these social issues, environmental protection has generated some of the most intense activism, and the environmental NGOs (ENGOs) have become the most vibrant and influential grassroots organizations in China today. According to a 1998 report by the China Environmental Protection Foundation, China had approximately 1,600 NGOs related to environmental protection (CEPF 1998), yet the majority of the organizations in this official statistic are governmentally initiated. The first real grassroots ENGO was Friends of Nature, established in 1994 (FON). Among the ENGOs that followed the FON's footsteps are the Global Village of Beijing (GVB), the Green Earth Volunteers (GEV), Green Home, Green Web, Beijing Environmental Volunteer Network, Greener Beijing, and China Wildlife Protection Association. Tellingly, FON now has some seven hundred dues-paying members, plus thousands of affiliated students organized in local clubs.[10] It is linked to like-minded organizations abroad. The GVB has grown into an institution with 14 staff members and over 4,000 volunteers all over the nation, while Green Home has recruited 30,000 members.[11]

With their relatively small numbers and limited resources, the major contribution of the grassroots ENGOs to China's environmental future is not their hands-on, problem-solving programs; rather, the significance of these organizations is their vision, strategy and method of educating the public about China's environmental problems and mobilizing them to act, both individually and collectively. In recent years, ENGOs have also become an effective impetus and institutional platform for cooperation among government, businesses, communities, media, NGOs in other fields and international organizations. Many environmental activists know each other, and they co-organize or join in activities such as the Earth Day China Action. These collaborations have created a profound societal influence beyond environmental conservation. Elizabeth Economy, an expert on China's environmental situation, states that ENGOs in China "are at the vanguard of non-governmental activity" (Economy 2004a: 131) and they have engaged in every aspect of environmental protection (Economy 2004b). She is convinced that an environmental movement impelled by the ENGOs is emerging in China (2004b).

Many reasons explain why ENGOs are able to take such crucial roles. First and foremost, the devastating deforestation, industrial pollution and abusive extraction of natural resources since the reforms have created grave environmental crises (Zheng 2001; Economy 2004a). Environmental destruction has taken an incredible toll on the economy and human lives, making it an urgent problem that the CCP state must deal with to obtain sustainable development and political stability. For example, about 4–6 percent of GDP is lost each year due to the environmental degradation. Over 64 percent of Chinese cities cannot pass the air quality test, and 300,000 people have died as a result of water pollution (Zhang 2004; Economy 2004b). Historically, the Yangzi River flooded once every few decades, but in the past decade it has flooded every year. The devastating flood of 1998 took 30,000 lives and created economic losses upwards of 300 billion RMB. Even though the government took some imperative actions that same year, strictly prohibiting logging in upper Yangzi Valley, it was too little, too late (Zheng 2001: 20–2). Some China scholars point out that "China has promulgated an extensive body of environmental law that is impressive in comparison to that of many other developing nations" (Alford and Shen 1998: 405–6); however, "most environmental policies are too complex, long-term, and deeply enmeshed in competing with economic interests to be effective" (Lieberthal 1998).

As in many other fields, the government is desperate for help from society, and is encouraging the public to join forces in the environmental actions. In 1996, the same year that MOCA tightened NGO registration, China's Vice-Premier, Song Jian, praised the positive roles of ENGOs at a national environmental conference and promised the government's support for all kinds of ENGOs (Song 1996: 2). Thus, the seriousness of environmental problems has provided the ENGOs more space and influence on policy-making than other types of NGOs. While this encouragement stimulates ENGOs by legalizing them, however, their activities are still circumscribed by government control and the absence of funding as well as legal and institutional mechanisms for environmental lobbying. Furthermore, whilst the central government earnestly addresses the importance of environmental protection, local governments continually prioritize economic development ahead of environmental protection, regardless of environmental laws (Economy 2004b).

Thus, ENGOs in China must navigate a narrow course within politically tolerated zones. In his study of ENGOs' survival strategy, Guobin Yang borrows Kevin O'Brien's notion of "boundary-spanning contention," the area "located near the boundary between official, prescribed politics and politics by other means" and that therefore may be "arguably legal, permissible in some eyes but not in others." Yang argues that ENGOs take advantage of political gray zones to advance contestable claims and extract concessions; often, as O'Brien describes, they employ "the rhetoric and commitments of the powerful to curb political or economic power" (O'Brien 2003: 53, quoted in Yang 2005). And he concludes, "Under the protective umbrella of the state policy of sustainable development, ENGOs promote an environmental discourse of democratic values and citizen participation" (Yang 2005: 52).

Recognizing the government's mixed attitude towards NGOs, the ENGOs pragmatically choose not to directly confront authority. Instead they push environmental protection and assist in the implementation of environmental laws via cooperation with official environmental bureaus or officials who are environmental protection enthusiasts. This cooperative strategy is evident in their program choices, which are politically feasible and less controversial,[12] and in their claim of apolitical motives for environmental remediation (Ho 2001: 916). For example, the key program of FON is public education, an activity deemed unthreatening by the government and a practical alternative to lobbying.[13] From 2000–01, FON's mobile environmental education groups visited over 120 elementary and middle schools in Beijing, Inner Mongolia, and Hebei Province, teaching youngsters and training teachers.[14] Other programs like the environmental summer camps, Earth Day China Action, Green Hope, tree planting and bird watching have not only attracted many participants, but have also done much to educate the public about the severe deterioration of China's environment and the devastating consequences for everyone.

The significance of the ENGOs' education programs is its challenge to China's current mainstream aspirations for commercial and material wealth and American standards of living. As Katrin Fiedler once wrote, "In many societies, NGOs play the role of advocates of 'alternative' development, with a special emphasis on values. In the current process of rapid globalization, the value-oriented nature of NGOs will gain importance as a counterweight to this trend of extreme market-orientation" (Fiedler 2002). Liao Xiaoyi, the founder and director of GVB and the 2000 winner of a prestigious environmental award, the Sophie Prize, called for the establishment of a value system that combines democracy, science, and harmony [with nature]. She also advocated a national spirit that treasures resources, simplifies lifestyles, raises goals, and respects all living things (Liao 2004). In a society hungry for material gain in a new era of economic freedoms, these voices provide a reminder of social and moral values. As indicated by the action of ENGOs, Chinese NGOs indeed represent efforts for alternative choices.

To an impressive degree, these activities *have* succeeded in raising people's awareness of environmental problems and their social and moral responsibility. In a survey adopting the standards of the Global Environmental Survey (GOES), the majority of urban residents prioritized environmental protection over economic development, and the great majority in the age group under 30 believed that individuals were the most responsible for environmental protection (Ma and Guo 2000: 201–10). Applications to join FON arrive weekly from all age groups and professions, and these speak powerfully of the organization's impact. Inspired by FON's activities, these letters strongly express people's realization of and deep concern about the extent of China's environmental degradation (Liang and Liang 2000: 431–94; FON Newsletters 2001). In another case, when Wang Yu was a student at Yunnan University, Liang Congjie's lecture at her university, in her own words, "Planted a green seed in her heart." Later, she organized an environmental group at the university, which several hundred students joined, and now she is a core officer at the Center for Biodiversity and Indigenous Knowledge, a well-known Kunming-based ENGO.[15]

The case of ENGOs also points to the idealism and activism of the next generation. While there were only eight student environmental groups in 1995, an impressive number of student environmental groups have surfaced since 1999, such that by 2001 most major universities had some kind of environmental organization, with at least 184 college environmental organizations in China (Yang 2005: 50). Some are organized by members of FON or other ENGOs; others are completely self-run. Impressively, these college groups have thrived under the CCP's strict supervision of student organizations after the 1989 student democratic movement.[16] Environmental protection gives college students a legitimate reason to organize activities beyond academic matters and campus walls.

Especially since the early 2000s, the ENGOs have increasingly become a major catalyst of cooperation among governmental agencies, NGOs, communities and the business sector. Liao Xiaoyi emphasizes that in building a greener China the most important factors are cooperative partners and citizen participation (Liao 2004). The GVB's experimental green community program provides a convincing example. The GVB's efforts are aimed at mobilizing society and one of its slogans is "Turn ideals into reality." The

120 *Social capital*

GVB launched its first green community on a street in Xuanwu, a district in Beijing. This program requires the formation of a joint committee including representatives from the Environmental Bureau, municipal government, Women's Federation, Office of Water Frugality, the GVB, the community residential committee, and residential property management and service companies. Each partner is a relevant stakeholder with the necessary authority and responsibility, participating in larger projects as a whole while leading their own activities. Much of this cooperation relies on the energy of resident volunteers, and the most profound accomplishment of green communities is changing residents' mentalities and lifestyles. At the pilot site in Xuanwu, 90 percent of the families converted to using economical light bulbs and water faucets; they sort and recycle garbage and batteries, plant grass and trees, and reduce noise pollution (*Beijing Evening News*, February 24, 2001: 4).

Although ENGOs avoid becoming political organizations, environmental protection *is* a political issue. Not only do the ideas and activities that ENGOs promote have deep political implications, but environmental interests often conflict with immediate economic and political interests. In the long run, as experiences in Taiwan and other parts of Asia demonstrate, civic self-empowerment through environmental movements creates a major impetus for broader, systemic reforms (Alford and Shen 1998: 419–20). Such phenomena have taken place in China since the early 2000s, as evidenced, for example, in environmental organizations' anti-dam actions. The first action was around the Three Gorges Dam, a controversial project with serious environmental and social consequences. Given the domestic and international outcry, it immediately became an extremely sensitive issue that was politically taboo to discuss or investigate (Dai *et al.* 1998). Nevertheless, open criticism of the Three Gorges Project is increasingly prevalent on the Internet and among university student environmental groups.

The controversy of the Three Gorges Dam and the global anti-dam movement galvanized Chinese ENGOs to respond to other dam projects. In 2003, when the central government approved the Yunnan government's proposal to build a huge dam on the Nujiang, which runs through southwest China, the Green Home, Yunnan People's River Valley, and FON immediately took action. Via workshops, forum discussions, TV programs, newspaper reports and calls for attention at international and UN conferences, these ENGOs generated a great deal of public support around the protection of Nujiang's ecosystems. After a half-year campaign against the Nujiang Dam Project, the ENGOs finally convinced the central government to stop construction for now, the first case in China where ENGOs significantly affected a government decision (Cao 2004).

In 2004, similar actions took place. In opposing a dam project on the Minjiang, another southwestern river, ENGOs launched an Internet petition against the Minjiang Dam to which 15,000 supporters signed their names online. The campaign reached China's premier, Wen Jiabao, who then admitted that this project had not gone through the environmental bureau's examination and approval process (Economy 2004b). Around the same time, to stop a huge dam project on the upper valley of the Yangzi River, nine NGOs, including GEV and FON, petitioned Premier Wen. The petition reads, "We call on the authorities to fulfill the vision of science-based development . . . to balance the human interests against nature, in order to leave our precious world heritage . . . to the world and to future generations" (Becker and Howden 2004). According to a report dated October 16, 2004, Wen agreed to suspend 13 dams on the Salween River in 2004, in response to protests from Burma, Thailand, and Chinese environmentalists (Becker and Howden 2004). This is a victory for ENGOs, and no doubt these actions will have a political consequence. Wu Dengming, the president of Green Volunteer League of Chongqing, states clearly: "This is a long-term struggle, and our organization's deepest purpose is to try to build a civil society and promote democracy" (Pomfret 2003a: 15).

One should not, however, exaggerate either the quantitative growth of NGOs or the scale of their influence at the present stage. In comparison with China's vast population, rapid economic development, and enormous environmental and social problems, the growth of grassroots organizations, active and fast growing as they are, is far from sufficient. Nor have the civic associations of other types generally developed sufficient horizontal linkage outside of their own networks and become an integrated non-profit sector. As other chapters have discussed, many hurdles slow NGO growth and hinder their full functionality. The adversity grassroots Chinese NGOs countered in the past decade forced them to become strong and resourceful; their development in number, range of programs, and social impact, as evident in the growth of ENGOs, has been substantial. Not only have they played a major role in advocating public interests and representing disadvantaged groups, but their actions have also started to influence governmental policy-making and implementation. As a result of grassroots efforts, a notable change has taken place in people's perceptions of environmental and social problems and their personal responsibility.

Dynamics and leadership of grassroots NGOs: the role of Chinese intellectuals

The forceful leadership of individuals in initiating and building NGOs has been a major reason for the success of these organizations. For instance, Liang Congjie (FON), Liao Xiaoyi (GVB), Wang Xingjuan (Maple Women's Hotline), Xu Jianchu (Center for Biodiversity and Indigenous Knowledge), Zhang Kailin (Yunnan Reproductive Health Research Association), Guo Jianmei (Peking University Women's Law Studies and Legal Aid Center), Wang Yongchen (Green Home), Wan Yanhai (AiZhi Action), Shang Yusheng (NPO Network), Xu Yongguang (China Youth Development Foundation), Huang Haoming (China Association for NGO Cooperation), He Zhonghua (Lijiang Minority Gender and Development Research Center), and Gao Xiaoxian (Shaanxi Association for Women and Family Research), among many others, all demonstrated incredible courage, vision, creativity and devotion in establishing organizations that championed their respective passions.[17] They are the main reason that these organizations were founded and survived. To understand the value and meaning of China's new organizations and their future directions, we must examine the dynamics of their leadership. This section focuses on China's NGO leaders and addresses the motivations that attract individuals to NGOs, the factors that help them succeed, and, most of all, the significant role that the personal traits of leaders plays in the growth of their organizations.

Among all the social, political, or economic forces, Chinese intellectuals and newly emerged private entrepreneurs have been the most significant driver behind China's associational revolution in the past two decades. While the next chapter will discuss the role of the latter in the formation of private chambers of commerce and trade associations, this section explores the role of scholars and intellectuals in the growth of grassroots NGOs through institutional cases and individual portraits. In analyzing what makes intellectuals particularly prime candidates to lead NGOs, the social capital framework again proves useful. Bourdieu, in his elaboration of social capital, argues that there are other forms of capital, including monetary capital, cultural capital, and social capital. Cultural capital relates to an individual's formal educational credentials and the more intangible complex of values and style in demeanor (Bourdieu 1997: 47–51). One of Bourdieu's major contributions to the social capital concept is his insight that social capital is interchangeable with money capital and cultural capital, and that such trades are actually requisite for development (Portes and Mooney 2002: 305). He further explains that the volume of social capital possessed by a given agent depends on the size of the network that he or she can effectively mobilize and the amount of other forms of capital he or she possesses (Bourdieu 1997: 51). Social capital is not a given, Bourdieu emphasizes, but rather "the product of investment strategies, individual or collective, consciously or unconsciously aimed at establishing or reproducing social relationships that are directly usable..." (Bourdieu: 52). In other words, social capital is acquired with the "investment of some material resources and the possession of some cultural knowledge, enabling the individual to establish relations with valued others" (Portes and Mooney: 305). In the case of NGO development in China, we see clearly how the cultural capital possessed by intellectuals has helped the success of pioneering NGOs, and, in many cases, how those intellectuals are skillfully trading their expertise, social networks, and social, even political, status in exchange for other forms of capital.

In comparison to the other socio-economic strata, Chinese intellectuals are the most able to lead NGOs; it was this elite, after all, that first introduced the concepts of civil society and NGOs to China. As the following cases demonstrate, the intellectuals' perception of China's current political, economic and social issues and the way they see the state and the non-governmental sector have greatly shaped the mission and role of the NGOs. Furthermore, in running the independent organizations, they have demonstrated strong governing ability, resourcefulness, knowledge of global civil society and NGO practice; moreover, their language skills and educational training enable them to communicate with INGOs. These qualities, as well as the social networks of the educated elite, comprise the most valuable cultural, personal, and even political capital in gaining the trust of donors, society, and their constituents. The inchoate state of institutionalized civic associations in China further underscores the influence of leadership on the survival and success of grassroots NGOs.

As discussed earlier, it was a deep-rooted tradition that Chinese intellectuals perceived their social responsibility as a mandated duty. This tradition has continued, as one can see in the 1980s students' democratic movement and the intellectuals' searching for civil society in the 1990s (Chapter 1). In his account of Chinese political elites and intellectuals, Joseph Fewsmith argues that this traditional role of intellectuals has significantly eroded in the 1990s, due to the change of political atmosphere and culture; yet he admits that the concerns of intellectuals continue to play a sociopolitical role by reinforcing, pressuring, or even ignoring the government (Fewsmith 2001: 10; see also Ding 2000: 111–40). Today, while many intellectuals continue to see themselves as society's conscience, they have also embraced new values of personal fulfillment and self-development. To various degrees, the emergence of NGOs in China presents great opportunities for motivated intellectuals who are quick to perceive and critique economic and social problems, yet who cannot challenge the status quo or be professionally challenged themselves at state institutions. By acting through NGOs, intellectuals simultaneously fulfill both their social responsibility and personal ambition.

It is worth noting, however, that loosened control over state employees and a more flexible private job market have also permitted intellectuals to work for NGOs and state institutions simultaneously. This has become one of the unique features of intellectuals' involvement in NGOs.[18] For example, university full-time professors can run their own non-governmental research centers; in many cases, their appointed teaching positions have nothing to do with these centers. Technically, they can only use their spare time to carry out research for NGOs; yet, in practice, the line between paid and spare time is often blurred. Although universities do not pay for the outside research that scholars carry out for their centers, the latter often are able to raise grants for their projects from outside funding resources. Under the current system, universities and other state research institutions encourage scholars to obtain outside funding, because those institutions charge overhead fees. Both teaching and research institutions require scholars to complete one or two articles a year, and yet, in most cases, the research done with outside grants and for the independent centers is acceptable to fulfill the research requirement.

124 *Social capital*

This situation leaves scholars with a great deal of time and freedom to undertake research or service projects of their own choosing. Additionally, to varying degrees, scholars can apply the resources from a state job, such as access to the library, office space and supplies, computers and, most of all, intellectual networks, to their own NGOs. Thus, amphibious personnel go far in explaining why so many independent research and service organizations have been established by scholars in the state institutions, and why most of these entities continue to exist. While relatively low salary levels and lack of credentials often prevent young professionals from working full-time for NGOs, this is not an issue for scholars whose primary professions place them very much at an advantage to run NGOs.

The following case studies highlight the significant contribution of intellectuals and the positive impact they have had on the growth of NGOs; yet, the purpose of this section is neither to idealize nor simplify their influence. The intellectuals' roles in NGO development are very much shaped by both China's current political culture and those intellectuals' personal interests. To begin, after the 1989 democratic movement when Chinese intellectuals examined the way they pursued China's modernization and future political reforms, many intellectuals concluded that radical actions could only lead to social instability and damage economic prosperity. Thus, when the CCP used economic development and social stability to rationalize the delay of political reforms, the mainstream intellectuals were supportive.[19] Equally important, Chinese intellectuals in general are beneficiaries of the economic reforms, and since the 1990s their social, political, and financial conditions have been improved greatly.[20] And this has no doubt decisively affected their attitude towards the state-led reforms.

Within this broad and complicated context, the Chinese intellectuals have presented a different view of NGOs rather than seeing the NGOs as a confrontational force against the state or an instrument of democracy. In the debate over civil society in the early and mid-1990s, many intellectuals addressed China's unique historical and political conditions and agreed with the notion of a "constructive (non-confrontational) interacting relationship between the state and civil society" (Chapter 1). In practice, the NGO leaders have been cooperative with the government, and are willing to compromise under the government's pressure. While NGO leaders indeed address the importance of autonomy and organizational independence, they do not confront the government for their rights. Instead, many intellectual NGO leaders use their social status, reputation, and social or even political networks to build good relations with the officials so that they can get things done.[21] Nor do the majority of NGO leaders publicly criticize the official NGO policy or assert NGOs' role in policy-making. As mentioned earlier, some NGO leaders openly address their apolitical mission and avoid becoming involved in political matters. Certainly such a stance is a means of survival; nevertheless, these views and practices have set the basic tone of China's current NGO–state relations, and, by and large, they have led to the fatal weakness of Chinese NGOs: the lack of political voices and real independence.

In the meantime, the commercialization of Chinese culture has also greatly changed intellectuals' behavior. After Deng Xiaoping's 1992 South Tour speeches, China's economic reforms were put into high gear. The whole country was in the mood for making money, and for the first time since the CCP came to power, intellectuals had the opportunity to exchange their knowledge and expertise for money, power, and fame. Fewsmith observes that the professionalization of the bureaucracy turned some intellectuals into technocrats, and others turned to academic specializations. He further argues that "At the same time, the commercialization of culture challenged traditional understandings of the role of intellectuals from below" (Fewsmith 2001: 13). Not surprisingly, the great majority of intellectuals and new college graduates prefer working for the government or businesses to NGOs. And for those who do choose NGOs, the utilitarian motives can be an important part of the decision. For example, when many intellectuals use their training and expertise to run non-governmental and non-profit enterprises (NGNCEs), the line between non-profit and for profit often is quite blurred; the non-profit nature has become questionable for a large proportion of NGNCEs.[22] In other cases, the international funding is a major attraction for some to organize or participate in NGOs (Chapter 6). In short, the intellectuals have brought both positive and negative influences to China's NGO formation, and, taking China's reality into consideration, this is a complicated picture that makes sense.

The following sub-sections discuss intellectuals' efforts in NGO development from institutional and personal perspectives.

Independent research institutes in the economic realm

As China's reforms began in the economic realm, economists were therefore among the first intellectuals organized outside of the state system, starting in the early 1990s. The Beijing Tianze (Unirule) Institute of Economics is one such successful case.[23] As depicted by *Business China*, Tianze exemplifies "a new breed of independent economic research institute staffed by researchers who include former government economists and overseas-trained PhDs. This small group of independent think-tanks is forcing a greater exchange of ideas between China's government and its academic community" (June 26, 1996: 7–8). Established in 1993, Tianze's five organizers were all renowned economists whose academic achievements and reputation gained them much trust and attraction. This was the primary reason that a private cultural company was interested in investing in Tianze. It was a mutual understanding that the company would invest monetary capital and that these economists would bring their personal and cultural capital into Tianze.

By its third year, over fifty researchers around the country and some international scholars had contracted with the institution, building a mutually beneficial relationship. This scholarly expertise has earned the institution many research contracts and projects, which allow Tianze to maintain financial independence. Furthermore, its founders' insistence on Tianze having an independent voice on China's economic policy and developmental strategy has garnered the institution widespread recognition and trust. Zhang Shuguan, one of the founders, states that freedom of thinking and freedom of exchanging ideas should be the principles of academia. He argues that, as think tanks, these independent research institutions should be "society's conscience" and independent from both the government and business sector so that they can objectively critique government policies (Zhang 2002). This mission is reflected in the pioneering research Tianze has undertaken on important economic issues – with resultant analyses that sometimes differ from official views – and its bi-weekly forums that have become Tianze's landmark feature. Its independence and high caliber research have made Tianze one of the most esteemed institutes of its kind, and its clients now include Chinese government agencies, major Hong Kong companies, the Asian Development Bank, the Ford Foundation, and Washington DC's Institute for International Economics.[24] Tianze is only one example, and in recent years more and more economists have launched their own independent economic research institutes (DWN 2003).

Intellectuals and the development of Women's NGOs

The rise of women's grassroots organizations since the mid-1990s provides another cogent example of intellectuals' important role in NGO development. Chinese women and their organizations were an indispensable force behind China's modernization movement and women's liberation during the first half of the twentieth century, from anti-foot-binding to promoting women's education and rights. From 1919 to 1949, 53 women's organizations were established in Beijing alone (Liu *et al.* 1994: 2). On the eve of the establishment of the PRC, some women's organizations jointly established the All-China Women's Federation (ACWF; see Chapter 3), which eventually became the only women's organization left in China. This situation ended after the reforms in the mid-1980s when some intellectuals founded independent organizations focusing on women's studies and issues, making scholars and intellectuals once again the most important force in promoting grassroots organizations.

Generally speaking, the growth of women's NGOs has been on two fronts: first, research centers pioneering women's and gender studies and, second, non-profit service provision specifically for women and children. To begin with, until the early 1980s, no Chinese university offered courses or conducted research on women's studies. Li Xiaojiang, who majored in contemporary European literature in college, was the first Chinese scholar devoted to women's studies. In 1985, she organized the Henan Women's Studies Association and China's first conference on women's studies. Two years

Social capital 127

later, Li established China's first women's and gender studies center at Zhengzhou University. Between 1987 and 1999, scholars at 36 universities established similar centers. Yet, women's studies continued confronting serious bias against them, and the traditional departments in those universities deemed research on the subject as having "no future" or to be "not proper subjects" for study (Li, Xiaojiang 2000: 3–28; Du 2000: 90–4). These universities neither funded nor staffed women's studies centers (Du: 90–1).

Ironically, these challenges stimulated scholars who were interested to change the situation. Many women scholars participated in the fourth WCW in Beijing in 1995, and the conference was an important factor that inspired those women's NGOs. Among the 36 university women's studies centers extant in 1999, 31 were organized around or after the fourth WCW (Du: 90). According to a survey by ACWF in 1999, the total number of women's research centers of all kinds increased to 80 nationwide (Liu 2000: 112). The NGO status of these centers allowed scholars to take on research projects without the approval of their universities, and also helped them to raise international funds. After the conference, INGOs became increasingly active in supporting Chinese NGOs, granting many centers research funds or having them participate in training workshops on the empowerment of women and other international conferences sponsored by INGOs.

As some of those women NGO leaders recalled later, these experiences taught them new theories, methodologies and vocabulary, new knowledge that far exceeds scholarship and academia.[25] These studies have changed China's traditional, authoritarian view on women as held by the CCP. These scholars argue that women are no longer merely the force of revolution and that their identity, history, and liberation are not merely bound solely to their social standing. Rather, women have their own unique identities, values, and needs. To promote these ideas, scholars now offer courses on women's physiology, culture, history, economy, medicine, family, and marriage. In turn, this teaching and research has profoundly influenced China's current women's movement. To a great extent, these studies have given a theoretical basis to the corresponding efforts to improve women's rights and living conditions in the country (Li, Xiaojiang 2000).

On the other hand, the development of a market economy in China has generally placed women at a disadvantage. Economic and social dislocation hit families hard, and violence against women and children soared after the reforms. A series of other problems followed: female unemployment rose; female university graduates had more difficulties finding jobs; in poor rural areas, large proportions of girls lost their schooling; the smuggling of women and children also increased, as did the violation of female migrants' rights and cases of prostitution (Liu 2000: 109–14). And yet, the government has paid little attention to these problems and is ill equipped to deal with them.

On the contrary, since the 1990s, an impressive number of women's NGOs have risen to the challenge. Again, most of the organizers are intellectuals.

128 *Social capital*

Their contributions include hotline services for physiology consultancy, women's health, sexually transmitted diseases, and lesbians and gays. Elsewhere, legal assistant centers support victims of domestic violence and child abuse; schools and clubs educate female rural migrants as well as disabled children; clubs support single women and mothers; centers teach sex workers about AIDS prevention; and shelters care for homeless children. The most well-known such NGOs, among others, are Maple Women Hotline, Jinghun Family Center, STD Hotline, Yunnan Reproductive Health Research Association, Peking University Women Law Research and Legal Aid, Shaanxi Women Legal Aid Center. Also, scholars in Kunming are investigating and helping sexual workers on Yunnan border regions with Thailand and Burma.[26] These non-profit private institutions address needs that the state has not yet addressed, and often their services are the only ones available of their kind. Yet, without any government monetary or other forms of support, and given the serious discrimination against these marginalized and disadvantaged groups, these groups and their organizers have had to work under extremely difficult conditions.

Li Xiaojiang once edited a volume of the collected experiences of some scholars and practitioners who organize women's NGOs (Li, Xiaojiang 2000). From these touching stories, it becomes clearly evident that it was the moral character of these outstanding individuals, their perseverance, intelligence, vision, and resourcefulness that enabled them to overcome all the hurdles and build thriving organizations. Yet, it is also clear that external conditions were crucial to their achievements. These leaders, because of their educational background and careers, usually had widespread connections with the outside world and opportunities to study abroad or attend international conferences, from which they obtained insights, encouragement, and resources. Furthermore, as a new and small field, women's studies and service institutions have formed a close and active network, through which scholars and member institutions benefit from shared information, cooperation in research projects, curriculum development, conferences, and moral support.

Three portraits of the first generation of intellectual NGO leaders

The development of NGOs provides Chinese intellectuals great opportunities to fulfill their ideas, responsibility, and personal value. At the same time, the traits of many intellectual NGO leaders have become indispensable assets to NGO development in China. The following paragraphs provide sketches of three renowned Chinese NGO leaders who are pioneers in their respective fields and whose examples have inspired many to follow. With diverse backgrounds and personal experiences, they represent different generations of Chinese intellectuals, and their stories point to the various forms of capital and values that they brought to their organizations. Across developing countries, it is a common experience to see the rise of a first generation of grassroots leaders possessing great vision, strong capabilities, and personal charisma. This cult of the leader was the main reason why organizations in many of these countries survived and succeeded. After ten years of growth, however, most founders of China's grassroots organizations are still holding on to their power and not passing the leadership to a younger generation. This situation can be attributed to a number of reasons. On the one hand, China's NGO sector is still underdeveloped and no decent program exists to train NGO leaders; thus finding new leaders who are visionary, capable, and driven can be difficult. On the other hand, after devoting many years of hard work to their organizations, the first generation of NGO leaders have become too attached to let go and allow a younger leadership to develop. The lack of employment mobility across sectors further impedes changes in leadership and staff. Thus, the Chinese NGO sector faces the challenge of regularizing term-limited leadership and recruiting more capable and devoted people.

Liang Congjie[27]

Liang Congjie is the founder and director of Friends of Nature (FON) and the winner of the 2000 Ramon Magsaysay Award for Public Service. His grandfather, Liang Qichao, was one of the two best-known leaders of the 1898 Reform Movement in the Qing Dynasty. Though he fled imperial suppression after the Reform Movement failed, Liang continued to advocate reforms and modernization.[28] He became a famous thinker and productive writer during the late Qing and early Republic, and his thoughts on building a new nation and a new people inspired China's first generation of modern intellectuals. Liang Congjie's father, Liang Sicheng, and mother, Lin Huiyin, received Western educations in the United States and England and were China's first established modern archeologists. With their family background, education, and personal charm, this couple became the most elite and romantic figures of China's intellectuals during the 1930s and 1940s. In the early 1950s, Liang Sicheng, then the vice-mayor of Beijing and a professor at Tsinghua University, was one of the two archeologists who stood up against Mao Zedong's decision to tear down the ancient Beijing city walls, gates, and other architectural structures. Tragically, his courageous voice was repressed, and he suffered a great deal of political persecution ever after and died at the height of the Cultural Revolution (Wang 2003: 73–122).

This is a glorious yet heavy heritage for Liang Congjie, who told me with a sense of humor that "I have been known as Liang Qichao's grandson and Liang Sicheng and Lin Huiyin's son for my entire life. When I visited my daughter in America, I was recognized as her father." Behind these humorous words lay his soul searching for his identity. Liang said, "If I inherited anything from my grandfather and parents, it is the faith that a person should have social responsibility" (Pan 2002). Environmental protection was the social responsibility Liang finally found. Facing people's ever-growing desire for consumption and the rapid degradation of natural resources, Liang and his friends often felt frustrated and powerless. In a public speech, he cried out, "A person should have a spirit and a dream, and in this world, we can choose another lifestyle" (Pan 2002). As a university history professor, Liang could have enjoyed an early retirement and an easy life; yet, he chose to challenge convention and fight for a better future for his country, people, and for his own conscience. Even in his seventies, he participates in all kinds of voluntary programs, from planting trees in Inner Mongolia to teaching children in Mobile Environmental classes. Liang and other members of FON pledge to make a personal effort on behalf of China's environment. He still prefers to ride a bicycle. And at home, Liang and his wife, an educator, recycle water in every possible way, and when FON people eat out, they bring their own chopsticks so that they do not have to use the disposable ones.

No doubt, Liang's personal traits and charisma are precious assets to FON. At the same time, Liang's political status brings to the environmental movement another form of capital. Liang is a member of the Standing Committee of Chinese People's Political Consultative Conference (CPPCC), a prestigious political organization representing, mostly symbolically, the voices of democratic parties and other political organizations. With such a position, Liang has been able to push for investigations on environmental law violations and, via CPPCC's personal or institutional channels, put forward reports and suggestions to the State Council and provincial governments on environmental issues or cases of law violations. Unfortunately, many of these efforts have never gone anywhere; however, Liang considers himself lucky to have such channels through which to get the message across.

His legendary family background, his social and political status and, most of all, his work for FON have made him a high-profile ENGO leader in China. When US President Bill Clinton visited China in 1998, Liang Congjie and Liao Xiaoyi were the two representatives of Chinese ENGOs who met him. During China's campaign for the 2008 Olympics, Liang was ordered by the government to represent NGOs in the Beijing Application Committee, as the International Olympic Committee requires such a figure, even though in his own opinion China should not hold the Olympics while its youngsters do not have playgrounds and sports fields. Yet, Liang's own example is a more powerful inspiration than his status or background. In many ways, Liang represents the best values of traditional Chinese intellectuals, which is that the educated people take responsibility on behalf of public good and that one should walk the talk. Liang brought those values into FON, and it is his spirit, character, and, most of all, devotion that has attracted so many Chinese people, young or old, to take up environmental protection.

Xu Jianchu[29]

Dr Xu Jianchu is the founder and leader of the Center for Biodiversity and Indigenous Knowledge (CBIK) in Kunming, Yunnan, a pioneering NGO in this field. Xu grew up in a rural town and graduated in 1986 from prestigious

Nanjing University, with a degree in botany and outstanding records in both academic performance and student leadership. Declining the university's offer of a teaching position and disregarding his family's opposition, Xu chose to work for a research station in Xishuangbanna, a minority region in the southern tip of Yunnan Province. At that time, Xishuangbanna had no running water or electricity, and many university graduates abandoned the area for cities. In contrast, Xu stayed and met his mentor Pei Shengji, the founder of Chinese ethnology. Under Pei's supervision, Xu eventually completed his MA and PhD in natural resource management.

Timing and location could not have been better for Xu Jianchu's academic ambitions. Yunnan, China's ecological and ethnic capital, has become a focal place since the 1990s for many international environmental organizations and natural scientists. The Ford Foundation entered the region as early as 1989 by launching four experimental sites for upland poverty alleviation. Later, the Ford Foundation and Winrock International, upon the invitation of the Yunnan Provincial Poverty Alleviation Office, sponsored the Yunnan Upland Management Project. From 1991 to 1994, this project sent thirty individuals from participating units in Yunnan and Sichuan to selected universities in Thailand and the Philippines for training in environmental sciences, natural resources management, social forestry, and agricultural systems (Mas 1999: 65). Xu was one of the trainees, and it was through this program that he first learned about participatory approaches to development. Again in 1994, Xu had the chance to learn firsthand about non-governmental work in Vietnam when he was a research fellow in an environmental NGO there. Frequent contact with the Ford Foundation, World Wild Fund for Nature (WWF), and the institutions and scholars of Southeast Asian countries opened his eyes to a new field, that of environmental NGOs.

With the financial support of the Ford Foundation and WWF, Xu established CBIK in 1995, with Pei as the chairman of the board of executives. At the time, CBIK had only one part-time and two full-time employees, and all researchers participating in CBIK's research projects, including Pei and Xu, were actually employed by the state institutions. After ten years of hard work, CBIK now has about twenty full-time program officers and staff members, and it also subsidizes the participation of ten to twenty Chinese and international scholars, foreign graduate students, and volunteers in its programs. At present, CBIK's research and programs focus on biodiversity conservation, community livelihood development, documentation of indigenous knowledge, and technical innovations related to resource governance at community and watershed levels. Several pilot or project sites operate simultaneously in each of these areas, and many of these programs are pioneers in terms of scientific focus and methodology, as well as building new pathways of interaction between Chinese and international practitioners, and between projects and local communities. In comparison to state research or poverty alleviation institutes that are better equipped and funded by the government, CBIK's programs have reached to the lowest level of communities in remote regions where there is no government program. Without multi-tier bureaucracy, CBIK's programs are often more effective and efficient than those of the state institutions.

Xu's leadership is reflected in his vision of CBIK. While some grassroots organizations focus their efforts on getting funding, Xu has a different perception of the long-term development of Chinese NGOs. He defines the unique role of NGOs as forces of social transformation rather than grant-seeking organizations. He insists that CBIK must represent people's interests, scientific principles, and environmental conscience. These principles have become the cornerstone of CBIK's success. Xu is also a strong group leader. He not only convinced many young people of the importance and value of environmental causes, but also brought out the best qualities and creativity of his team. Xu's leadership has earned him the trust of people at CBIK. One program officer quit his job at a government agency to work at CBIK, and he told me that "I came to CBIK because of Xu, and I agree with his ideals and admire his leadership." In the meantime, Xu realizes the importance of providing competitive employment conditions so NGOs can attract promising young people. Through his successful management, CBIK is now able to match state institutions in its staff salaries and benefits.

Xu has brought into CBIK various forms of capital, including his solid training in ethnology and natural resources management, ideas, his knowledge of international foundations and INGOs, his capacity to govern and market, his personal charisma, unusual energy, and his social connections with scholars, government officials, and international NGOs. All these have been the greatest force behind CBIK's success. Xu is well connected, not least with his early mentor, Pei Shengji. As he himself noted, "It was Pei who connected me to the outside world and to cross-disciplinary research." Furthermore, Pei was a member of the Yunnan Province People's Political Consultative Conference and, as honorary director of CBIK, he bestowed upon it much political protection. As a result, CBIK is one of the few grassroots institutions nationwide that is able to register as a corporate organization (*faren shetuan*).

At the same time, his years of working with international grant-giving and program-oriented institutions, as well as CBIK's own successes, have earned Xu trust from foreign organizations, which, by his own admission, is why they continually fund CBIK's work. While all Chinese NGOs are facing increasing competition for resources, especially foreign funds, from its establishment to the present, CBIK has completed dozens of research projects, 95 percent of which were internationally funded. Xu is responsible for raising around 80–90 percent of those funds.

As a leader, Xu recognizes the necessity of renewing leadership and absorbing fresh blood into CBIK. Over the years, he has repeatedly emphasized the importance of teamwork and nourishing young people by encouraging them to get advanced training and giving them opportunities to participate in decision-making and leading projects. In part, he is driven by a sense of responsibility for his own success; as he noted, "I should give the young people what Pei had given to me." His emphasis on fresh minds is also practical; Xu pointed out that "NGOs need new blood and new leadership. A mature organization ought to regularly renew its directors, and the director should not always hold on to the position." In the spring of 2004, Xu resigned from the directorship of CBIK, expressly for the purpose of transferring leadership to a younger generation.[30]

Wan Yanhai[31]

Dr Wan Yanhai is a prominent AIDS activist and educator in China and the founder of AiZhi Action, a non-profit organization devoted to AIDS awareness and education, and human rights for HIV/AIDS patients, homosexuals, and other marginalized groups. After graduating from the prestigious Fudan University Medical School in Shanghai, Wan joined the National Health Education Institute in 1988. With such an educational background and a promising start to his career, Wan could easily have become either a physician or a public health official. Instead, he chose a rough and bumpy road towards advocating public awareness of AIDS and the rights of marginalized peoples in China. The letter nominating Wan as the 2002 international recipient of "Awards for Action on HIV/AIDS and Human Rights" states, "Dr. Wan has been on the front lines of fighting an epidemic that Chinese authorities would prefer to sweep under the rug. He has taken extraordinary personal risk to break down the conspiracy of silence around HIV/AIDS in China and to ensure protection for persons at highest risk" (CHALN 2002).

Since China discovered its first AIDS case in 1985, the epidemic has rapidly spread, especially after the mid-1990s. In western China, the mode of transmission of HIV is intravenous drug use and prostitution; in central China it is blood collection and transfusions; and in coastal regions and cities, it is prostitution and a combination of other factors. Some studies predict that by 2010 ten million Chinese will be infected with HIV (Chen, X. 2002). In early 1990, Wan was assigned by the Ministry of Public Health to set up China's first official program to provide information and counseling on HIV/AIDS. Yet, Wan soon found that his ideas on fighting the epidemic directly conflicted with the health authority's policies. At the time, the government believed that China could control AIDS from spreading by preventing HIV-infected people from entering the country and isolating HIV carriers within China. Wan, on the other hand, perceived the prevention of AIDS in China very much as a political and human rights issue. In 1992, he opened China's first hotlines providing information on HIV/AIDS in Kunming, Shanghai, and Shenyang; he also organized "Men's World," a grassroots group for promoting gay men's health education. Wan openly advocated the rights of homosexuals, sex workers, and intravenous drug users and urged them to organize their own self-support groups. In a 1992 article, Wan wrote,

> People with AIDS and those in high-risk groups are entitled to form their own organisations and participate in planning, AIDS prevention, and control. Since China is a populous country and has a large high-risk group of gays, prostitutes and intravenous drug users, and since it has been proved many times that there is serious discrimination against people with AIDS and high-risk groups, there is an urgent need to develop non-governmental organisations which can provide consultations for people in high risk groups and help for those who have AIDS.[32]

Wan's views and actions directly confronted the CCP's human rights policies and anti-homosexuals stance. One year after the opening of AIDS hotlines, the government shut them down; a year later, the Ministry of Public Health accused Wan of promoting homosexuality and prostitution, and dismissed him from his job. As Wan was nevertheless determined to continue fighting for those most at risk from the AIDS epidemic, it became clear to him that NGOs were the answer. He perceived the cooperation of high-risk populations as a crucial factor in preventing HIV from spreading, and in this, NGOs have an irreplaceable function. He thinks that grassroots organizations are not only community-based and close to the people they serve, but are also trusted by those that they serve. These target groups believe the sincerity of their work, in contrast to their perception that governmental institutions merely go through the motions. These organizations are also much quicker and efficient in addressing crises than are government organizations, which Wan notes must go through the whole process of conducting studies, strategic planning, budget setting, application, approval, funding appropriation, and participant organization.

In 1994, Wan founded his own grassroots NGO, called AiZhi Action, a name that sums up its mission: Ai, to love, and Zhi, knowledge. Wan explained that, in China, the obstacles of fighting AIDS come not just from the government's irresponsible policies, but also from serious discrimination among the Chinese against HIV/AIDS victims, sex workers, and homosexuals. "These people need love and care," Wan said, "and they also need knowledge. In fact, not just these high-risk groups; the Chinese public in general needs knowledge and information about AIDS and homosexuality." Since the mid-1990s, AiZhi Action has made it its mission to tackle widespread ignorance about HIV/AIDS and to expand prevention efforts in China through education, counselling, opinion polls, research, publishing articles, and conferences aimed at drawing up policy recommendations for the government. AiZhi and its volunteers also visited Henan villages, documenting the extent of HIV infection. Because of their dedication, the Chinese public and outside world have begun to perceive the true picture of how far the AIDS epidemic has spread and gain the first glimpses into China's gay population and its health needs.

Wan and his colleagues have overcome many hurdles, including government regulations, attempts by local authorities to cover up the rural HIV/AIDS epidemic, widespread social prejudice against victims of the virus, ongoing police harassment and threats from government officials, and, especially during the early years, unstable funding for their programs. For a long time, Wan was not allowed to take any action in Beijing, and was watched and followed by police. On July 1, 2002, after a UN report announced that AIDS had become a serious disaster in several Chinese provinces, the Chinese government forced AiZhi to shut down its Beijing office and detained Wan. Under international pressure, the Chinese government released Wan a month later, and AiZhi was thus able to register at the Bureau of Industry and Commerce as a for-profit institution (HRW 2002).

Indeed, it took great courage to face the political risks and challenge the authorities, and yet Wan insisted that he only did what he was supposed to do. In our interview, Wan said, "I was trained in public health and was working in a national institute on health education. I have the knowledge to educate and help people, and most of all, I have the responsibility to do so." Growing up during the Cultural Revolution, Wan was disturbed by and disliked many unjustified and inhumane things that happened around him. In university, even though he was majoring in medicine, he read a great number of books written by Western thinkers and philosophers in the post-Enlightenment era. He also participated in the student democratic movement in the late 1980s. These experiences nourished his value of humanity, human rights, and social responsibility. To use Wan's own words, "It is not difficult for me at all to choose the cause as I did, but it would be very difficult for me to give it up."

To conclude, millions of Chinese are participating in some sort of formal or informal network that has helped them improve their personal lives as well as get involved in public affairs. It is true that networking for personal purposes does not always directly benefit the public good or influence government policy; social networks can also bring negative consequences to society. However, the foremost significance of civic engagement is the exercise of the right of association, which had been denied the Chinese for so many years. Another direct consequence of the upsurge of associations is the increase of social capital, civility, and citizenship among ordinary people. From participating in civic associations, they learn to interact with each other and with the state. In the past ten years, the Chinese civic associations have planted seeds of human rights, social responsibility, volunteerism, humanity, and democracy in the hearts of Chinese people. Today, more and more people are aware of their right to a voice in private and public affairs. Grassroots NGOs have become platforms and institutional channels for the expression of their interests and involvement in decision-making. After thirty years of dictatorship, these changes are profound, and they are nourishing a civil society in the country.

5 Corporatism vs civil society
NGOs in the economic realm

The NGOs discussed in this chapter include trade associations (*hangye xiehui*) and chambers of commerce (*gongshanglian* or *shanghui*).[1] When the Cultural Revolution (1966-76) ended, NGOs in the economic realm were among the earliest associations to be revitalized and organized, and they have since become the most rapidly rising type of NGO. Given the remarkable growth of non-state-owned enterprises in China's market economy, the trade associations and the chambers of commerce that serve as nongovernmental intermediaries require special attention in our study of Chinese NGOs and civil society. Two distinct growth patterns have emerged from the experiences of economically oriented NGOs. The first is a bottom-up pattern, in which enterprises, mostly private, create chambers of commerce or trade associations to protect and represent their interests. This has occurred most significantly in some coastal cities, exemplified by Wenzhou, a medium-size city in Zhejiang province, southeast China. Elsewhere, changes follow a top-down model, in which the government assumes primary responsibility for the organization of industrial and trade associations.

By examining both growth models, this chapter will demonstrate the significant roles of both the government and private entrepreneurs in the development of NGOs in the economic realm. It argues that the government, driven by the need for non-state, intermediary management for China's market economy as the state apparatus contracted, has systematically transformed a large proportion of industrial bureaus into trade associations; consequently, it has substantially enlarged the size and resources of the non-governmental sector. Although this transformation is not yet complete, the most difficult and decisive step – the separation between the state and trade associations – has been taken. The study further argues that the bottom-up model reveals the potential as well as the limits of the role of private entrepreneurs in China's civil society evolution. On the one hand, the private chambers of commerce have displayed obvious features of autonomous associations; on the other hand, the entanglement of political and economic elites has raised serious doubts about the willingness or ability of private entrepreneurs to influence China's future political reforms.

This chapter includes three sections: a brief summary of the theoretical debate over China's associational growth, a discussion of four types of groups in the top-down model, and a case study of the bottom-up model – private chambers of commerce in Wenzhou.

Simultaneous development of corporatism and civil society

Previous studies of China's surge in associations have debated whether the concepts of civil society or of corporatism best describe the changes in China's associational landscapes. This chapter argues that China's associational revolution has occurred along the lines of civil society and corporatism simultaneously, as clearly evidenced in the distinctive growth models of bottom-up and top-down. Corporatism and civil society approaches help us understand the differences in non-governmental organizations' power arrangements with the state as well as in their specific organizational features. The experience of Chinese associations indicates that the state has generated new institutional mechanisms for adopting profound economic and social structural changes, and in corporatist relations the state still holds control. At the same time, associations, bottom-up ones in particular, are raising their voices in the implementation and even making of policy; there are clear indications that a civil society is evolving.

The concept of corporatism

The depth of Chinese government interference or even control of non-governmental organizations and the absence of the latter's voice in government decision-making processes has led some Western scholars to question whether the civil society approach is appropriate for the study of Chinese state–society relations. Instead, they believe that corporatism is a much more accurate framework in which to explain what has happened in the past twenty years. In China, as elsewhere, not all associations facilitate civil society or democracy. While it has adopted a more supportive policy towards NGOs, the Chinese government also has defined non-governmental associations as bridges to reach out to society and extend state power. Two groups of social organizations in China present clearly corporatist relations with the government: trade associations and well-established national organizations. The former emerged under the government's economic institutional reforms and are relocated ex-governmental managerial agencies. The latter, as discussed in Chapter 3, were founded long before the Cultural Revolution and usually have extended vertical networks nationwide. This chapter will primarily examine trade associations as a measure of corporatism.

Corporatism refers to the power and interest arrangements between the state and associations, such as unions and employers' associations. Scholars offer different interpretations of this theory. According to Charles Taylor, corporatism indicates an integration of civil society and the state, as exemplified in Sweden, Holland, Germany since the 1980s: "an interweaving of society and government to the point where the distinction no longer expresses an important difference in the basis of power or the dynamics of policy-making. Both government and associations draw on and are responsive to the same public" (Taylor 1991: 118). In other words, corporatism indicates a balanced and integrative relationship between the state and interest groups in Western societies where civil society has evolved fully. Most social scientists who have adopted a corporatist approach to China's NGOs, however, accept the definition of corporatism put forward by Philippe Schmitter. According to Schmitter, corporatism is

> [a] system of interest representation in which the constituent units are organized into a limited number of singular, compulsory, non-competitive, hierarchically ordered and functionally differentiated categories, recognized or licensed (if not created) by the state and granted deliberate representational monopoly within their respective categories in exchange for observing certain controls on their selection of leaders and articulation of demands and supports.
> (Schmitter 1974: 93–4)

This system, as Schmitter points out, presents "a particular modal or ideal-typical institutional arrangement for linking the associationally organized interests of civil society with the decisional structures of the state" (86).

Accordingly, in corporatism, the state and institutional interests (associations) join in a cooperative and mutually beneficial relationship. Both the active intervention of the state and the monopolistic practices of the associations are essential to any arrangement between the two. The state recognizes the authority of licensed associations in their respective categories, and its protection of such authority allows the associations to incorporate and exert control. In return, the associations serve as intermediate mechanisms between the state and its constituents. Schmitter and Jurgen R. Grote note that in some countries agreements between governments and interest groups, like employers' associations and trade unions, can be stabilized even while the political or institutional conditions for corporatism are not mature (Schmitter and Grote: 1997: 171–5). During political and economic transformations in Eastern Europe, for example, nations engaged in experimental corporatism. The rise of corporatism in Eastern Europe depended on the state's leadership and the trust it received from the interest organizations (175–80). To a great extent, the Eastern European case mirrors the rise of China's associations. As the following examples show, not only do the majority of the associations depend on the state's leadership, but the state also receives the trust of those associations.

Corporatism in China

Susan Whiting was the first American scholar to adopt the concepts of "pluralism" and "corporatism" in discussing Chinese social organizations since the 1970s. "Pluralism," Whiting argues, "is not an adequate framework for understanding the role of NGOs in the Chinese case." Instead, "a corporatist framework is useful in that it highlights the mechanisms which the state can use to limit and control the political impact of NGOs" (Whiting 1991: 20). Later, Jonathan Unger and Anita Chan reached a similar conclusion in their study of corporatism in China (Unger and Chan 1996: 95–129). They adopt a model of corporatism based on Schmitter's interpretation that features a single organization at the national level "as the sole representative of the sectoral interests." Their definition highlights the state's decisive position in the relationship, because "[t]he state determines which organizations will be recognized as legitimate and forms an unequal partnership of sorts with such organizations." Even the associations get channeled into the policy-making processes, Unger and Chan point out, as they often help implement state policy on the government's behalf (95–6). Unger and Chan go on to divide corporatism into two variants: liberal/ societal and authoritarian/state.[2] They are convinced that state corporatism provides a more accurate description of the events unfolding in China than does a civil society approach, because the latter "assumes too much independence in associational life in Deng's China" (106).

Questioning the corporatism approach, Gordon White, Jude Howell, and Shang Xiaoyuan argue in their study of Chinese civil society that there is no "systematic and clear-minded attempt to establish a form of socialist corporatism as part of the reform programme," even though, to a certain extent, the experiences of some social organizations reflect a conscious response on the part of political and administrative elites to the new economic climate created by market reforms (White *et al.* 1996: 211–15). Their observation may well describe the situation in 1980s China; nevertheless, this has no longer been the case since the early 1990s. As the next section will discuss in detail, the development of trade associations demonstrates a consistent and systematic multi-level effort by the government to rely on associations as a crucial part of administrative and industrial management reforms.

These newly created, top-down associations present several distinctive features that are identical to corporatism. The first is their monopolistic nature. In each industrial sector or trade at a given geographical region or administrative level, the government allows only one trade association. This regulation also applies to bottom-up autonomous associations. In fact, by systematically transferring official bureaus into top-down associations, the government has largely blocked the possibilities for bottom-up associations to grow. Such regulations have caused problems. When private businesses and other social organizations try to establish their own associations, they cannot register because of presence of the top-down associations.[3] The authority of these top-down trade associations is owed not to their constituency but to state recognition and government prohibition of competitors.

Secondly, according to White *et al.*, "corporatism is usually a matter of institutional design by state elites with certain conscious aims" (White *et al.*:

140 *Corporatism vs civil society*

212). Many top-down associations in China are indeed established to carry out certain missions or even government functions as specifically defined by the government. As shown in the case studies below, the Federations of Industry and Commerce act to unite private entrepreneurs, while the Self-employed Laborer Associations aim to control individuals who do not have a working unit (*danwei*) to oversee their behavior. Clearly, the large-scale promotion of trade associations is the state's attempt to create new managerial mechanisms for an increasingly market-oriented and pluralized economy.

Thirdly, the majority of top-down trade associations are organized into nationwide, hierarchically ordered systems. Governmental regulations of NGOs normally do not allow social organizations to have local branches, and only a handful of people's organizations have nationwide vertical networks (Chapter 2). However, the trade associations play a role unique among social organizations: they are an indispensable instrument of the government's macro-management of the economy. Currently, the newly established industrial management follows two major hierarchical systems. The first system is based on the industrial sector, with the industrial federations (former industrial ministries) on top and trade associations of individual enterprises at the bottom (see Figure 5.1). This system is a transformation of the old industrial bureaucratic hierarchy, and so far it continues to carry on government functions, especially at the upper level. In contrast, the second system – the industrial economic federation system – is newly founded according to administrative regions, and focuses on providing professional services such as policy study, information collection, and

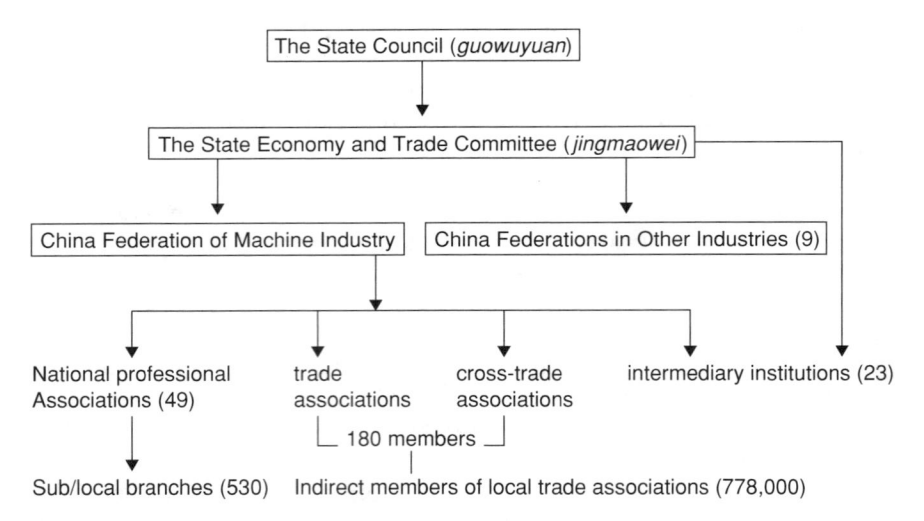

Figure 5.1 The managerial system of trade associations in the machine industry.
Sources: Interview with an officer of the Office of Management of Social Organizations in the Ministry of Machine Industry, 1996; Xue 2003: 484–97.

domestic and international market development.[4] These hierarchically ordered systems, via different channels, link the government at the highest level to individual firms at the bottom. State corporatism appears in these hierarchies quite clearly, especially in the first system where federations still hold power over members at the lower level.

Finally, even though the former industrial bureaus have been transformed into non-governmental associations, they retain many ties to the state system. At various times, government bureaus and trade associations have shared the same offices and personnel (*yitao renma liangkui paizi*). Using a contemporary Chinese political saying, this is called "buttocks command heads" (*pigu zhihui naodai*): when their positions switch, the officers involved change their opinions and methods accordingly.[5] In the mid-1990s Unger and Chan observed that "different genres of corporatist organizations all still largely operate within the 'state-corporatist' mould, still dominated by the central state or by the local government that initiated them" (Unger and Chan: 128–9). The observation remains largely true today.

Thus, the corporatism approach helps us explain certain features of the current relationship between trade associations and the government. Yet one must notice that the circumstances under which such a relationship emerged is rather different from what Schmitter and Grote depict as the precondition of corporatism. In their view, corporative relations are a result of the differentiation of interests and interest groups, and an important purpose of corporatism is to avoid further competition and to deliver order and agreement. In other words, competition and conflict among interest groups make state intervention necessary (Schmitter and Grote 1997: 171–5). Despite the twenty-year development of a market economy, however, interest splits and conflicts in China have not yet developed to a point that this issue becomes the primary motivation for state intervention. Nor have the interest groups accumulated enough political power to become equal partners in negotiations with the state. On the contrary, the state is pushing enterprises, state-owned ones in particular, to survive market competition and interest differentiation. In this sense, China approaches state corporatism "not as a mechanism for yet further strengthening the state's grip over the economy and over society, but rather the reverse, a mechanism through which the state's grip could be loosened" (Unger and Chan: 105).

The loosening of the government's grip on economic management is a logical cause of the fundamental change from a totally state-planned and state-controlled economy to today's "socialist market" economy. The establishment of corporatist relations, to a great extent, allows the state to continue its power over an increasingly privatized economy while it theoretically recognizes trade associations as corporative partners rather than subjects. This dual nature is reflected in the trade associations' function of "serving both the government and their members" (*shuangxiang fuwu*). In the past, top-down associations largely focused their attention on following the government's interests. If we accept the notion of "state-corporatism," we can identify most top-down associations with this concept. Even Unger and Chan agree, however, that some organizations "are gradually coming under the influence of, and beginning to speak on behalf of, their designated constituencies" (Unger and Chan: 128–9).

Civil society approach

In dissenting from the corporatist approach, White, Howell, and Shang argue that the decline of government control and the increasing diversity and effective expression of social interests support the idea that civil society provides a useful framework for thinking about China's social organization sector (White *et al.* 1996: 3–4). Howell points out that civil society

> implicitly assumes an oppositional and conflictual relation with the state, neglecting the cooperative dimensions ... Discussion about civil society was and still is largely concerned with the desire to limit state power. Civil society has been seen as a crucial ingredient for democratic life.
> (Howell 1996: 107)

To avoid such a narrow approach, White *et al.* propose a "sociological definition of civil society" that they distinguish from a political conception of civil society. They see the latter as equating "civil society" with "political society" in the sense of a particular set of institutionalized relationships between state and society based on principles of citizenship, civil rights, representation, and the rule of law. The sociological conception, on the other hand, involves an intermediate associational realm situated between the state on one side and the basic building blocks of society on the other (individuals, families, and firms). The associational realm comprises separate social organizations formed voluntarily by individuals to protect or extend their interests or values and that enjoy some degree of autonomy from the state (White *et al.*: 208–9). With this understanding, White and his colleagues identify a strong and growing sphere of social association in China which exhibits, albeit to widely differing degrees, the organizational features of a civil society: voluntary participation and self-regulation in their activities, and autonomy and separation in their relationship with the state (208).

While corporatism may explain power and interest arrangements, it does not account for the political, economic, or social structures in a given society. It is the civil society approach that enables us to see structural changes in the past two decades. The upsurge of private civil associations indicates substantial structural reforms, and serves, along with grassroots organizations, as powerful evidence of civil society evolution in China. Since the late 1990s, accelerated institutional reforms have reoriented the relations of top-down associations with the state and their constituencies. More organizations have recognized the crucial role of their members' well-being to the organization's future.

Until recently, the great majority of top-down associations consisted of current or former state-owned firms. With the growth of the private economy, however, increasing numbers of private firms have joined these associations. Even an association such as the China Grouping Companies Promotion Association (CGCPA, the translation original), an organization of large state-owned companies, is now open to the private sector and its rising number of large companies and grouping companies.[6] In exchange for their support, private companies ask associations to consider their interests and serve their needs.[7]

In some large industrial cities and certain industries, reforms that entrust managerial responsibilities to trade associations have occurred quickly. In 2001, for example, the Shanghai municipal government decided that all trade associations should become financially self-sufficient within the next three years, a policy called "three-year weaning" (*sannian duanna*).[8] The majority of trade associations in the machine industry no longer receive any government funding; their income comes mainly from membership fees, paid services, or profits from their businesses.[9] Of course the cut-off of official funding has affected the government–association relationship. The case studies below show clearly that governmental control over the top-down associations declines as official funding shrinks. To cite an example, the government requires associations to send out its documents and propaganda materials to members. In the past, this did not pose a problem when the government provided funding, but now the associations ask, "Who should pay the postage?"[10]

This is a legitimate question, and it carries broader implications for the state–association relationship. Asking the government to pay for services it requires of non-governmental associations changes the nature of relations between the two. When official funding supports association operations, the government acts like a parent toward the recipients.[11] In recent years, the government has cut funding but continues to ask associations to provide all kinds of services. Eventually, it will need to pay fees for services. When that day comes, the government will become a client of these organizations rather than a parent. Furthermore, the self-sufficiency policy has put enormous pressure on the associations and has forced them to reassess their relations with constituents. Now that more and more associations depend largely on membership fees and service charges, they are taking members' needs seriously. The trend of top-down associations becoming constituency-oriented is clear and inexorable. It is true that the government maintains considerable control over these economic associations; nevertheless, it is only a matter of time until the non-governmental sector takes over decision-making power fully. Thus this study disagrees with the notions that "economic development is not yet leading to demands for greater autonomy by entrepreneurs" and that "most individuals and groups in China do not seek autonomy but rather closer embeddedness within the state" (Dickson 2003: 133–4).

When we look at bottom-up organizations, we see more profound progress in the evolution of civil society. As discussed in Chapter 2, since the 1980s the private economy has become the most vibrant and fastest growing part of China's economic development. Entrepreneurs have come to realize their common interests and have become increasingly active in organizing their own associations. The case study of Wenzhou below provides convincing evidence. The self-supporting and self-operating chambers of commerce in Wenzhou have created an indispensable space where their constituents' interests can be expressed and met, and where they can interact with the government. Wenzhou's independent chambers of commerce have become an influential example for all kinds of aspiring associations; many trade associations and other NGOs nationwide have visited these organizations.[12] Such institutional channels between the state and society did not exist prior to the reforms, and such autonomous associations and their energetic performance seriously challenge the top-down pattern.

Undeniably, the private entrepreneurs in Wenzhou have prompted the upsurge of civic associations, and such actions carry clear political impact. Nevertheless, one cannot assume that the entrepreneurs are or will become a powerful force for political reform by the CCP. To understand the political role of private entrepreneurs, we need to examine their perspectives on the official reform policy and their relationship with China's political elites. Private entrepreneurs have benefited from the state-led economic reforms; indeed, their social, financial, and political conditions have improved substantially in the wake of the reforms. The great majority of today's entrepreneurs come from meager social, cultural, and financial backgrounds, and it is the reforms and open policy that have made possible the opportunities to become rich and successful.

The rapidly increasing size and collective wealth of China's new economic elite has caused the CCP to change its attitude towards them substantially. The most convincing evidence is Jiang Zemin's landmark speech of the Three Represents (2001), which laid a theoretical base for recruiting entrepreneurs to the CCP. And within a year, 100,000 entrepreneurs flocked to join (Young 2004: 45). The party's intention to draw the newly rich under its wings was further revealed in the National Assembly of the Chinese People's Congress in 2003, when the number of representatives of private entrepreneurs jumped to five times that of the previous Assembly. So much discussion on adding "protection of private property" into the Constitution occurred in both the Congress and the Chinese People's Political Consultative Conference that some media cynically called these two organizations "the clubs of the wealthy."[13] When the daughter of Hu Jintao, China's president and the secretary general of the CCP, secretly married the wealthy owner of sina.com, China's biggest Web portal, Nick Young, a China expert, called the union an emblem of the growing alliance between political and economic power in China (Young 2004: 45). The "marriage" between China's political and economic elites will have a strong role in determining China's political power structure in the near future (Fewsmith 2004).

Understandably, the entrepreneurs' own interests align them with the CCP leaders' view that economic growth and social stability are paramount national concerns, and in general they support the state-led reforms. In his survey (1997–99) of 524 entrepreneurs and 230 party and government officials in China's four provinces, Bruce Dickson found that entrepreneurs unanimously prefer the state leadership without input from below in economic reforms and that they show as little interest as government officials in opening political reform efforts to the wider population (Dickson 2003: 135). So far, private entrepreneurs have lacked the vision and motivation to seek strong political roles in China's ongoing transformation. Thus, while the growth of civic associations in the economic realm is one of the few watershed events in the development of NGOs and civil society, one must also recognize the Chinese characteristics of this evolution. The rise of economic and even political influence among entrepreneurs does not confirm a general assumption that the development of a market economy in a socialist country necessarily leads to political reforms. In China's situation, we see a more complicated picture.

Four categories of top-down associations

The top-down and bottom-up models represent the responses of the government and the private business sector to the challenges imposed by the market economy. The major distinction between the two models is the nature of organizations' relations with the state. The following discussion examines four different categories of top-down associations with examples. It highlights the diversity of top-down associations in their founding, functions and, especially, their relations with the state. This study finds that the government has, in different periods and through different policies, turned to non-governmental mechanisms to implement its reform agenda and achieve what it could not do by official decree. Thus the development of top-down associations presents a convincing case of corporatism in the relationship of the state and the private sector. This section also concludes, however, that these organizations are acquiring various degrees of operational autonomy.

The top-down model describes state initiative and degrees of control in establishing and directing organizations. Official funding and an employment quota (*shiye bianzhi*) are the two major indicators of these organizations' relationship with the government.[14] Accordingly, the great majority of top-down trade associations have existed within the state system and are only recently moving out from under the wing of the state. Having not yet fully obtained the power and autonomy promised them by the reforms, these organizations cannot function effectively, nor do they have financial independence. To variable degrees, the top-down associations continue to need government assistance for staff benefits and office supplies.[15] A 1998 investigation revealed that one-third of trade associations in the survey performed poorly due to insufficient funding and personnel (CIEAS 1998).

Consequently, most former government employees and well-educated young people prefer not to work in top-down associations, which in most cases cannot afford to hire full-time employees with competitive benefits. For instance, the staff of the Shanghai Federation of Industrial Economy (SFIE) consists mainly of retirees, with half of their incomes paid by their original work units as part of a pension plan, and workers borrowed temporarily from other institutions. By comparison, the average age of trustee members in Wenzhou Garment Chambers of Commerce (WGCC) is 41.[16]

This study classifies top-down trade associations into four categories based on their history and the way the government initially organized them:

1   "non-governmental" organizations that existed before the Cultural Revolution to carry out political or economic functions assigned by the government and that have been revitalized since the economic reforms;
2   civic associations newly founded by the government to fulfill certain managerial functions or economic needs in the new market economy;
3   professional associations (*xiehui*) established by professionals who work within the state system; and
4   trade associations that have been transferred systematically from former industrial bureaus.

Category 1

This category contains governmental organizations established before the Cultural Revolution. Few in number, this type of organization often served symbolically as representative of different social forces, and these organizations carried specific missions designated by the government. For example, the federations of industry and commerce were the membership organizations of private entrepreneurs, and the friendship associations with foreign countries served as "private channels" to help the Chinese government communicate with the outside world when the CCP government had only limited relations with other countries. With such a historical background, these organizations maintain close ties with the government.

One best understands this model through its most representative example, the All-China Federation of Industry and Commerce (ACFIC) and its local branches (federations of industry and commerce, FIC). The historical roots of civic associations in the economic realm date to the first half of the twentieth century when, as Chapter 1 discussed, a large number of chambers of commerce, trade associations, and other private economic organizations were active in China. During the Liberation War against the Nationalist Party (1945–49), the national bourgeoisie was not an enemy of the CCP's revolution. But after 1949, the CCP quickly changed its political promises and policies towards this social class, and almost all chambers of commerce and trade associations vanished during the Socialist Reform of Industry and Commerce in the 1950s.

To replace the former organizations of private businessmen and still to "represent" their interests, as early as 1951 the CCP government started to organize local FIC. In 1953 the ACFIC was established, with a multi-tier national system down to the county level. As described by an FIC official, its function is to help "the government hold the capitalists" and "reform the capitalists."[17] Since then, the FIC have become a major political tool of the CCP's united front to connect the government to private entrepreneurs. Before the Cultural Revolution, they were subsumed into the administration (*xingzhenghua*) and became a part of the government apparatus. Under the state-planned economy, the only function left for the FIC was to assist the CCP's united front. In exchange, the ACFIC, along with eight other national people's organizations, enjoyed special political and material privileges (Chapter 3).

Since the urban economic reforms launched in the early 1980s, however, the FIC's role has changed dramatically. When the door finally opened to private businesses, the older generation of businessmen – although not many survived the thirty years of harsh political conditions – was now much in demand. The government expected the FIC to serve as an instrument in guiding and helping private enterprises in the new economy and redesigned it as an organization that mainly provides services and forums to private entrepreneurs, those with large businesses in particular. Prior to the open policy, given the scarcity of non-state-owned businesses, the FIC had gradually come to include state-owned or collectively owned enterprises. In 1991, the CCP's Central Committee issued a document to announce that the FIC's mission should now focus only on private entrepreneurs and recruit enterprises in the non-public sector.[18] The existing state-owned firms were shipped out of the FIC, and today only private businessmen and their firms can join the FIC at the national, municipal, or county levels.

By 2002, China had 2,800 FICs at the county level or above, consisting of over 1,600,000 federation members, including enterprises, institutions, and individuals (ACFIC 1996; *People's Daily*, November 23, 2002). With their multi-tier organizational system, the FIC function as channels to increase communication between the government and the newly rich. While the primary task of the FIC is to furnish private entrepreneurs with professional, financial, and information services, their duties also include generating private monetary and business resources for public interests such as charity and social development. Furthermore, the FIC are responsible for assisting and guiding entrepreneurs to keep in line with the CCP's political principles.

Since the FIC had been established and tightly controlled by the government for over thirty years before the reforms, the process of differentiating them from the government has been slow. Influential figures in the ACFIC are advocating more autonomy, however, and Unger's study of FIC argues that even though the FIC remain under the close supervision of the party, "there are indications that at the municipal and especially district levels the

Federation branches have become attuned more to the interests of their constituencies than they are to the interests of the state" (Unger 1996: 815).

The government, too, has gradually perceived and encouraged the increase of the FIC's private role, noting that this is also in the state's interest. An example of the government's new attitude is the recurrence of the name "*shanghui*" (chambers of commerce), a term related to capitalism that had disappeared from China for more than thirty years. In a meeting of the CCP's Central Secretariat in 1987, the party proclaimed that FIC were private chambers of commerce in both domestic and international matters (WFIC 1999: 1). In his 1994 visit to the ACFIC, Jiang Zemin inscribed the words "People's Chambers of Commerce" with the intent of highlighting the non-governmental nature of the ACFIC (ACFIC 1996); soon thereafter, local FIC also renamed themselves as chambers of commerce.

Yet, the autonomous nature of the FIC remains a controversial issue. Reversing the trend, in the congratulatory letter of the CCP and the State Council to the 9th National Assembly of ACFIC Representatives (November 2002), the federation's nature as "united front, economic and non-governmental" was reannounced (*People's Daily*, November 23, 2002). During the meeting, Wang Zhaoguo, minister of the CCP's Department of the United Front, once again defined the FIC as the

> people's organizations and private chambers of commerce under the leadership of the Chinese Communist Party. They are the bridge and communication-belt between the party, government and the people in a non-public-owned economy. They are also assistants of the government in governing a non-public-owned economy.
>
> (*People's Daily*, November 23, 2002)

Over the past decade, however, growing numbers of private entrepreneurs have become involved in the initiative and governance of the FIC. In the most recent national representatives' assembly in 2002, private businesspeople constituted 56 percent of the 412 members of the ACFIC executive committee (*People's Daily*, November 23, 2002). Moreover, successive chairmen of the ACFIC have been members of so-called democratic parties, some of whom have experience running private enterprises, and the leaders often hold high positions in the National People's Congress and the Chinese People's Political Consultative Conference. As another example, the best-known project initiated and promoted by the ACFIC and their members is Worthy Causes (*guangcai shiye*, "the glorious cause"). In 1994, ten successful private businessmen who were also executive committee members of the ACFIC called on private enterprises to invest in economic and social development in impoverished areas. This new project was headed by Wang Zhaoguo, endowed by the government, and established in cooperation with the China Promotion Association of the Worthy Cause. With 8,846 private entrepreneurs holding over 22.9 billion RMB, it launched 5,744 Worthy

Cause projects within seven years. These projects have hired over one million people and helped some 2.6 million poor people (*People's Daily*, April 14, 2002). In promoting the Worthy Cause, the FIC at all levels have cooperated and furnished crucial services to entrepreneurs, free of charge.

Prior to the passage of the Donation Law (LD 1999), there were no tax exemptions for charitable donations, and thus entrepreneurs had little incentive to donate money to public causes.[19] Through the Worthy Cause projects, the FIC inspired a social conscience among business owners and mobilized their desire to improve private businesses' low public standing.[20] Furthermore, the FIC helped many to find appropriate partner projects and obtain *Xinghuo* funds, a governmental loan for development in poor areas. Meanwhile, these private businesses made healthy profits (*People's Daily*, April 14, 2002). Private money is a weighty bargaining chip when FIC members advocate for more autonomy. While the FIC have encouraged their constituencies to serve the best interests of the public as well as the private sector, their relations with the government have gradually shifted from taking orders to acting with initiative.

Even so, the FIC have a long way to go to become autonomous. Although the executive board of the ACFIC now has more businesspeople than ever before, when the ACFIC assembly adjourns, the standing executive body, all on the government payroll, runs the daily operation. Employees of the FIC still enjoy treatment as state employees in terms of their health insurance and retirement plan, and new employees must pass the civil servant examination before they can work at the FIC.[21] The officials of the FIC are entitled to official ranks, with the president of the ACFIC equal in rank to the State Council minister (*buji*), and the head of the Beijing FIC equal to director of an under-ministry bureau (*juji*). Furthermore, the chairmen of the ACFIC and local FIC often are not CCP members and hold only nominal power; in general, it is the vice-chairmen or secretaries general – often governmental officials – who wield the real power.

Category 2

Another type of top-down association was founded by the government after the 1980s to meet the needs of economic development. In the aftermath of the reforms, new issues related to an increasingly market-oriented economy surged; yet no institutional mechanisms existed to deal with these problems. Consequently, new institutions were rapidly established to fill this gap, and most of them have been classified as non-governmental in their legal status. For example, the China Consumers' Association (CCA) was established in 1984 to participate in the International Federation of Consumers, an international non-profit organization. Since China does not have a government institution to enforce the Law to Protect Consumers' Interests and related regulations, the CCA is entrusted with seven duties that it could not fulfill were it not to enjoy certain governmental power.[22]

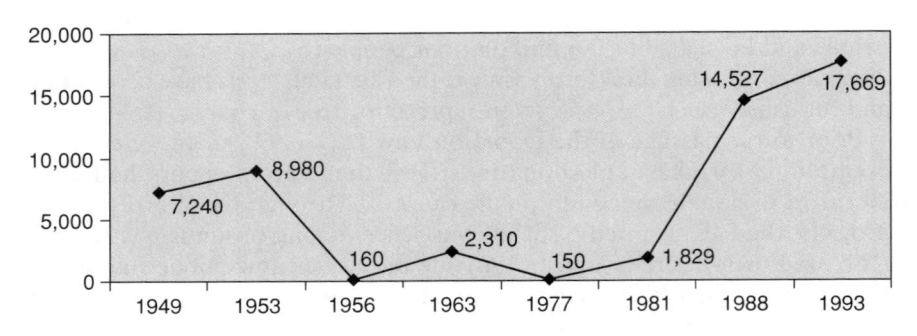

Figure 5.2 Self-employed laborers in urban China (1949–93) (thousands).
Sources: Statistics of the National Bureau of Industry and Commerce, in CSELA 1994: 16–23.

Other organizations that fall under this category, such as the Private Entrepreneurs' Associations (PEAs) and the Self-Employed Laborers' Associations (SELAs), were founded in the mid-1980s to supervise or even control workers at non-state-owned businesses. Unlike the usual control of state employees through work units, since the members of these organizations would be non-state employees, the government decided that non-governmental institutions would better serve its purposes.

The SELAs provide a good example through which to analyze the nature and function of this type of NGO. At the establishment of the PRC, over seven million non-agricultural, self-employed laborers (SELs) lived in urban areas and several tens of millions in the countryside. As the economy developed during the early 1950s, this number increased; however, when the Socialist Reform Movement of Capitalist Industry and Commerce ended in 1956, the total number of SELs dropped sharply (Figure 5.2). From then until the beginning of the Cultural Revolution, due to a modification of the CCP's economic policy that loosened control of individual businesses in the early 1960s, the self-employed population grew as they catered to people's daily needs. Nevertheless, as the "tail of capitalism," the SELs were a constant target of Mao Zedong's continuing revolution, and by the end of the Cultural Revolution in 1977, the total figure for SELs had reached the all-time low since the founding of the PRC. The disappearance of SELs and their services created enormous difficulties in the daily lives of urban dwellers. For example, in 1949 Beijing had about 15,000 restaurants but by 1976 only six hundred were left. As a resident of Beijing at that time, I remember vividly how difficult it was to eat out.

In order to relieve the tremendous pressure for merchandise and services, in the early 1980s the government gave the green light to private businesses and encouraged self-employed laborers. The chief concern of this new policy, however, was to employ the mounting number of jobless urban and rural populations. As Figure 5.2 shows, in the 1980s the SELs made their most impressive increase. The state soon became seriously concerned about this highly scattered, mobile, and unstable labor force. In an educational document written in 1994 by the government-run China Self-employed Laborers' Association (CSELA), a frank description of SELs revealed the government's opinion of these people and its real intention in founding CSELA. The document refers to self-employed laborers as "a unique social group that is large, complicated, with little education and poor personal quality as a whole; they are loosely organized and badly disciplined, and they do things very much as they please" (CSELA 1994: 68). Without work units to supervise the self-employed laborers, the government felt compelled to "found an association to enforce official stipulations of SELs, and mostly, to educate and control this group politically and socially" (CSELA: 68).

In 1980, one year prior to an official document that permitted the self-employed to form associations, some self-employed people in Harbin, a large city near China's northeastern border with Russia, organized the first bottom-up SELA for their own interests, and by 1986, in 27 provinces, over 24,000 local SEL associations had emerged (CSELA: 50–3). However, these originally bottom-up associations soon came under the government's tight supervision. The establishment of the national association (CSELA) for the SELs in 1986, with high governmental officials on its board of directors and executive body, demonstrated clearly that this institution would become the most important instrument for the government to control and reach out to the self-employed. This situation continues; in 2004 the vice-director of the National Bureau of Industry and Commerce still held the post of the director of CSELA.[23]

Local SELAs have the following duties: maintain an orderly market, collect SEL taxes, manage fair product prices, provide birth control for SELs, encourage good hygiene and prevent epidemics, and assist the police in maintaining public order. Since the main mission of SELAs is to oversee every laborer, it is not surprising that SELA membership is mandatory. Individuals will not receive business licenses if they do not join SELA,[24] and they automatically become SELA members when they register with the Bureau of Industry and Commerce (BIC) to obtain business licenses (CSELA: 65–9). In defining NGOs' voluntary nature, Mark Lyons, an Australia sociologist, points out that

> a few third sector organizations succeed in requiring everyone who belongs to a certain profession or works for a certain company or attends a university to join a professional organisation, a union or a student union. This does not make them any the less third sector organizations. Rather, it testifies to the success of past political activity and is likely still to be contested.
>
> (Lyons 2001: 2)

According to Lyons, such organizations are still voluntary because "those who are active in directing the organisation are still volunteers in the

152 *Corporatism vs civil society*

conventional sense" (2). Clearly, this is not the case in this instance, where government agencies, namely the BIC, use their power in issuing business licenses to force self-employed people to join SELA. This is rather unusual even among new associations initiated by the government. Furthermore, directors of SELAs are not elected by the members but are government appointees, with staffs on the government payroll.

Another unusual feature of SELAs is their subservient position to the BIC, whereas other types of social organizations have more of a guidance-and-supervision relation to their mothers-in-law. The revenues of SELAs at the county level come almost entirely from managerial fees paid by the self-employed laborers to BIC (CSELA 1994: 86–7).[25] In the areas where the private economy is rudimentary or the number of self-employed is small, SELAs' sustenance has become a serious challenge; according to an official estimate in 1996, one-third of SELAs at the county level are in this condition.[26]

As Figure 5.3 illustrates, SELAs have a comprehensive structure from the national CSELA to the member groups in neighborhood communities. For example, according to a field investigation conducted by Jonathan Unger in the Chaoyang district of Beijing, the Chaoyang SELA was divided into 28 association sub-branches to cover all the neighborhoods and market areas. These sub-branches have been further divided into about 1,000 member groups, each containing around twenty members (Unger 1996: 799). By

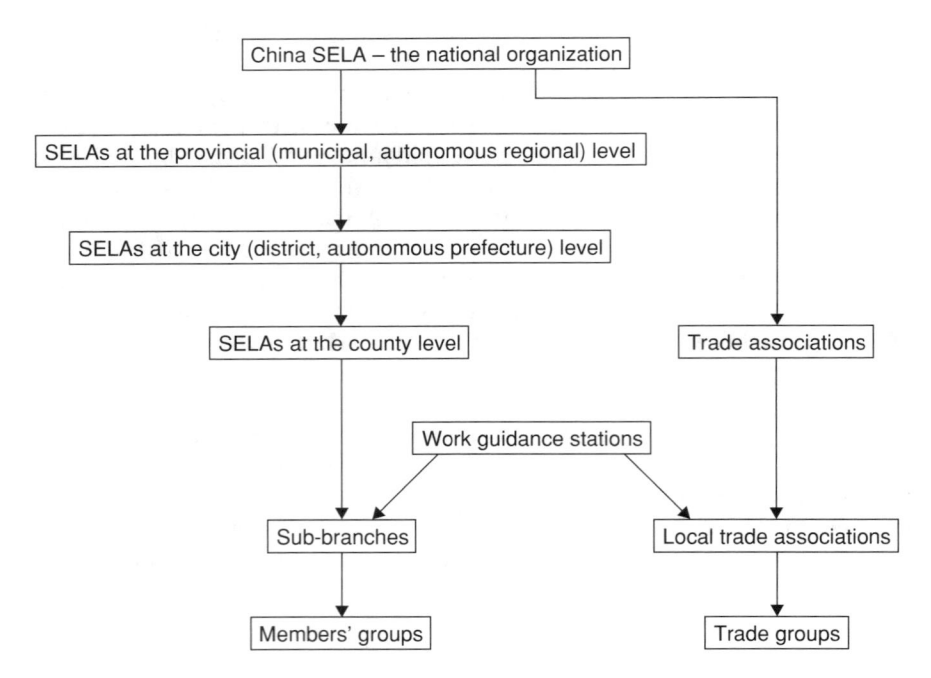

Figure 5.3 The organizational structure of the Self-employed Laborers' Association.
Source: CSELA 1994: 79.

1993, thirty provincial SELAs and 2,881 county SELAs had been organized with 29,136 sub-branches and 306,993 member groups (CSELA: 52). Of all the newly established social organizations, SELAs are now one of the most thoroughly organized. The real power of SELAs lies in the networks designed to reach every self-employed individual. The motive behind the network is obvious: SELAs are the only institutional channel the government has that can reach the multitudes of self-employed, and the government has much reason to be concerned about such a large and rootless labor force.

According to the CSELA Charter passed in 1991, the most substantial task of the association is "to protect SEL's legal rights and interests, and to deliver their reasonable opinions and requests" (CSELA: 205–6). A large gap persists between rhetoric and reality, however, for SELAs are tightly controlled by the BIC. This grip further hampers their ability to self-organize, already made difficult by the diversity and disorganization of the many individual SELs. Most seriously, a vast majority of SELA members receive little education and do not know their rights, let alone how to use the SELA to protect their rights.[27] In addition, SELAs must assist the BIC, the Bureau of Tax, the Bureau of Hygiene, and Bureau of Foodstuffs; indeed, some officials in these bureaus are members of SELA committees. When corruption or other abuses of power take place, as they often do, people in small businesses cannot count on SELAs for assistance. Unger concludes that "Beijing's vendors and petty entrepreneurs are too weak and too low in status to hold any influence at all over the officials who are supposed to administer their activities" (Unger 1996: 802–3).

Category 3

The third group of associations consists mostly of professional organizations organized by individual office holders and professionals who represent their respective governmental institutions in those associations. By 1994 these groups represented 22 percent of social organizations (Ma 1999: 310). An interesting feature of this type is that the constituents include almost all the state-owned firms; yet the organizations themselves are run by elected members who usually have a free reign. A few of these associations existed before the Cultural Revolution, but the great majority were founded after the reforms. The basic difference between professional and trade associations is that the former are not concerned with any managerial issues, while the latter are involved greatly in managerial matters such as price or quality control and the approval of business licenses to new firms. In general, most of the income of these associations comes from membership fees. Although the government does not fund this type of organization, other government aid is available, such as office space, conference expenditures, and research grants.

The China Grouping Companies Promotion Association provides a representative example of associations in this category.[28] Officially registered with the MOCA as a national social organization in 1994, the CGCPA was started in 1987 by several CEOs of large state-owned industrial companies at a time when state-owned companies were falling behind and had difficulties adapting from a state-planned to a market-oriented economy. Beginning with just fifty companies, CGCPA has since tripled its membership, drawing from almost all regions in China, and in such areas as machinery, military industry, energy, light industry, agriculture, transportation, medical equipment, pharmaceuticals, construction, and domestic and international trade. Given this cross-section of economic situations and geographic localities, the only thing these members have in common is their large size and their being state-owned.

To sustain and develop themselves, these enterprises desperately needed not only knowledge about the market, but also new managerial mechanisms and communication channels. Furthermore, separation from the government has created conflicts of interest with the government and between different businesses. Even though many large enterprises are still state-owned, they feel an ever more urgent need to express their opinions on policy and protect their own interests. In 1995, for example, the State Council's institutional reforms directly affected the interests of CGCPA members, who rightly feared that the government might take back the authority granted to enterprises or co-opt property rights. This conflict of interest was only one manifestation of a much larger issue – the control of state property – that had become an ever more sensitive and complex problem as reforms deepened. Yet no individual company had the courage to confront the State Council.[29]

To solve this dilemma, CGCPA organized a policy investigation into the issue. Eight economic experts were invited, and their efforts resulted in three workshops and seven reports. The reports not only analyzed existing practices and problems, but also suggested certain solutions to the government. After a hearing attended by its members and state officials, CGCPA submitted its reports to the State Council. Some of the suggestions were espoused by Zhu Rongji, then vice-premier, and later enforced. Between 1998 and 2001, CGCPA submitted sixteen reports involving government policy-making, and the influence of its members on China's state economy has made CGCPA a high-profile association and prompted many large companies to join. CGCPA, a non-governmental intermediary, was able to participate in and affect national policy-making. As their slogan proclaims, "we can do what individual enterprises want to do but cannot do or do well, and what the government does not want to do or has no time to do" (*Economic Daily*, 经济日报, June 6, 2001: 1).

Nevertheless, the autonomous nature of CGCPA is still contestable; according to the paradigm NGO definition, CGCPA is not a legitimate, autonomous organization. CGCPA was established by the initiative of its constituency and it has managed to be financially self-sufficient throughout its existence. However, not only are group members all state-owned enterprises, but the directorship also overlaps with the office holder status of the CEOs. Such an overlap in leadership benefits the association in many ways. Since CGCPA receives no direct government funding, an important component of its income is donated by the company that the director heads. The CEOs also bring valuable social capital to CGCPA through their political and social connections. When the head of CGCPA has access to an important decision-making body in the central government, the association's voice is more likely to be heard. As this case illustrates, the nature of the state–NGO relationship involves a web of connections among the elite.

During these years, CGCPA has not only established an impressive relationship with the media, but also regularly works with eighteen government bureaus and six national NGOs on the economy, as well as with over fifty experts in some twenty universities, research institutions, and consultant companies. All of these, in CGCPA's own words, are "intangible capital and important conditions for our success" (CGCPA 2001). CGCPA's achievement is significant in that an intermediary social organization stood up to protect its members' interests and effectively influenced government policy. This role is one that neither individual enterprises nor government agencies can play.

Category 4

The final but most prominent group comprises the trade associations. As China's economy becomes increasingly market-oriented, a fundamental change in managerial structure is inevitable. The Chinese government has concluded that establishing macro-management with non-governmental trade associations to mediate between the state and enterprises is a key step in the economic transformation (Lü 1999: 18). The government has gradually yet systematically adopted non-governmental institutions to replace the old state-planned industrial management. This is almost like killing three birds with one stone. By turning a large segment of the intermediate official bureaus into trade associations, the government quickly created a much needed intermediary mechanism for the market economy. These top-down associations allow the government to retain a strong grip on the private sector while also suppressing the emergence of bottom-up associations. In addition, since legally the trade associations are no longer governmental agencies, the transformation trimmed the industrial administrative body significantly. This experience was unprecedented and is unique among all types of NGOs in China.

The first official encouragement of trade associations came in 1982 with the approval of the State Council, and the first group of national trade associations emerged. Since then, the development of trade associations has gone through roughly three periods. From the early 1980s to 1988, the trade associations made relatively promising progress. For example, the State Council started an experimental reform in the machine industry, and from 1984 to 1988 over a hundred trade associations appeared in the Ministry of Machine Industry.[30] The second round of reforms (1989–92) was deeply affected by the student demonstrations in Tiananmen and the suppression that followed, as were all social organizations in China. Around that time the Ministry of Civil Affairs (MOCA), which had taken over responsibility for social organizations, began to tighten controls over the registration of new organizations. The growth of trade associations stopped until Deng Xiaoping's speech on his tour to South China in 1992.

Since 1993, the government has worked to complete its theoretical discourse on the promotion of trade associations. This marks the third period in the rapid development of the trade associations. At the Third Plenum of the Party's 14th Central Committee in 1993, Jiang Zemin, Li Peng, Zhu Rongji and other high-ranking officials repeatedly emphasized the importance of trade associations as social intermediaries, as well as the need to nourish and develop a market economy within a socialist system (DBP 1999: 1–7). This occasion marked the CCP's decision to "utilize the market's intermediary institutions and to bring their roles in service, communication, notarization, and supervision into full play." The document also called for "the development of chambers of commerce and trade associations" (DBP 1999: 2). Soon thereafter, the State Economic and Trade Commission held three high-level seminars on trade associations that helped the central government determine its policy towards trade associations and other intermediary institutions. As never before, an impressive number of official documents provided details on the roles and responsibilities of trade associations, and on the improvement of their legal, financial, and personnel conditions.

Through these efforts, the government arrived at a clear definition of the trade associations' roles in the transformation of economic structures in the short term and the establishment of a market economy in the long term. As described in a 1997 document by the State Economy and Trade Commission, the mission of trade associations is as follows:

1 establish a self-disciplinary mechanism, standardize enterprises' self-governance, promote fair competition, and protect the benefits of all players;
2 help the government registration bureaus screen new enterprise registration applications;
3 participate in making and implementing technological, managerial, and quality standards; issue product certificates and assist the government in improving and correcting unqualified products;
4 guide, supervise, and regulate product prices and arbitrate price disputes; prevent monopolies and protect fair competition and lawful trade;
5 collect and analyze statistical data on trade for the government;
6 conduct research on investment, reform, or development; promote domestic and international technology exchange as well as new hi-tech products and technology. (DBP 1999: 32–9)

After the establishment of these guidelines, an energetic promotion of trade associations followed. Aimed at transforming departmental management into trade-oriented management, the government decided to transfer a large number of intermediate industrial bureaus at the mid- and local levels into trade associations. A vigorous campaign was launched in 1997 in 23 trades in Shanghai, Guangzhou, Wenzhou, and Shenzhen. This effort escalated dramatically when Zhu Rongji became premier and in the late 1990s instigated the largest ever State Council's institutional reforms. In 1998, ten industrial ministries were first recreated and reduced to state bureaus under the State Economic and Trade Commission before being completely dismissed in 2001 (*People's Daily*, February 2, 2001: 2 and March 3, 2001: 5). In their place, ten general trade associations at the national level (*zonghexing hangye xiehui*) were established to coordinate and provide services to enterprises in their respective industries, with government functions placed under the State Economic and Trade Commission. According to Du Juezhou, the new chair of the China Federation of the Textile Industry and former director of the State Bureau of the Textile Industry, "the dismissal of the state industrial bureaus symbolizes the end of the era when the state controlled industry" (*People's Daily*, March 3, 2001: 5).

These general trade associations are officially classified as NGOs and must register with the MOCA and its local branches. Before 2001, the industrial ministries and their subordinate offices served as the mothers-in-law for these NGOs; now, the State Economic and Trade Commission supervises the ten general trade associations, and these in turn supervise the trade associations in their respective industries or businesses (*People's Daily*, February 20, 2001: 2).[31] The government's forceful promotion of the trade associations was definitely the most dynamic force behind the rapid growth of the top-down civic organizations in the economic sector. While the total number of social organizations declined in the late 1990s as a result of Jiang Zemin's 1996 decision to consolidate non-governmental entities and tighten official control (Figures 5.4 and 5.5), the trade associations made impressive progress (Figures 5.6 and 5.7). The experience of the trade associations illustrates the decisive influence of governmental policy towards NGOs on the growth patterns of different types of social organizations.[32]

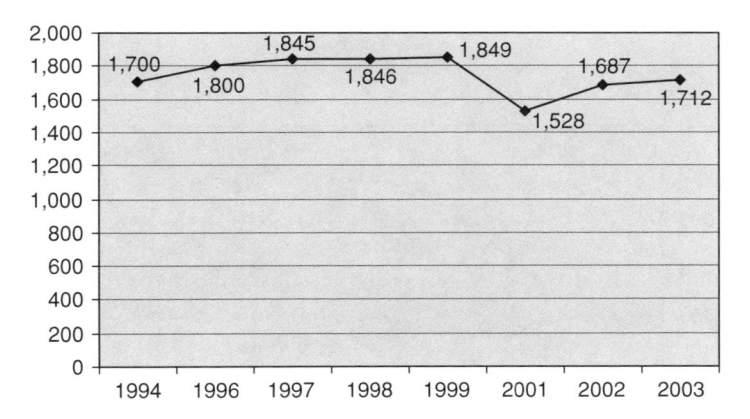

Figure 5.4 Growth and decline of national SOs (1994–2003).
Sources: NBS 1998: 274, 1999: 192, 2002: 102; Rong 1996: 64; Zhang Zhigang 1999.

158 *Corporatism vs civil society*

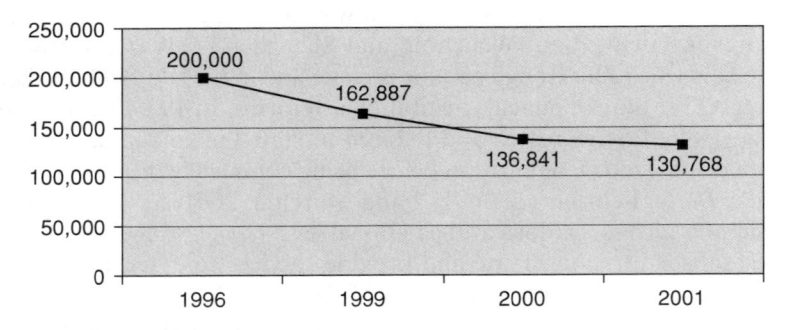

Figure 5.5 Decline of all types of SOs nationwide (1996–2001).
Sources: see Figure 5.4.

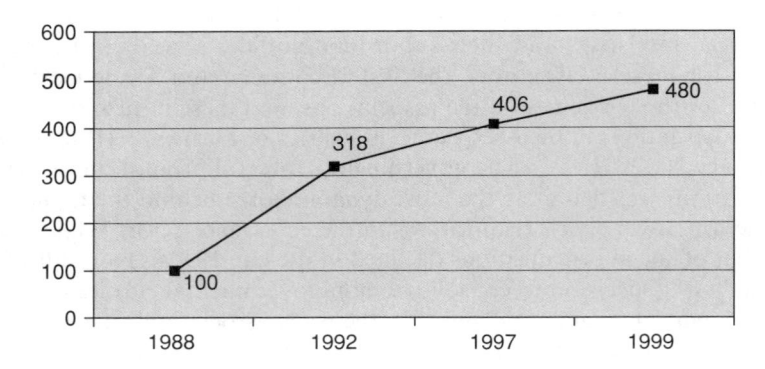

Figure 5.6 Growth of national trade associations (1988–99).
Sources: see Figure 5.4.

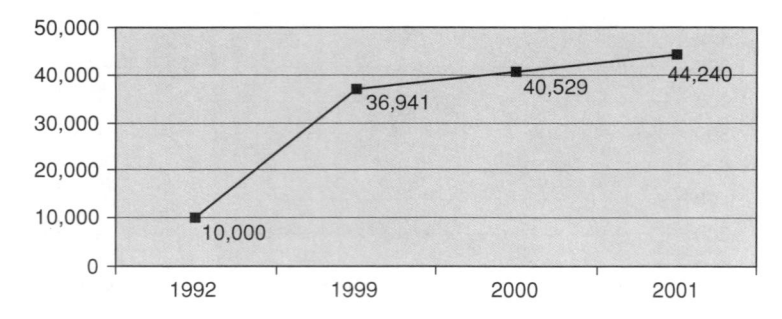

Figure 5.7 Growth of trade associations nationwide (1992–2001).
Sources: see Figure 5.4.

Bottom-up pattern: the chambers of commerce in Wenzhou

Simultaneous with the development of the top-down associations, another distinct growth pattern in the economic realm emerged, that of the bottom-up non-governmental organizations, in which enterprises themselves, mostly private ones, created chambers of commerce or associations to protect and represent their interests. This pattern appeared most significantly in the southeastern coastal provinces, most notably in Wenzhou, a medium-sized city in Zhejiang Province, Southeast China. These bottom-up organizations demonstrate features different from those of the top-down models in governance and in relations with their constituents. Their role in economic and social development is becoming increasingly vital.

Wenzhou was among the first fourteen coastal cities opened to the market economy. Its geographic location, tradition of private business, and the municipal government's reform dynamics have promoted its market economy and private enterprises most impressively. From 1980 to 1996, as state-owned and collectively owned businesses declined, otherwise owned and private enterprises increased more than a hundredfold. Around the late 1970s, Wenzhou had only 6,477 businesses: 302 state-owned, 4,801 collectively owned, two other ownerships, and 1,372 private enterprises at the village and township level. By 1996, the total number had increased to 117,829, and of these, 112,232 (95 percent) were private businesses (Zhang Zhenhai 1999: 182). From 1979 to 2000, the Wenzhou economy grew at an average rate of 15 percent a year, and the total industrial output increased from 1.12 billion RMB in 1978 to 203 billion in 2001 (Zhan and Zhang 2002). In 2000, the private sector made up 85 percent of Wenzhou's domestic output value and 95 percent of the industrial and retail value (Ma 1998: 23; Chen, M. 2002). By 2001, state-owned businesses further declined to only one percent of the total output value of the city.[33]

It is within this context that the bottom-up, private, non-profit organizations emerged. From 1992 to 2004, under the supervision of the Wenzhou Federation of Industry and Commerce (WFIC, also named Wenzhou General Chamber of Commerce), 114 private chambers of commerce in Wenzhou (WCCs) were established, covering almost all important businesses in the greater Wenzhou area. In addition, since 1995, Wenzhou businesspeople have started 93 WCCs in other cities to promote and protect their interests (Cao and Zhang 2004: 2).

Several characteristics differentiate WCCs from the top-down associations:

1 they were initiated by private entrepreneurs;
2 they are self-sufficient, self-managed, and self-recruiting, with no funding from either the Wenzhou government or county governments;
3 memberships are voluntary, and private companies join because they consider these chambers of commerce to work for their interests;
4 private entrepreneurs, often the most outstanding ones, make up the executive boards and the boards of trustees, and they are directly elected by the members of their respective organizations.

It is notable how these new chambers of commerce present strong similarities to their precursors in the late Qing and early Republican period, especially in governance structures, leadership election, and the patriarchal role in arbitrating and supervising member firms' operations (Chapter 1).[34]

A prime example is the Wenzhou Garment Chamber of Commerce (WGCC).[35] Since its founding in 1994, 330 of the 1000-odd fashion companies in the city and surrounding counties, among them most of the well-known companies, have joined the WGCC. As its charter announces, "The WGCC insists upon the principle of voluntary membership, self-election of leadership, self-hiring, self-sufficiency, and self-management. It also upholds the policy of self-governance, self-service, self-adjustment, self-discipline, and self-education" (WGCC 2000a). All of WGCC's income comes from private sources such as membership fees, private donations, and service fees. The membership fee is 800 RMB/year; to become a trustee, vice-president, or president, one is expected to donate 2,000 RMB (board member), 5,000 (standard board member), 10,000 (VP), or 30,000 (president).

Despite these fees, many entrepreneurs compete for the posts because to hold one points to the good reputation of their firms in their field. Signs showing that the stores are members of WGCC or board members of WGCC, usually hanging in the most noticeable spot in the store, earn customers' trust in the products. WGCC is also organized and run by entrepreneurs elected by their fellow businessmen. In elections, multiple candidates vie for each post. Among the 18 members of the board, fourteen are entrepreneurs, and the other four are the secretaries-in-general of WGCC – full-time employees – of the local chambers of commerce. These people understand the importance of the WGCC's services to the success of their own companies; thus they willingly devote time, money, and energy to the WGCC's work. When Chen Min, the owner of a garment company worth 500 million RMB, was elected president of WGCC in 1999, he resigned his CEO position so he could better serve WGCC. Now he spends half of his time working at WGCC without pay, and in 2000 he donated 200,000 RMB to WGCC. Total donations by board members in 2000 came to 433,000 RMB, over sixty percent of WGCC's total income that year (WGCC 2000b). WGCC illustrates the major features of all WCCs: monetary donations to the organization by its leaders are usually far larger than membership fees, and democratic elections are widely practiced.

So far, no other area in China has developed such pervasive and active organizations for private entrepreneurs. The distinctiveness of the Wenzhou model owes much to its unique historical tradition and to recent economic developments that shaped its culture and the traits of its people. A brief examination of these factors will illuminate the conditions that have nurtured bottom-up, private chambers of commerce and trade associations.

Today, Wenzhou spans over 11,784 km^2 and is home to 7.15 million people. Surrounded by mountains, it has very limited arable land. In 1978, one-third of the land was agricultural and the per capita land tenure was only 0.53 *mu* (less than 0.04 hectares). On the eve of Deng Xiaoping's reforms, Wenzhou had a surplus of over one million agricultural laborers (Chen and Zhou 2002b). Furthermore, as Wenzhou is situated on the Taiwan Straits, the pre-reform government considered it a military front against Taiwan and thus too risky for infrastructural investments. In the 1950s, Wenzhou was similar in economic size and composition to Ningbo, a city on the northern coast of Zhejiang province. Between 1949 and 1978, total state investment in building Wenzhou's infrastructure was less than 60 million RMB, only one-seventh the average national state investment (Chen, M. 2002). In contrast, state investment to Ningbo in the same period was 600 million RMB.[36] Thus, before 1978, the state-owned economy contributed only 36 percent of Wenzhou's industrial output value, far below the national average of 78 percent (Ma 1998: 1).[37] Limited natural resources and the lack of government investment forced Wenzhou's people to seek other means of livelihood. During the thirty years of state-planned economy from 1950 to 1980, even when political persecution reached its peak in the Cultural Revolution, Wenzhou's underground family-based private businesses never ceased.[38] Right after the reform and open policy, these family businesses became essential instruments that facilitated Wenzhou's private economy.

Wenzhou's residents like to say, "The unique natural environment nurtured the nature of the Wenzhou people." Wenzhou was called an ocean culture: frequent migration since ancient times, ocean trade, and the lack of strong ties with any inland cultural center nurtured an independent, diligent, creative, practical, and adventurous people. After the 1980 reforms, these traits have been put to good use. Wenzhou's utilitarian culture has a historical origin. As early as the Tang and Song Dynasties, Wenzhou – then known as "Ou" or "Yongjia" – had become a prosperous manufacturing and commercial port in Southeast China. Far from the capitals of imperial dynasties, Wenzhou enjoyed a relatively isolated cultural environment. Against the mainstream of Confucianism, the "Yongjia School" in South Song and the "Three Scholars of East Ou" in the late Qing were well known for their advocacy of business and economic development. In the Song Dynasty, mainstream scholarship and philosophy was the school of *Li, Xin* and *Qi* (universal order, human nature, and energy matter). This philosophy, also representing a Chinese Zen school, strongly opposed materialism and human desires, and greatly influenced contemporary scholars. Opposing the mainstream teaching at its height (1150–1223 A.D.), the Yongjia School emphasized utilitarianism and strongly criticized "meaningless discussion of human nature (*kongtian xinxing*), of repressing commerce and emphasizing essence [i.e. agriculture]" (*yi mo hou ben*). It advocated "promoting commerce and supporting manufacturing" (*tongshang huigong*) and believed that utilitarianism should exist equally with humanity and virtue (*gongli yu renyi bingcun*) (WDC 1995: 464). Again, in the late nineteenth century, Chen Qiu, Song Shu, and Chen Fuchen (Three Scholars of East Ou) called strongly for the establishment of commercial law and official support for business, manufacturing, and agriculture (Ma 1998: 3; Chen, M. 2002).

When I visited Wenzhou in 2001, everyone I interviewed, from office holders to old businessmen, told me about these ancient scholars and their influence on Wenzhou's culture. No doubt, Wenzhou people are very proud of their unique cultural tradition. The long absence of orthodox ideology in Wenzhou was an important factor in cultivating Wenzhou scholars' utilitarianism, and its traditions in commerce and manufacturing continued even after the establishment of the PRC. Thus, it comes as no surprise that, immediately after the open policy, Wenzhou's private businesses began to grow like mushrooms after a summer rain.

A major feature of Wenzhou's private economy is its small size and family-based operation. This was especially true at the outset of the private economy. Family businesses were competing mostly with state-owned factories that had government funds and technological resources, and the family enterprises desperately needed capital. Wenzhou people refer to the 1980s and even the 1990s as "the period of primitive accumulation of capital." During this period, Wenzhou businesses would do almost anything that would help them make money; most notoriously, they sacrificed quality for profit. The lack of sufficient supervision and regulation of private businesses led to chaotic, fraudulent practices and suicidal competitions, and the resulting damage to the private economy in general was devastating.

To many Wenzhou business people, the most humiliating moment came on August 8, 1987, when over 5,000 pairs of Wenzhou-made shoes were publicly set on fire in Hangzhou, the capital of Zhejiang province, by the official bureau on product quality. These shoes were nicknamed "week shoes" because their soles consisted of paper and could last only a week (Li 2000: 520–1). For a long time, "Wenzhou" was synonymous with "forgery and poor quality" (*jia, mao, wei, lue*). In 1990, the province and local governments sent out quality-inspection groups to investigate electrical products in 14 towns in Wenzhou. During this examination, 49 companies "voluntarily suspended themselves," and the government shut down 255 family workshops for making forged products (*People's Daily*, January 26, 2001). Without question, the shoddy merchandise hurt Wenzhou's private businesses badly, and the scandal made Wenzhou's private entrepreneurs recognize the importance of product quality to sustainable growth.

Meanwhile, private businesses felt a great need for legal and government protection. These family-based businesses concentrated on light industries and small products, and the technologies and skills needed to produce them usually were simple and easy to copy. Often, when new products came onto the market, counterfeit copies appeared almost immediately. Consequently, the downward-spiraling price competition made almost all companies lose money, a problem only exacerbated with the entrance of more and more companies. Thus, individual businesses sought an institutional mechanism to implement copyright regulations and eradicate forgery and substand products. On top of this, as was discussed earlier, the government did not provide services such as market information and business training to private companies. Without these services, local private businesses hardly had a chance to compete in the national market, let alone the international market. Yet neither the state system nor the newly emerged private sector had the kind of managerial and service instruments these private businesses were requesting.

Not surprisingly, Wenzhou businesspeople took the initiative. Starting in the late 1980s, and especially in the 1990s, private entrepreneurs organized associations and chambers of commerce to save their business reputations and protect their rights; they also managed to persuade the government to recognize them as legitimate business intermediaries.[39] Chambers of commerce (also called *tongye gonghui*) were not foreign to Wenzhou, and they numbered 198 at their peak (Ye 2000). 98 WCCs still existed on the eve of the establishment of the PRC in 1949. Some of their leaders went on to lead WFIC in the 1950s, and a few still alive by the end of the Cultural Revolution even became involved in the recovery of WFIC. When I was in Wenzhou in 2001, the officials of WFIC introduced me to three of the original WFIC leaders, who told me a great deal about their lives and work before and after the PRC, including the organization of WCCs in the 1930s and 1940s.

Building upon this historical and cultural background, the private WCCs have accomplished a multitude of tasks.[40] First, they furnish their members with business services previously very much needed but unavailable. They offer training workshops on marketing, sales, technology, and management, and some also regularly publish newsletters on market information, new business trends, and activities of their trades, free of charge to all the members. They help members open new markets and create new products, and now assume full responsibility in attracting foreign and other regions' investments to Wenzhou. For example, the WGCC has held conferences and exhibitions to help over 2000 garment companies and workshops develop marketing strategies. In 2001, it organized 21 member companies to attend the China International Fashion Fair. In addition, it also organized visits by its members to fashion industries in Hong Kong, Paris, Italy, and Germany. In another instance, since its establishment in 1994 the Wenzhou Optical Industry Chamber of Commerce (WOICC) has organized visits by its members to the United States, Brazil, Italy, Japan, and Taiwan to learn new technologies and products. It has also brought members to the Hong Kong International Exhibition each year, and WOICC contributed three-quarters of all Chinese products in the 1999 exhibition. Total sales in these exhibitions increased from 15 million RMB in 1995 to 88 million in 1999. Without the chambers of commerce, individual companies would have neither the capacity to open their own exhibitions nor the ability to participate in national or international exhibitions.

Secondly, the WCCs play an important role in protecting members' interests and rights. To begin with, to protect the general interests of the trade, these organizations discipline members in good business behavior and management, including quality control and copyright protection. As charters of chambers of commerce are approved by member assemblies and membership is voluntary, members agree to the charter upon joining the associations and in general follow the regulations. To protect the copyrights of member companies, for example, since 2001 the WCC for Hardware has handled 280 cases against counterfeit products (Cao and Zhang 2004). Meanwhile, the chambers of commerce represent their constituents' interests to the government and protect them from abuses of power. For example, a Wenzhou business in Baotou was frequently harassed by the local Bureau of Industry and Trade and Bureau of Taxation and could do nothing about it until the WCC in Baotou stepped in and stopped the abuse after the business joined the chamber (Cao and Zhang 2004). In 2002, WCC for Cigarette Lighters collected about a million RMB to help member firms fight the EU's anti-dumping lawsuit against Wenzhou cigarette lighters. It won the case, the first such victory since China joined the WTO (Cao and Xiao).

The most notable accomplishment of the WCCs involves quality control and building an excellent reputation in their brand names. These associations recognized that product quality had become a fatal weakness in their businesses and made quality their first priority, epitomized in the slogan, "quality up, trade up." WCCs not only actively assist the governmental quality control agencies and establish quality examination centers, but they also frequently invite renowned national or provincial experts to examine the quality of their products and ask for advice. By the late 1990s, Wenzhou had become a city famous for its high-quality, fashionable clothing and shoe industries. It was also the biggest producer of China's optics, low-pressure electrical products, and cigarette lighters. On December 15, 1999, another shoe torching took place in Hangzhou, but this time Wenzhou's shoe companies and the government burned thousands of counterfeit shoes that had used Wenzhou's brand names. Wang Zhentao, known as the King of Shoes in China, said at the site, "The fire of 1989 woke us up, and it made us realize the importance of quality and a good brand name ... Today, we simply want to let the world know that Wenzhou also hates forgery and poor quality" (Li, H. 2000: 520).

In comparison with the top-down associations, leaders of WCCs are much closer to their businesses and constituents; therefore, they are well aware of problems and can usually bounce them back to the government fairly quickly. For example, around 2000, WGCC asked the government to reconsider or revise its policy on three major issues: bestow real estate property rights to private factories, end unfair taxes on Wenzhou's chain stores in other cities, and reduce the severe fines and suspensions imposed by uninformed official quality examinations.[41] Many associations have won the trust of their constituents, and more and more private entrepreneurs now come to their associations for help when they have difficulties.[42] This explains why participation in some associations approaches eighty percent, especially with small businesses. The WCCs in Wenzhou and those in other cities have become a home for their constituents, and the most frequently used words in describing the power of these associations are "cohesion and affinity of the chambers of commerce to their members." Similarly, since the leaders of these organizations are democratically elected and are usually the most respected in their trades, their arbitration of member disputes or discipline of wrongdoing is effective.[43] Autonomy and members' support make success possible; after all, the destiny of these associations is closely bound up with the prosperity of their trades and the well-being of their constituents.

With all the autonomy that WCCs enjoy, however, these organizations remain under various degrees of state control. Legally, they fall under the supervision of both the Wenzhou Bureau of Civil Affairs and the WFIC, and in other regions they also need the approval of respective local bureaus of civil affairs.[44] Although the Wenzhou government has been relatively open-minded and supportive towards the private sector, its policies are not always approved by the central government.[45] In recent years, local governments in both Wenzhou and other regions have become more and more supportive of WCCs, recognizing the economic influence of those organizations. For instance, since 2001, WCCs in Liaoning, Xin Jiang, Yunnan, and Sichuan have brought several tens of billions RMB investment from Wenzhou to those regions (Yu and Xiao 2004). The former mayor of Wenzhou called the WCCs "the thermometer of Wenzhou economy" (WFIC 1999: 7).

Politically, however, the WCCs do not represent an independent voice. Indeed, even as the establishment of WCCs indicates the success of private entrepreneurs' collective efforts, it does not mean the WCCs have the power to negotiate with the government. As a high official in the Wenzhou government candidly said, "If they want to negotiate with the government, the government will shut them down."[46] Currently, the WCCs do not want to participate in any political activities that are not in line with official policy. "The purpose for us to organize is," the president of WCC in Guangzhou stated frankly, "making money, making money, and making money" (Yu and Xiao 2004). A 2004 report on WCCs concludes, "Non-governmental initiative, governmental acquiescence, and non-confrontation (against the government) have become the tacit agreement between these organizations and the government" (Yu and Xiao 2004). Once again, the case of Wenzhou chambers of commerce reveals the complications of autonomy for Chinese NGOs.

In short, the development of economic NGOs over the last two decades has presented two growth patterns: top-down and bottom-up, and they reflect the simultaneous evolution of corporatism and civil society. Under China's current political system and the history of thirty years of a state-planned economy, it is not surprising that the top-down model is the more prevalent. Only in areas or trades where the private economy has become a major player can private associations emerge. Despite the current scarcity of such associations, given the rapid growth of the market and private economy, they have high potential. To a great extent, development patterns of NGOs in the economic realm reflect the general situation of NGOs in China as the most profound transformation in Chinese history continues. Given the tremendously unbalanced economic and social development going on throughout China, there are, and will be, more than one type of state–society relationship and NGO growth pattern.

6 "It takes two to tangle"
International NGOs in China and their impacts

After the open and reform policy, the phrase *yu guoji jiegui* – literally, "connecting [Chinese railroads] to international tracks" – became a catchword in the Chinese political vocabulary. This phrase is often translated into English as "catching up with international standards" or "communicating with the international community," and conveys the Chinese government's strong desire, after thirty years of isolation, to open itself up not only to foreign businesses and international aid, but also to the rules of the game as played by the outside world. The process was initiated at the urgings of the United Nations Development Programme (UNDP) in 1984, at which time the government started to reach out to the international non-governmental sector (Huang 2000: 3).

China's economic reforms, which have made a significant impact on the world economy, have also generated political and social consequences that have attracted much international attention. Non-governmental organizations (NGOs) in particular have shown an enormous and ever-growing interest in China's current transformation. Though communication between foreign organizations, the Chinese government, and Chinese NGOs was slow at first, the turning point in the involvement of international non-governmental organizations (INGOs) in China came at the 4th World Conference on Women of the United Nations in Beijing, 1995.[1] The conference came at a time when the global civil society was emerging, and there was a surge in local and national NGOs throughout the world. This trend and the conference decisively influenced INGO work in China. Since then, INGOs have become increasingly active and their programs approach a wide range of economic and social development issues. Hosting the conference also gave Chinese scholars, the government, and NGO practitioners a great opportunity to perceive the meaning, magnitude, and role of NGOs firsthand. The positive impact of the conference is manifold, foremost that it helped open China to global civil society.

This chapter studies the role of INGOs in China's NGO development and focuses on three aspects. First, it looks at INGO involvement in China as a part of globalization and the emergence of a global civil society. Second, it approaches the Chinese government's attitude towards foreign NGOs in light of China's economic and social transformation and its policy towards domestic organizations. Third, it analyzes the impacts and limitations of INGO operations in China against the current conditions of local NGO development. By analyzing these issues, this study argues that both the Chinese government and international community have strong desires to open China's market and society to international aid and involvement. Again, both recognize the necessity of cooperating with each other to achieve goals in economic, political, and social reforms, despite the dissimilarity between their goals and approaches. As the title of this chapter suggests, the involvement and influence of INGOs in China can only flourish when China's own conditions are ready. The readiness includes both the government's tolerance of international influence on political issues and, more importantly, initiatives of indigenous organizations on social, economic, and maybe eventually political issues.

The chapter concludes that the rapid growth of Chinese NGOs and their urgent need for international aid have permitted the rise of international influence. In the past ten years, INGOs have become an indispensable factor in first supporting and strengthening local and grassroots NGOs, and then uniting these local efforts into coalitions with regional and even international actions. To most small and independent Chinese NGOs, foreign funding has been their only resource. INGO programs for economic and social development have introduced new ideas, approaches, and methods to their Chinese counterparts. INGOs helped Chinese NGO leaders open their eyes to what is happening in global civil society and connected them with their international counterparts, a crucial step in getting China to become a part of the global civil society. By funding research centers in China's prestigious universities and exchange programs, international foundations also have played a crucial role in research, such as studies on NGOs, rule of law, political reforms, and human rights. Facing China's vast needs, INGOs have increasingly concentrated their limited resources on nourishing domestic leaders and organizational capacity in an effort to maximize their influence in China.

Nonetheless, since many independent organizations depend on foreign support to operate, their independence may well become a question in the long run. The study further argues that, despite their limited number and operating purview, INGOs have become, especially since the mid-1990s, a powerful and even crucial instrument in facilitating the growth of autonomous and grassroots Chinese NGOs. Yet, due to cultural, ideological, and political differences, theories, approaches, and programs introduced by international organizations are not always suited to China's reality. Often, these NGOs' own agendas and preferences prevent them from better understanding indigenous people and their organizations.

The impact of globalization and global civil society on China

Globalization, with its profound impact on the economic, social, and environmental spheres, has changed the world, and China, changing in turn, has come to shape the world. China has transformed itself from a command to a market-based economy, and it has become an enormous market for foreign goods and technology, as well as a major exporter of a wide range of products. China's energy policy, for instance, affects prices in the world's oil market, and the sustainability of its economic and social development in general has been closely watched by governments, businesses, and non-governmental organizations around the world (Economy and Schreurs 1997). The environment is a convincing example. China's air pollution, brought on by rapid industrialization and increased use of automobiles, is no longer simply a domestic issue, and coal-fired power plants in Beijing contribute not only to local air pollution, but also to acid rain in Japan and global climate change (Economy and Schreurs: 5). By the year 2020, China will be the world's largest producer of CO_2 gases; therefore, "any meaningful multilateral efforts to reduce the global emissions of greenhouse gases will require China's cooperation" (Johnston 1998: 555). In fact, the impact of China's economic development goes beyond environmental issues. Harry Harding, Dean of the Elliott School of International Affairs at George Washington University and a trustee of the Asia Foundation, forthrightly pointed out that, "American interests in economic prosperity apply at home and around the world. It is in American interests to see China's vibrant economy, and its political and social stability" (Harding 1997: 2–3). At once shaped by global standards and markets, China's importance in many international affairs has increased significantly, since its political, economic, and social problems now also carry much greater consequences worldwide.

As a result, globalization has created growing pressure on the Chinese government to seriously consider international factors in its policy-making. In his book on globalization and state transformation in China, Yongnian Zheng concludes,

> [G]lobalization has posed serious challenges to the Chinese state. Nevertheless, the Chinese leadership has regarded globalization as a unique opportunity to rebuild the Chinese state... While nationalism is directed at building a strong and wealthy China, Chinese leaders recognized that such a goal could only be realized by integrating the country into the global community.
>
> (Zheng 2004: xvi)

Globalization thus has pushed Chinese leaders to seek membership in the international community and accept international rules. For example, since 1981, China has signed eight international environmental agreements. More significantly, after fourteen years of negotiation, China finally became a member of the World Trade Organization (WTO) in 2001. A milestone in China's relationship with the international community, this entrance is seen by some international observers as a triumph since its membership falls "under terms that hewed closely to the long-term Western goal of bringing China into the world trading system on 'commercially viable terms'" (Lardy 2002: 2). However, many others, including scholars and decision-makers around the world, raise serious concerns about China's role in international affairs, since China's intentions internationally remain unclear (Moore 2002: 5).

China paid a high price to join the WTO. It "promised not only to reduce significantly tariff and non-tariff barriers but also to open up long-closed sectors such as telecommunications, banking, insurance, asset management, and distribution to foreign investment" (Lardy: 2). Nevertheless, China's top leaders were determined. In the wake of the Asian crisis, they were convinced that "there was no viable alternative to the globalization of production and that, indeed, China through WTO membership would benefit from greater participation in the trend" (Lardy: 20). As discussed in Chapter 2, China's CCP leaders understood that economic growth was the crucial condition for the legitimacy of their power. In the attempt to continue delivering better living standards to its population, the CCP leadership accepted the stiff demands of the international community (Lardy: 11).

This was the broad context in which China's top leaders decided to allow international involvement in China's economic, social, and even political reforms. This involvement comprised three different but entangled trajectories: bilateral or multilateral cooperation at government levels or between the Chinese government and UN organizations; donations and other kinds of support for Chinese charitable organizations by foreign private businesses; and the international non-profit sector operating in China. This chapter mainly discusses the international NGOs and perceives their presence in the country as a direct reflection of the surge of global civil society.

After the resurfacing of this concept in the 1980s in Latin America and central Europe, "the civil society idea has been spreading like wildfire" (Anheier et al. 2001: 15). The 1990s witnessed

> the emergence of a supranational sphere of social and political participation in which citizens' groups, social movements, and individuals engage in dialogue, debate, confrontation, and negotiation with each other and with various governmental actors – international, national, and local – as well as the business world.
>
> (Anheier et al.: 4)

The discussion of "global civil society" or "civil society at the global level" indicates that "civil society is no longer just that slice of associational life that exists between the individual and the state within a country but also across national boundaries" (Hyden 1997: 18).

Salamon, Anheier, and their colleagues believe that this "global associational revolution" is due in large part to the "crisis of the state" in both the so-called North and South, and this questioning of the state has focused new attention, and new expectations, on the civil society organizations. This reawakening has also been stimulated by the communications revolution of the past two decades (Salamon *et al.* 1999: 4). Despite the controversy over the extent and potential of civil society, especially at the global level (Edwards *et al.* 1999: 119), it has nonetheless become quite clear that "the urgency and the magnitude of the problems that confront humanity and nature in the world" require civil society organizations around the world to play a central role (WSSD 2002). NGOs in both developed and underdeveloped nations, regardless of their disagreements,

> all agree that there are increasing opportunities to work together across institutional boundaries in order to influence the forces that underpin poverty and discrimination, finding partnerships and synergy where few existed before, and molding not just a strong civil society but a society that is just and civil in all that it does.
>
> (Edwards *et al.*: 120)

It is within this global trend that NGOs, international or single-nation, have launched their operations in China.

Chinese government policy towards INGOs

Chinese government policy towards international organizations is a key issue affecting their operation in the country. In 1979, the Chinese government took the initiative in reaching out for international assistance through cooperation with the UNDP, and since then an increasing number of foreign and international organizations have come to China. And yet as late as 2004, the government still has not promulgated a unified policy on the legal status of these organizations. This section analyzes the government's general attitude towards INGOs using the most up-to-date information as of early 2004, and explains why the official regulations of INGOs have been contradictory and inconsistent, varying at different times and in different regions.

To discuss China's official INGO policy, one must understand two rather conflicting influences that have shaped this policy. The first is the CCP's general distrust of, and at times hostile attitude towards, Western countries. Rooted in China's contemporary history of humiliation and defeat by foreign powers since the Opium War in 1840, such attitudes were strengthened by the CCP's political and ideological stances. To a large extent, this attitude has continued after the reforms and opening policy. The past twenty years have witnessed how the sweeping tide of Western culture has profoundly changed Chinese public opinions about the outside world and about China's own culture. This has substantially undermined the CCP's ideology and is the price that the regime has paid for economic development. Fighting the tide, the CCP has constantly resorted to nationalist sentiments and the memory of China's humiliation in contemporary history to strengthen its ideology.

Such a perpetuation of communist ideology and propaganda has prolonged the distrust of foreign countries and organizations. Even though the government is now encouraging all types of foreign aid to China's economic and social development, suspicions towards the motivation behind foreign organizations cast a big shadow over the official attitude. While a small number of foreign NGOs, including American organizations, entered China right after Deng Xiaoping launched his reforms at the end of the 1970s, the government's concern over INGO influence on Chinese people has actually increased since the 1990s, since people are now allowed to found their own organizations.

Secondly, however, the economic reforms since the late 1970s have created intense pressure both from within the party and from society to push China to open to the outside world. As Hao Yufan, a Chinese political scientist, points out, one consideration that shaped China's current attitude towards the international community is the government's strong desire to "reaffirm China's leadership role in the Third World in negotiations with technologically advanced states over international environmental obligations" (Hao 1992, in Johnston 1998: 557). In her study of China's official stance towards its responsibility and promise to international environmental protection, Alastaria Johnston argues that Chinese leaders can be particularly sensitive towards external criticism or praise of China's behavior in the international arena, and it is crucial for them to preserve a favorable image as a responsible major power (Johnston 1998: 558–9, 563–4). Balanced against this desire for respectability is the vigorous campaign for international funding, resources, and access to information and technology on the part of the Chinese government, as well as special interest groups and NGOs (Johnston: 586). Most of all, the Chinese government is convinced that the international involvement in China's domestic development is an indispensable compromise for China to catch up with international standards and, in exchange, to obtain urgently needed international aid: science and technology as well as funds. The primary purpose of the government is to get foreign investment, private or governmental, and scientific and technological assistance for China's economic development. This objective was clearly reflected in its handling of foreign private organizations. While the government has still not been able to issue a policy applicable to all types of INGOs in China, it did promulgate, as early as 1989, a regulatory document specifically for the foreign business organizations.

"Temporary Regulations on Foreign Chambers of Commerce" (1989) was China's first official document regarding the management of foreign organizations in China. Though pressured by all INGOs for a policy on their legal status, until early 2004 only the foreign chambers of commerce received the "privilege" of being registered under the Ministry of Civil Affairs (MOCA). According to this regulation, before a foreign chamber of commerce can register with MOCA, it must be approved by the Ministry of Foreign Economy and Trade (MFET). This dual approval procedure is similar to the one required of Chinese NGOs, with one fundamental difference. MFET only serves as an approval agency to chambers of commerce, and does not act as a supervisory agency. In other words, unlike Chinese NGOs, foreign chambers of commerce do not have mothers-in-law to watch over their daily operations. As a former director of MOCA's Division of Social Organizations states, the purpose of this regulation is to make it convenient for foreign business firms and business people to invest and do business in China. "It promotes international trade and exchange of economy and technology... It benefits our open and reform policy, and improves China's investment environment" (Chen 1997: 15). This statement explains quite bluntly why the Chinese government was so interested in propagating a regulation specifically for business-related organizations only.

In March 2004, the government revised the registration regulations of foundations, and this document is applicable to both domestic and foreign foundations in the country, the first time in China's official regulations of NGOs since the 1950s. However, the chambers of commerce and foundations constitute only a small fraction of the foreign organizations that have entered China since 1978. To the great majority of INGOs, the official attitude towards their legal status in the country is neither clear nor consistent. The ambivalence between political wariness and economic motivation has resulted in a hot and cold official policy towards INGOs that is not always encouraging. Aside from the regulation for business associations and foundations, the Chinese government has failed to actively form a clear and unified regulation on international NGOs' legal and taxation status in China, in contrast to the establishment of clear and strict guidelines for Chinese NGOs in 1998. Such ambiguity towards INGOs has certainly brought negative consequences and difficulty to their operations in China. The cause lies in the Chinese government's overall attitude towards NGOs as well as its ignorance about INGOs.

Furthermore, the Chinese government also needs to found new institutional mechanisms to deal with foreign organizations. In the past, under the CCP's dominant ideology of anti-"American imperialism" or "Soviet Revisionism", the government adopted a principle that drew a clear line between domestic and foreign affairs (*neiwai youbie*). Any matter involving foreign affairs was handled with special caution and was strictly controlled by a handful of government agencies such as MFET. Prior to the reform era, the government kept communication channels with foreign non-governmental organizations in developed countries open. For example, the Chinese government was frequently in contact with a wide range of Japanese NGOs or political parties not in power during those years when the two countries did not have formal relations. Some Chinese "non-governmental organizations", such as the China Friendship Associations to the Foreign and the provincial branches were established by the government not only to receive information but also to create an image of communication at the non-governmental level. During the height of the Cultural Revolution, many foreign NGOs became crucial information and communication channels.

After the reforms, while these governmental agencies continued to function, it gradually became clear to the government that, in order to attract INGOs and international private funds, it needed non-governmental intermediary institutions to assist in their operation. Influenced and supported by the UNDP, the Chinese government sent out in 1984 its first delegation to four European countries to investigate INGOs and search for possibilities and opportunities for collaboration (Huang 2000: 1). This investigation resulted in the establishment of the Division of International NGO Liaisons in 1985 and the China Association for NGO Cooperation (CANGO) in 1992. Both are supervised under the China Exchange Center for International Economy and Technology (CECIE), a governmental agency under MFET.

CANGO was registered with MOCA as a non-governmental, non-profit, and voluntary membership organization operating nationwide. However, up until 2002, its expenditures, from office to staff salaries and benefits, were entirely funded by the government,[2] and, as will be discussed later, one can clearly see the strong government influence on its work. Yet, CANGO is the first national organization of this sort in China and its appearance heralds the new way in which the Chinese government is managing foreign organizations. CANGO's mission is to create a strong, empowered network of Chinese NGOs to address poverty alleviation and environmental protection by acting as an intermediary agency that partners international and Chinese NGOs to enhance fundraising, provide technical support, and build the capacity of grassroots social organizations in China. Between 1985 and 1999, CANGO cooperated with over 120 INGOs and multilateral institutions to bring over 240 million RMB (equal to USD$30 millions) of international aid and grants to hundreds of projects in over twenty provinces (Huang 2000: 2).

Eventually, similar NGOs were founded by the government at the provincial level to deal with INGOs working in their respective regions, and here the government control is even heavier. For example, Yunnan Provincial International Non-governmental Societies is directly controlled by the province's Bureau of Civil Affairs, whose director is concurrently the head of the Societies. Such administrative constraint also transfers into the range of activities that such national and provincial organizations cover. Although INGOs come to China bearing a wide array of missions, domestic organizations such as CANGOs are disproportionately devoted to key themes like economic development, a theme heavily promoted by the government.[3] This leads to a less diversified body of institutions, which are also less able to match or partner with INGOs in their proposed projects.

The absence of a uniform regulation on INGOs and the insufficient institutional mechanisms to support as well as supervise foreign organizations has made their operation a controversial and complicated matter for both the government and INGOs. The government officials who are directly in charge of INGOs are often extremely cautious.[4] Not only do they not have a clear rule to follow, but they also do not want to be blamed in case anything bad happens with INGOs. This attitude has made the latter's effort to obtain legal status in China very difficult. Renee Hsia and Lynn White's study vividly illustrates how sometimes INGO registration in China can be a nightmare. In order to obtain official approval, the INGO in question submitted the organization's charts, application, and financial forms from the US Internal Revenue Service to the Provincial International NGO Society (PINGOS) only to find out that this agency was not the only one whose consent was needed. While PINGOS handled the legal matters of the NGO's residency in that province, it was MFET's Relations and the Foreign Enterprise Service Corporation that was in charge of allowing the NGO to hire local Chinese employees. Furthermore, since this organization's mission was to train people working in healthcare, it had to walk the extra miles to get permissions from the public health and education bureaus (Hsia and White 2002: 340–1).

In contrast to this "passing the buck" registration process is the lack of government supervision of INGOs. On the one hand, allowing and supporting INGOs to carry out their programs in China, the Chinese government has given these foreign organizations a wide range of opportunities to get involved in China's economic and social development. On the other hand, the depth and weight of the foreign influence brought on by such involvements are literally beyond the government's control or even knowledge. For instance, the only time MOCA's annual statistics revealed the number of NGOs from Taiwan, Hong Kong, and Macao operating in China was 1990, and it has never given any number for foreign organizations in the country (NBS 1990–2003).

In another example, micro-credit projects have become very popular in China, especially since the mid-1990s, and enormous amounts of foreign funding have poured in for these projects. Introduced by the international NGOs, these programs aim to elevate deprived rural regions as well as urban disadvantaged populations. Yet, how many micro-credit projects supported by foreign funding are launched in China? How many foreign and domestic institutions are engaging in these projects? Where are they located, and what kind of work are they conducting? No governmental agencies can answer these questions, nor can the Chinese researchers.[5] In fact, some Chinese NGO leaders criticized the current government attitude towards international organizations as being unfairly soft compared to the strict registration rules against Chinese NGOs.[6] A local official study of the management of INGOs admitted that "the government only paid attention to the resources they brought in, and in fact we know little about these organizations' missions, organization headquarters and registration" (NYNGOs 2003: no. 7–8).

As the next section will discuss in more detail, the majority of INGOs have successfully stayed in China for years without any formal registration, and there are many ways to do so. Even though registering with MOCA or BOCA is almost impossible, these organizations often find that obtaining sponsors from governmental institutions and local governments to permit them to operate in China is fairly easy. The reason, to borrow words from the same official study, is that "Cooperation with INGOs brings certain financial benefits and social effects; thus, many governmental bureaus want to seize the power to manage or control them" (NYNGOs: no. 7). A large number of the projects conducted or sponsored by INGOs are in cooperation with the Chinese government, especially at the local level. For example, all the Salvation Army's China programs are operated together with the government.[7] Such cooperation is mutually beneficial. Official approval and institutional support help INGOs carry out their projects smoothly, while government or governmental organizations receive overhead fees for their sponsorship and access to technological and monetary resources.

In short, the absence of regulation on foreign NGOs has created confusion and difficulties for both government and foreign organizations. Pressure is mounting from Chinese and international NGOs, as well as official agencies in charge of NGOs, to formulate a unified and clear INGO policy. Around late 2003 and early 2004, news from insiders has confirmed that the Chinese government has decided, at long last, that all types of international organizations will receive a legal status similar to their Chinese counterparts in the still pending new revision of the "Regulations for Registration and Management of Social Organizations".[8] This is a significant change in the official INGO policy, in terms of providing a legal base for both official supervision and INGO operation. The slow development of these documents reflects a deeper conflict within the CCP's reform policy. The regime understood the political risks and consequences of an open policy; yet, it needed the outside world for China's development and wanted China to play an important role in the international community.

The current state of international NGOs in China

Foreign organizations re-entered China soon after the 1978 reforms commenced. Historically, foreign institutions, missionary or secular, had established themselves long before the CCP took national power in 1949. The earliest modern private hospitals, schools, and other charitable facilities, numbering in the thousands, were founded in China by Protestant and Catholic missionaries almost two centuries ago. Since then, Western private organizations and individuals, with all kinds of missions or reformatory ideas, have rushed into the country. At the turn of the twentieth century, China was, in the minds of many Americans, not only a great market and an extension of the domestic frontier, but also "a market for all types of early twentieth-century progressive American reform. It was this idea of

China as a *tabula rasa* for American reform interests that provided a most revealing link between domestic and diplomatic attitudes" (Israel 1971: xi).

The Rockefeller Foundation was the first American private foundation to enter China, and in 1915, it launched the most advanced medical project – the Peking Union Medical College (PUMC) in Beijing, China. The PUMC is by far the Rockefeller Foundation's single most expensive project abroad, and, unlike their missionary predecessors who tried to convert the Chinese to Christianity, the foundation's ambition was to reform China through modern medical science and scientific methodology (Ma 2002b: 159–83). Some American scholars see today's growing number of foreign entrants into China as a continuation of "the desire of contemporary Westerners to 'rescue' China – which resembles the mentality of Europeans and colonialists from earlier centuries" (Hsia and White 2002: 330).

The PUMC was decried as a symbol of cultural imperialism in the early years of the People's Republic, along with missionary educations, medical institutions, and charitable organizations. These groups withdrew from the country soon thereafter. Between the 1950s and late 1970s, there were literally no private, foreign institutions operating in China. The Ford Foundation and the Asia Foundation, two American private foundations with large China operating budgets, were among the few Western NGOs that entered the country after 1978. Since then, a large number of foreign private organizations and international NGOs with programs from poverty alleviation, education, health care, and environmental protection to human rights and legal system reforms have become established in China. Forced by the lack of consistent registration policies to be resourceful in gaining legal operational status, INGOs have developed the following methods:

- Establishing Hong Kong or Macao-based headquarters or branches through which their programs are run in the mainland, e.g., OXFAM, Salvation Army and Asia Foundation.[9]
- Opening representative offices in Beijing, with a government institution as a supervising agency, e.g., the Ford Foundation. Beijing is the most difficult location in which to obtain permission to open an office as it is under the closest watch of the central government and is the most politically sensitive spot in China.
- Opening offices in cities other than Beijing, and registering with local bureaus of civil affairs, e.g., Kunming, the capital of Yunnan Province, now has the largest number of INGO offices.
- Opening program offices, which are not required to register with the government.
- Registering with the bureau of industry and commerce as a business company, such as US Nature Conservation.
- Operating cooperative programs with Chinese NGOs or governmental agencies, thereby avoiding registration.

178 "It takes two to tangle"

- Obtaining an "International Expert's Service Certificate" from the State Bureau of Foreign Experts.
- Signing an "Agreement Memorandum" (*liangjie biwanglu*), e.g., over ten INGOs have signed such a memo with Yunnan Provincial International Non-governmental Societies.

There are no official statistics on foreign NGOs in China. The *China Development Brief*, a private newspaper registered in the United States and focusing on Chinese NGOs, has published the *Directory of INGOs in China*, which offers certain organizational information such as entry date, country origin, mission, budget, and operational conditions. Accordingly, there were 150 INGOs operating in China in the early 2000s.[10] Though this list does not include all INGOs in the country, it is by far the most widely available, updated compilation on this subject. Based on the data provided by the *Directory*, the INGOs' operations in China demonstrate several features.

First, the statistics indicate a steady growth in the numbers of new INGOs entering China since 1978, with an even faster rate since 1996. By 2001, out of the 137 INGOs that provided an entry date, about 40 percent came to China after 1996 (Table 6.1). These figures support the conclusion of this study that INGOs have shown more interest in China since the fourth UN World Conference on Women in 1995, which opened the door and facilitated their entry.

Second, the great majority of the INGOs are program-operating organizations, and the statistics point to the strong presence of American NGOs. For instance, among the earliest foreign organizations re-entering China from 1978 to 1980, almost 80 percent were American organizations. As Table 6.2 shows, 38 percent of the total number of INGOs came from the United States, by far the best represented country. There are 64 organizations listed that have a regular annual China budget, half of them are over US$500,000. The largest three are the Ford Foundation ($9 million), Hong Kong Red Cross ($8.8 million), and the Asia Foundation ($4.3 million). Nearly 30 percent of the groups in this funding category are American organizations. Of the 17 NGOs with budgets over one million US dollars

Table 6.1 Number of INGOs entering China since 1978, by time period

Entry year	1978–80	1981–85	1986–90	1991–95	1996–2001	Unknown	Total
# INGOs	14 (11 U.S., 3 HK)	15	25	29	54	5	142
Percentage	9.9	10.6	17.6	20.4	38	3.5	100

Source for Tables 6.1–6.4: *Directory of International NGOs in China*.[i]

[i] *Directory of INGOs in China*. Not all INGOs in the Directory provide complete information about their entry date, country of origin, and operating situation.

Table 6.2 Country origins of INGOs currently in China

Countries/ Regions	North America	Europe and Australia	Taiwan, Macao, and HK	Asia	International	Unknown	Total
# INGOs	57 (54 U.S.)	32 (18 UK)	29 (26 HK)	6	17	1	142
Percentage	40.1	22.5	20.4	4	12	0.7	100

Table 6.3 INGOs' organizational status in China

Status	Beijing office	Beijing representative	Office in other cities	Non-HK NGOs w/HK office	Unknown	Total
# INGOs	14	18	39	7	64	142
Percentage	9.9	12.7	27.5	4.9	45	100

per annum, 41 percent are American. The total budget for all the American organizations reached US$23,178,000 in 2002, the largest amount from any single country.

Third, NGOs from Hong Kong have played a unique and influential role in the development of the non-profit sector in China. Even though Hong Kong returned to the mainland in 1997, NGOs in Hong Kong are still categorized by MOCA as international organizations. To a great degree, they are autonomous from the central government's control. The number of HK NGOs running programs in China, 26 in 2002 according to the *Directory*, is impressive. These were the only organizations, along with American NGOs, that went to China before 1980 (Tables 6.1 and 6.2). These NGOs also provide a large amount of funding for their operations on the mainland, totaling US$15,694,460 in 2002, second only to the United States. Hong Kong's unique geographical location and its active civil society make it an ideal place from which international organizations can launch their programs in China (Table 6.3).[11] Furthermore, due to HK's cultural ties with the mainland, these organizations have an advantage over all other INGOs. Their contributions to mainland organizations are not limited to monetary, technical, and volunteers' assistance. As there is no language barrier and since people in HK generally have a better understanding of the mainland's political and economic situations, HK NGOs tend to be more effective and pertinent in terms of project selection and communication with local people and organizations.

Finally, given the fact that the government did not have a consistent and clear policy towards INGOs and that it was very difficult for INGOs to obtain legal status and offices, especially in Beijing, it is impressive that many of the INGOs have established formal operations in China. As of 2001, 56 percent of the INGOs had either offices or representatives in China

Table 6.4 Major foci of INGOs in China, by organization

Focus	Health AIDS/HIV	Environment and agriculture	Education	Charity	Human and social development
# INGOs	18	25	21	23	28
Percentage	12.7	17.6	14.8	16.2	19.7

Focus	Women and children	General	Other	Total	
# INGOs	18	4	5	142	
Percentage	12.7	2.8	3.5	100	

or Hong Kong (Table 6.3). Sixty organizations had regular staff working in China, and the most staffed organization, Tibet Heritage Fund, had 187 national and international staff members (CDB 2002). Most importantly, many of the programs these organizations run are not in traditional areas like charity or education; rather, they strive to meet China's new social, economic, and political needs brought on by the profound changes of the last two decades (Table 6.4).

The role of international NGOs in China

Though few NGOs are international, "one of the hallmarks of contemporary NGO activity," as a study of the global environmental movement concludes, "is the extent of coalition activity not just within countries but at a transnational level" (McCormick 1989: 136). This section discusses how INGOs have become an indispensable factor in first promoting and strengthening local and grassroots NGOs, then uniting these local efforts into coalitions with regional and even international actions. The INGOs have, via grants, training workshops, conferences, and their own programs, brought ideas and programs adopted from the global civil society movement to Chinese NGO leaders and assisted them in connecting with their international counterparts, a crucial step in getting China to become a part of the global civil society. To analyze these developments, the following discussion focuses on three aspects of INGOs' role: the emergence of NGO study in China, the introduction of new approaches and methodology, and INGOs' monetary resources and experts' assistance. It also provides three case studies to illustrate the arguments. World Wide Fund for Nature (WWF) is the first INGO invited by the Chinese government to operate environmental programs in China, and its China efforts are not just in environmental conservation but also in promoting cooperation among the government, businesses, and NGOs. The NPO Network is China's first NGO aiming to strengthen communication, information sharing, and governance of NGOs, and its founding was only possible with INGOs' assistance. The Ford Foundation is by far the largest grant-giving institution in China and has been an important actor in promoting especially grassroots organizations. As this section discusses the impact of INGOs, it is of note that these organizations would not have played an impressive role without the upsurge of Chinese NGOs and the relaxation of China's political environment.

The international impact on the emergence of NGO study in China

The birth of the study of NGOs in China came along with and is an important part of the growth of the non-governmental sector in China. It has since become a forceful advocate for NGO development in China. An impressive proportion of NGO scholars have been NGO activists themselves, and throughout their early stages, these two groups maintained close contact with each other.[12] The discussions among Chinese scholars on civil society and theories have introduced to China the very ideas and approaches that have nourished NGOs around world. It is not an exaggeration to say that this field's emergence in China is the direct result of INGO scholarship. Especially after the 4th World Conference for Women, international civil society scholars have shown enormous interest in Chinese NGOs, and foreign foundations also have provided many grants to facilitate exchange between Chinese scholars and their international peers. For example, the Ford Foundation and Asia Foundation were the major sponsors for the first two international conferences on NGOs held in Beijing in 1999 (Chapter 2).

The theories that have been debated internationally have supplied Chinese scholars with the theoretical tools to define China's new institutional landscape and associations. In addition, as a study of the global influence on China's social change suggests, "under conditions of growing global communications, local actors may seize on exogenous idioms to legitimate principles of equality and participation already 'present' in social practice . . ." (Hefner 1998: 22). On the one hand, because of China's current political situation, most Chinese scholars tend to avoid the subject of the potential conflict between civil society and the state. Some even omitted words like "China's pro-democracy movement" when they translated works of Western scholars on civil society.[13] On the other hand, the study of NGOs in China is largely based on Western theories and concepts, regardless of China's political conditions.

From the reappearance of NGOs in the late 1970s to their rapid increase in the late 1980s, neither the government nor scholars knew how to define these organizations and their legal status. The 1950 official regulations of SOs remained unchanged, and no serious scholarly work on this phenomenon was published at the time. This situation changed dramatically, especially after the 1995 WCW, when the term "non-governmental organization" was first introduced to China. The NGO Forum of the conference popularized the term and inspired the first generation of women NGO leaders and scholars in China. Prior to the conference, delegations of Chinese women's organizations participated in a series of international conferences and, as some later recalled, it was at this time that they came to realize the unique and influential role of NGOs in today's world politics. These women were impressed by the fact that NGOs have strong voices on many issues that governments or governmental organizations were reluctant to face.[14]

To prepare the conference and help Chinese women's organizations to understand the meaning and practices of NGOs, the All-China Women's Federation (ACWF) launched a campaign to train women leaders at all levels around the nation. Over 8,000 workshops and seminars nationwide have involved almost two million female leaders and activists, most of whom discovered "NGOs" for the first time.[15] While the ACWF was not an independent NGO and did not know about NGOs, both the organizers and participants in those trainings were atypical in that they represented a new generation of women who had received their higher education after the Cultural Revolution.[16] This campaign offered an unprecedented opportunity to hundreds of thousands of Chinese women to learn about NGOs. The conference and activities around it promoted a boom in Chinese women's organizations (Liu 2000: 109–14), and the term "NGO" entered formal Chinese political vocabulary (Chapter 3).

After the conference, the international exchange of NGO knowledge continued to shape the evolution of Chinese civil society. Since the initial delegation of Chinese NGO activists and officials visited the United States in 1995, Chinese NGO practitioners and scholars have frequently been in contact with international NGOs and research institutions. Scholars from Europe, North America, East and Southeast Asian countries, and Australia came to China, and vice versa. Now, the study of NGOs has become a hot research topic in China. It was against this backdrop that Lester Salamon introduced the internationally accepted interpretation of the term "NGO" at a conference on NGOs in Beijing, 1999. This definition (see the Introduction of this volume), now familiar among Chinese NGO activists and scholars, has reshaped the Chinese official classification and regulation of the non-government sector.

Realizing the importance of Chinese NGO leaders and scholars maintaining close contact with their international counterparts, INGOs have contributed much to this end. For example, from 1982 to 1997, the US–China Committee for Legal Education Exchange (CLEE), initiated and funded by the Ford Foundation, focused on building law faculties at elite government-designated universities and institutions of political science and law. CLEE was directly involved in training more than 250 young Chinese legal academics in either the PRC or the US, and in the promotion of many other scholarly exchanges between lawyers, university professors, and government specialists in the two countries. The Ford Foundation provided more than $4 million in grants to support these activities (Feinerman 2002: 60). In 2000, the Ford Foundation

"It takes two to tangle" 183

gave over five million USD to programs and conferences promoting communication and cooperation between China and rest of the world (FF 2000). Consequently, since the late 1990s, an impressive number of international conferences and seminars on NGOs, attracting scholars from many countries, have been held in China. International experts on NGOs have cooperated with Chinese research institutions conducting surveys on China's social and NGO conditions, and some of them have even become directly involved in the Chinese government's NGO regulation and legislation.[17]

International organizations and scholars thus directly influenced the growth of NGO study in China. Yet, many Chinese students of NGOs are clearly aware of the gap between Western theories and Chinese reality. The debate in the early 1990s among Chinese scholars on the applicability of civil society theories in China, as discussed in Chapter 1, indicated serious doubts about the pertinence of these Western ideas to our interpretation of and advances in the country's contemporary political reforms. China's current political reality and its history and tradition are, many argue, constraints on the emergence of civil society. As for the development of NGOs, some scholars see mere survival rather than confronting the state as the foremost priority for these organizations. Because of the limited purview of permissible activities in the non-governmental sector, Chinese scholars and NGO activists address the unique behavior of Chinese NGOs and the necessity of maintaining a close and constructive relationship with the government.[18] Chinese NGOs' specific features, some scholars conclude, make certain Western NGO research approaches and methodologies unsuitable.[19]

To a certain degree, the rise of the study of NGOs in China has generated government and public attention on NGO development, and the frequent contact between NGO scholars, Chinese or international, and activists with officials in charge of NGOs further magnified such an impact. Over the years, quite a few top Chinese NGO scholars as well as NGO activists have established fairly close relationships with officials in charge of NGOs, and, via these people, Western ideas and practices of NGOs and civil society have indirectly influenced official regulations over NGOs. A comparison of the government's 1989 and 1998 regulatory documents on NGOs in Chapter 2 reveals significant changes in NGO legal status and definition, indicating the impact of international NGO theory.

Again, as detailed in Chapter 2, the most significant progress in China's non-profit sector as a result of the 1998 NGO documents was the creation of the new term "non-governmental and non-commercial enterprises" (NGNCEs) for private, non-profit service providers. Since these service institutions had been denied existence as non-profits prior to 1998, many registered as for-profits, while others could not even exist. The new legal status provided them with an equal, legal position as social organizations, mimicking countries like the United States, where private, non-profit professional institutions, such as private schools, hospitals, nursing homes, research institutions, and museums, constitute the majority of the non-profit sector. For a long time, Chinese NGO scholars and activists had been using international practices as examples in their attempt to establish a legal status for increasingly active and numerous private professional institutions.[20] This was the first time in the history of the PRC that the government not only allowed a wide array of private, non-profit institutions to exist, but also provided them with legal protection. Today, their total number has exceeded social organizations and has become a major part of China's non-profit sector (Ma 2002a: 306).

New programs, new approach

Global civil society has become the expression of alternative visions that emphasize "democratization, participation and the empowerment of marginalized voices, justice and equity and a reclaiming of the local to counter the centralizing tendencies" (Elliott 1998: 131). It is these visions that have guided programs launched by INGOs and their Chinese partners in China especially since the mid-1990s. In line with the global civil society movement, programs aimed at providing mechanisms for sustainable development and escalating the capacity of less advanced people introduced new ideas and technology to Chinese NGOs, particularly local grassroots organizations. As the state–society relationship changed profoundly under the reform strategy of "small government, big society," the government has transferred ever more economic and social responsibility to society. Mostly, it is the NGOs and grassroots organizations in neighborhood communities and villages that are taking over these responsibilities. With very limited resources and experience, these organizations are facing enormous challenges in dealing with all kinds of problems, including HIV/AIDS, drugs, urban migrants, and environmental degradation, many of which are entirely new to both the government and society. Though this is not an uncommon challenge for developing countries, Chinese non-governmental organizations are fortunate that, in having entered the movement relatively late, they can be guided by the experience of civil society in other countries.

Thus, by building on past experiences worldwide and building on a global vision, INGOs have been crucial in connecting Chinese NGOs with the "railroad tracks" of global civil society. INGOs introduced Chinese people and their organizations to NGO theories, new approaches and methodology, programs addressing current social and economic problems, and access to international information and technology. Among the most popular ones are capacity building training, organizational capacity assessment (OCA), participatory approaches like participatory rural appraisal (PRA), the microfinance or micro-credit projects, eco-tourism, environmentally sustainable development, and good governance theories. These fresh ideas and methods have helped Chinese NGOs and local grassroots organizations establish their programs, especially in distinguishing themselves from the traditional top-down approaches that are still used by the governmental organizations.

Furthermore, one of the most significant new phenomena in the Chinese NGO sector is the rapid growth of cooperative activities among Chinese NGOs and their international counterparts. An impressive number of international experts, NGO practitioners, and volunteers from around the world are directly involved in programs at all levels, from national training workshops to rural community and village women micro-finance programs (Tang 2002).[21] Especially ten years ago, the majority of Chinese NGOs lacked any horizontal connections with their peer groups; while in contrast, with their abundant funds, expertise, and trustworthy reputation around the world, many INGOs were in a unique position in China to mobilize collective efforts. Since the late 1990s, INGOs have been using their ideas and resources to nourish non-governmental cooperation, in addition to uniting different sectors to work together for certain public causes. This role of INGOs is crucial in integrating Chinese NGOs into a collaborative and effective sector.

The following two examples, WWF and the China NPO Network, demonstrate the depth and breadth of the collaboration between Chinese NGOs, INGOs, and the government. Since 1985, WWF has invested over US$1,165 million in more than 11,000 projects in 130 countries, and its role in mobilizing global environmental conservation has been described as "banker, advocate, instigator, teacher, advisor, diplomat, planner and communicator" (Elliott 1998: 138). This is a good description of the role of WWF in China, where it is exemplary in its international initiatives and promotion of cooperation among Chinese NGOs, the government, and business sector in China.

As the first international environmental organization invited by the Chinese government to assist Chinese scientists in giant panda conservation, WWF's relationship with the government goes back to 1980. Today, WWF operates through its main office in Beijing and field offices in Changsha (Hunan Province), Kunming (Yunnan Province), and Lhasa (Tibet). Its thirty staff members work on over twenty projects in China, from restoring the Yangzi River wetlands to environmental education. In 1999, WWF's China expenditure was US$2,312,000, and the figure increased to US$3,025,000 in 2000 (WWF 2000). Although in many ways WWF pioneered environmental protection activities in China, it could not achieve what it did without the interaction with and cooperation of Chinese grassroots environmental NGOs. Perceiving the momentum, WWF designed its activities to assist and generate local environmental initiatives.

This study addresses the most important contribution by WWF to China's environmental movement and NGO development: its approach, which focuses on establishing cooperation among the Chinese government, corporations, and NGOs, as well as among NGOs themselves. It is widely accepted by Chinese officials and even environmental advocates that China should focus first on economic development which is more likely to lead to improvements in the environment over the long term. Many others even see development and environmental protection opposing each other (Johnston 1998: 567).

In a country where the state overwhelmingly dominates the inchoate civil society, the environmental organizations face a great challenge. Yet, WWF is convinced that "the very factors that appear daunting can also open up opportunities," and that "working directly with the government offers the possibility for rapid and widespread replication of new approaches in fields where cooperation is successful" (WWF 2000).

As stated in its annual report, WWF believes that Chinese partners from all sectors of society are the driving forces for conservation and development.[22] It lists 65 Chinese governmental and non-governmental institutions and organizations as WWF partners, including national and local government environmental bureaus, universities and national research institutions, and well-known environmental NGOs. Its monetary and expert resources, international reputation, and its long-standing working relationship with the government have no doubt made this approach feasible.

For instance, starting in 1997, the Chinese Ministry of Education, WWF and British Petroleum (BP) launched a two-stage program called "China Elementary and Middle School Green Education Action." This was the first such cooperation in China's education arena, and only because they had the government's participation could the first stage of the experiment involve 34 elementary and middle schools in ten provinces/cities, with four of the most prestigious normal universities establishing environmental education centers to facilitate the program. The program offered thirty workshops, and over 2,000 people participated, including 800 environmental heads in government organizations. In its second stage, this program has now expanded to over sixty schools and twelve universities, published various teaching materials, and involved various environmental programs in local nature conservation and community education in WWF training activities. Such an approach allows WWF China to influence, to a certain degree, official policy on the environment, which is a crucial function of NGOs. In 2002, after the first stage of the green education program successfully ended, WWF and the government worked together in making a national environmental education curriculum. With the government's approval, environmental education will become a required curriculum in China's secondary education, thus affecting two hundred million students.

The second example is a case in which a local initiative became successful, with international support, in promoting cooperation among Chinese NGOs.[23] The China NPO Network is a Beijing-based umbrella body that was established in 1998 by several Chinese NGOs whose leaders felt a need for communication among NGOs. The network's main foci are to provide information and consultation to all Chinese NGOs, and to facilitate information and other resource sharing. Initially, however, without government approval, necessary resources, or experience, their efforts failed.[24] Eventually, this idea of providing services and training to Chinese NPOs received international attention and support, resulting in an NPO Network that is a combined effort between Chinese initiative and international backing. The major financial resources of the network come from the World Bank, the Ford Foundation, and individual program funds drawn mostly from INGOs or foreign organizations. INGO leaders and scholars have given presentations in almost all network training workshops, and their expertise and moral support are undoubtedly very meaningful. With this support, the network has become one of very few institutions in China providing information on NGOs, consultation, and a forum for practitioners and scholars. By 2003, about 90 of the most active independent NGOs had joined the Network's Internet coalition.[25] A major organizer in Chinese NGO capacity building training, it is also currently launching China's first NPO organizational capacity assessment. Despite its mission and organizational structure, however, the network still cannot register with MOCA as a non-profit institution, because, failing to identify a "mother-in-law" to supervise the network, it has to register with the Bureau of Industry and Trade as a for-profit body.

In 2000, the network launched a two-year series of training programs entitled "Chinese NPO Experts Training," attended by over 400 NPO workers, government officials, and business people. Based on this training series, the NPO Network and Ford Foundation organized a conference in 2001 to further discuss the issues and experiences of NGO training. This was followed almost immediately by a three-year training series in 2002 on NPO capacity-building training. Subjects of these workshops, carefully chosen to satisfy the urgent needs of Chinese NGOs, include: leadership and development, NPO public management, management of participatory development projects, NPO CEO training, NPO governance, accountability, fundraising, taxes, and the public good. To facilitate the training, an impressive amount of teaching materials were written by Chinese and foreign experts in 2002, including the magazine *Training*. The NPO Network is not limited to Beijing, and as a joint effort between the NPO Network, Shanghai Green Roots Power Information and Consultancy Corporation, Shanghai YMCA, and Hong Kong Community Partners, an NPO training program was launched in Shanghai in 2003.

These workshops have furnished the embryonic Chinese NGO force with the most up-to-date knowledge and techniques in the NGO movement, and have also become communication fora for Chinese and international NGO activists. For example, the Resource Alliance, an international NGO specializing in training in participatory skills and capacity building, started working in the developing countries in 1991. The NPO Network's conference on Chinese NPO training caught the Resource Alliance's attention and led to communication during and after the conference between the two organizations and the British Council. This resulted in the Resource Alliance becoming the contractor for the network's second series of NPO capacity-building workshops and the British Council the sponsor of the training series (RA 2003).

In recent years, many leaders of Chinese NGOs have come to realize the importance of their own organization's performance and public image to the long-term development of NGOs. As the Network attempted ways of achieving NGO self-discipline and efficacy, it received support from Pact, an American NGO with expertise in NGO capacity building and assessment. Pact and the NPO Network reached an agreement for cooperation at the 2001 conference. Accordingly, they are undertaking the design of an organizational capacity assessment (OCA) framework, based on OCA experiences in over 300 NGOs in 20 countries, to suit the needs of the Chinese NPO sector. In 2003, the China OCA is piloting this framework with six high-profile organizations based in the Beijing area. Pact is convinced that this program will provide "deeper insights into and understanding of the dynamics, strengths and challenges of the NPO sector in China."[26]

International funding: the case of the Ford Foundation

In the past two decades, the international bilateral and multilateral organizations, as well as many independent foundations, have increasingly distributed their aid among NGOs. For example, in 1992, NGOs worldwide spent almost US$8 billion in providing humanitarian aid, development assistance, and technical support (Hsia and White 2002: 329). In 1995, Clinton's "New Partnership Initiative" announced that 40 percent of the United States Agency for International Development funding would be dispersed through NGOs (Hsia and White: 329–30). According to the Asia Foundation's 2003 estimation, over 500 international NGOs and foundations give more than $100 million each year for projects in China (Yuan 2003: 40). It is hard to exaggerate the impact of these foreign resources on both the Chinese government's attitude towards the international community and towards the development of Chinese NGOs. As noted earlier, downsizing made it very difficult for the Chinese government to reject international help in economic and social development, and it has therefore compromised its ideological and political stance in order to obtain aid and to establish China as a world power.

This section focuses on the features of foreign foundations' grant-giving and their impact on Chinese NGO development. Using the Ford Foundation as an example, the study examines the types of recipient organizations, projects and geographic regions through which the Foundation's money flows, in the hopes of illustrating how those organizations influence China's NGO landscape and its operations. It also seeks to answer how China's own political and social situations have shaped foundations' grant-giving behavior. The case study of the Ford Foundation is a comparison with other private foundations and the programs supported by the China Association for NGO Cooperation.

The Ford Foundation had a history of interest in China long before it came to the country in 1979, when it entered along with a few other foreign private organizations.[27] Prior to the opening reforms, the Foundation had financed study abroad programs at top American institutions for Chinese students, but it had never directly become involved in any programs in China. From 1979 to 1989, without an office in the country, the Foundation's funding to China-related programs, especially to Chinese institutions, was rather insignificant (FF 1979–88). For example, the Foundation's first major program in China was a two-year joint program with the Chinese Academy of Social Sciences, that gave a total of US$400,000 to five senior Chinese economists to study at US universities and one US economist to work in Beijing (FF 1980). Its main interest in Asia then lay with South and Southeast Asian countries. In 1986, the Foundation's funding to China was about US$200,000, compared with US$2.47 million to Bangladesh and US$7.88 million to India (FF 1986).

The turning point came in the late 1980s, when the Foundation successfully got the China Academy of Social Sciences (CASS) to be its sponsor and opened up a representative office in Beijing in 1988, a feat few foreign NGOs had been able to accomplish. The Ford Foundation's legal status in China is a unique case. As Tony Saich, the Chief Representative of the China Office at the Ford Foundation in Beijing (1994–99), recalls, the decision to place the Ford Foundation under the jurisdiction of CASS had gone through the top leaders of the CCP and the State Council, from Hu Yaobang and Zhao Ziyang to Li Peng and Hu Qiaomu.[28] No other foreign or international organization had attracted such attention from the government, and this indicates clearly the eagerness of China's top leaders at that time to invite important foreign institutions, especially those with deep pockets, to China. In 1989, the Ford Foundation's grants to China-related programs jumped to almost US$4 million (FF 1989). Since then, China has become a focus of the Foundation's Asia strategy. From the opening of its Beijing office to 2001, the Foundation spent a total of US$128 million on Chinese institutions and China-related programs.[29] According to the *Directory of INGOs*, around early 2000, the Foundation had the largest annual operating budget of all INGOs in China, US$9 million for 200–300 projects, and currently it is the biggest private grant-giving organization in China.

This sudden interest of the Ford Foundation in China is reflected in the burgeoning of funding from other US foundations. From 1994 to 1996, the total given by US independent foundations to China-related non-profits was US$77.77 million, of which US$31 million (40 percent) went directly to Chinese non-profits and other Chinese recipients. The largest US foundations in China are the Ford Foundation, China Medical Board of New York, the Freeman Foundation, the Starr Foundation, the Rockefeller Foundation, and the Henry Luce Foundation (Boisture 1998). The Ford Foundation's grants accounted for 29 percent of the total grants from the 15 US foundations in China (Table 6.5).

Over the years, the Ford Foundation's selection of programs in China has greatly broadened. The Foundation started its work focusing mainly on economics, law, and international relations, in an effort to accommodate

Table 6.5 Largest US funders of charitable activities relating to or in China (1994–96)

Foundations	Amount of grants	% of total grant
Ford Foundation	$23,081,628	29.32
China Medical Board of New York	$13,019,000	16.54
The Freeman Foundation	$9,364,500	11.90
The Starr Foundation	$8,863,000	11.26
The Rockefeller Foundation	$7,751,820	9.85
The Henry Luce Foundation	$7,353,250	9.34
John D. and Catherine T. MacArthur	$3,209,650	4.08
All others	$5,127,888	7.72

Source: Boisture 1998

China's reform agenda at the time (Table 6.6). When its understanding of the situation and involvement deepened, the Foundation gradually expanded its work into social and political arenas, going as far as the government allowed. In the early 2000s, the Foundation announced the following eight topics as its core China foci: economic and development finance; educational reform and cultural diversity; environment; governance and public policy; international cooperation; law and rights; civil society; and sexual and reproductive health (Table 6.6).[30]

The changes in funding are influenced by the Foundation's policy reorientation, trends in international civil society, and the recipient country's situation. For example, the Ford Foundation was one of the few foundations devoted to birth control programs in the 1950s. In the early 1990s, the Foundation decided to switch from population control to "a women-centered approach that sought to emphasize women's reproductive health, economic advancement, and role in policy making." This trend was further accelerated by agreements reached at the 1994 Cairo International Conference on Population and Demography and the 4th World Conference for Women in 1995 (FF 1995). In China, its support to improvements in women's reproductive health reached US$ 2.1million in 2000 (Table 6.6). The Foundation's work in China in the past ten years indicates a strong commitment to poverty alleviation, human rights, education, government reform, and civil society.

A comparison of the Ford Foundation's programs with those promoted by the Chinese government reveals the foreign independent foundations' unique position in addressing issues that are ignored by the state. The government, often via GONGOs, like CANGO, channels a great deal of international monetary and other aid to projects in selected regions in line with its political agenda. While the government still has a say in what INGOs can do in China, foreign foundations, especially those with a wealth of funds, manage to initiate projects as they will. For instance, the Ford Foundation's China programs and grants have never been interrupted or interfered with by the government.[31] Programs sponsored by INGOs are not

Table 6.6 The Ford Foundation-funded China-related programs (1986–2001) (in US$)

	1986	1989	1995	2000	2001
Rural development	183,838 (92.5%)	1,214,500 (30.9%)	1,995,000 (34.2%)	0	0
Law	0	1,123,210 (28.5%)	0	0	0
International relations/ cooperation	15,000 (7.5%)	1,537,150 (39.1%)	467,000 (8%)	1,647,500 (8.6%)	1,087,937 (8%)
Education	0	0	753,000 (12.9%)	2,644,989 (13.7%)	1,733,200 (12.7%)
Reproductive health	0	0	1,267,000 (21.7%)	2,130,914 (11.1%)	1,967,150 (14.5%)
Urban poverty	0	0	281,000 (4.8%)	0	0
Human rights	0	0	541,000 (9.3%)	2,069,235 (10.7%)	2,288,900 (16.8%)
Civil society	0	0	0	505,400 (2.5%)	702,600 (5.2%)
Governance	0	0	480,000 (8.2%)	2,388,000 (12.4%)	1,720,250 (12.7%)
Development finance	0	0	0	387,800 (2%)	965,500 (7.1%)
Community development	0	0	0	400,000 (2.1%)	0
Environmental development	0	0	0	3,777,002 (19.6%)	2,373,860 (17.5%)
Peace and social justice	0	0	0	1,527,000 (7.9%)	210,000 (1.5%)
Religion, society and culture	0	0	0	51,000 (0.3%)	0
Media, arts and culture	0	0	0	1,636,245 (8.5%)	476,400 (3.5%)
Others	0	61,000 (1.5%)	50,000 (0.86%)	100,000 (0.5%)	70,000 (0.5%)
Total	198,838 (100%)	3,935,860 (100%)	5,834,000 (100%)	19,265,085 (100%)	13,595,797 (100%)

Source: FF 1987, 1989, 1995, 2000, 2001

always to the government's taste, and they introduce approaches and technology that may not be familiar to either the Chinese government or indigenous NGOs.

In the case of CANGO, it is clear that the focus of its programs is economic development. As shown in Table 6.7, over 80 percent of CANGO co-sponsored projects during 1987–99 concerned rural poverty alleviation. When we include women's economic development, which also focused on rural areas, this figure reaches almost 88 percent. One of the top priorities of the government agendas is to improve economic and social conditions in old CCP liberation bases from the revolutionary period, minority-dominant

Table 6.7 A comparison of giving foci between China's CANGO and US foundations (%)

CANGO 1987–99	Poverty alleviation 80	Women's economic development 8	Community development 12			
Ford Foundation 2000–01	Environmental development 18.6	Human rights and civil society 17.6	Education 13.2	Reproduction health 12.8	Governance 12.6	Economic development 5.6	Others 19.6
US independent foundations 1994–96	Education 43	Health 24	Environment 6	Economic development 5	Social service 2	Others 20
US corporate foundations 1994–96	Education 41	Health 12	Environment 1	Others 46		

Sources: Huang 2000; FF 2000; Boisture 1998

"It takes two to tangle" 193

regions, and remote and impoverished areas (*lao, shao, bian, qiong*). Yet, over the same period, most projects CANGO co-sponsored with INGOs in fact went to regions of former liberation bases, e.g., Yimong Mountain, Shandong Province, Dabie Mountain, Anhui Province, North Sichuan Province, and North Shaanxi Province (Huang 2000: 105–35).

The Ford Foundation, in contrast, funds a greater array of projects. It has shown much interest in promoting Chinese NGOs, scholars and other professionals, and having them communicate with each other and with their international peers. Over 20 percent of its funding in 2000 was devoted to projects promoting international cooperation, communication, conferences, and workshops. In order to address the urgent shortage of operating funds for the independent organizations, the Foundation launched a program in 2003 to grant selected NGOs three-year "institutional development funds." This program is welcomed among Chinese NGOs.[32] Significantly, more than a quarter of its grants in 2000 went towards projects addressing civil society, human rights, governance, and legal or administrative reforms, arenas that are not being funded by the government. The Foundation clearly states that its civil society program works to

> increase the impact of citizens' groups working for peace and social justice, strengthen the philanthropic community that supports them, and encourage citizen oversight of the public and private sectors. We believe in the value of associational life and see the nurturing of strong, independent and democratic civil society as a goal in and of itself.[33]

Given that the Chinese government does not fund programs related to civil society and human rights, the Foundation's efforts in those areas are particularly important (Table 6.6). Furthermore, in contrast with the CANGO, the Ford Foundation's major interest area is in the Southwest, most notably the Yunnan Province where many ethnic minorities live. Over 80 percent of the Foundation's China grants in 2000 went to Southwest regions (Table 6.8).

Likewise, a comparison between foundation and foreign corporate giving also points to the diversified support given by foundations (Table 6.7). A study of US support of Chinese NPOs shows that, from 1994 to 1996,

Table 6.8 Geographical distribution of Ford Foundation's funding in China (2000), in US$

Yunnan	Southwest (including Yunnan)	All others	Total
1,715,447 (41.3%)	1,625,690 (39.1%)	811,700 (19.5%)	4,152,837 (100%)

Source: FF 2000

corporations gave a total of US$949,000 to Chinese non-profits (Boisture 1998); most of these donations, however, as Table 6.7 demonstrates, are towards charitable causes, especially those that improve foreign companies' public image and/or promote their products in China. For example, oil and automobile companies gave contributions to road construction projects and environmental education.

Over these years, the Chinese government has made it clear that it prefers foreign organizations to fund existing programs operated by Chinese organizations. As pointed out by *China Development Brief*, the easiest way to avoid bureaucratic obstacles in INGOs' registration in China is to find legally recognized Chinese agencies as INGO partners, reach an agreement, and then hand over the money.[34] Based on the difficulties INGOs confronted in obtaining legal status in China, one can well conclude that the government intentionally set up this matter with INGOs' cooperation with officially controlled or preferred organizations. However, grant-giving INGOs not only define their own policies according to their respective missions, but they also follow their respective countries' laws on grant-giving and donations. For instance, under US law, "when a foundation makes a grant to an organization that does not qualify as a public charity, the foundation must exercise a significantly higher degree of supervision over the use of the grant funds than is required for grants to public charities" (Boisture 1998). So, the Chinese government has to learn or may have learned that INGOs have their own policies and priorities in selecting which programs and institutions will manage their grants.

Nevertheless, one cannot ignore the fact that in its time in China, the Ford Foundation has indeed given impressively to Chinese government agencies and government-controlled organizations (Table 6.9). Its funding pattern is not unique among such organizations and can be explained in two ways. First, foreign grant-giving organizations are required or pressured to give grants to Chinese government organizations or distribute grants via government agencies. For example, the distribution of all grants of the China Medical Board of New York has to go through the Ministry of Public Health.[35] Over the years, the Ford Foundation has given an impressive amount of funds to the China Academy of Social Science that sponsored the

Table 6.9 The Ford Foundation's grants to different types of organization (1989–2000), in US$

Year	Chinese government organizations	Chinese NGOs	INGOs	Total
1989	1,356,330 (35%)	0 (0%)	2,579,530 (65%)	3,935,860
1995	3,796,400 (65%)	240,500 (4%)	1,796,500 (31%)	5,833,400
2000	7,843,901 (40%)	3,961,241 (20%)	8,046,625 (40%)	19,851,767

Source: FF 1989, 1995, 2000

Foundation's legal operation in China. Secondly, the Ford Foundation is convinced, as WWF is, that in China funding government programs can be an effective way to achieve its purposes, including influencing government policy.

Perhaps the most meaningful change in the Ford Foundation's giving pattern is the significant increase in grants given to Chinese NGOs (Table 6.9), which is a direct result of the growth of Chinese NGOs, as well as the Foundation's evolving orientation. Many high-profile, independent Chinese NGOs depend on international funding as their major source of income, and the Ford Foundation's annual reports show a list of all the familiar names of Chinese NGOs. The Chinese government does not fund independent NGOs at all and, up to the present, private Chinese resources are still quite limited. Thus, international support has been a key to the survival of grassroots NGOs in China, regardless of the fact that such dependency has a negative impact on their independence in the long run. To cite a few examples, in 2000, 85 percent of Global Villages and 52 percent of Friends of Nature's income came from international organizations like the Ford Foundation (Wang 2000: 151, 175). These are two of the most well-known environmental organizations in China, but although their reputations and social connections place them at a much greater advantage than the majority of small grassroots NGOs, even they cannot raise enough funds from domestic sources. Wuhan University Center for the Protection of Rights of Disadvantaged Citizens, Peking University Center for Women's Legal Aid, and Red Maple Women's Hotline, all pioneering NGOs in China, rely on the Ford Foundation for approximately 70 and 100 percent of their funds (Lee 2000: 381–2; Wang 2000: 218).

Limitations of INGOs' efforts in China

Despite the impressive achievement INGOs have made in China, one must recognize the limitations of their influence and the controversy regarding their operations in the country. The crucial factors that shaped INGOs' work in China are the conditions of indigenous NGOs and the government NGO policy – which has alternated between encouraging and restricting. Moreover, the missions and agendas of INGOs in China, along with their insufficient knowledge of the country and limited resources, have also limited or compromised their effectiveness.

Although official policy towards INGOs has become much more open and positive since the late 1990s, the Chinese government still has a say in what types of program INGOs can carry out in China and where they are allowed to work (Ma 2003; Simon 2003). While the government welcomes and even appeals for international help in areas such as poverty alleviation, education, economic development, and healthcare, certain subject areas, as well as geographic regions, are politically sensitive or even taboo for INGO operations. Foreign organizations, worried that they might jeopardize their work in the country, usually avoid direct confrontations with officials. If INGOs take a stand on politically sensitive issues, the consequences can be serious. For example, around 1996, the Chinese government was very unhappy with the Naunan Foundation, a German organization that also had an office in Beijing, because its headquarters in Germany held a conference on Free Tibet. To indicate its intolerance of the foreign organizations' interference in China's internal affairs, the Chinese government demanded that the Naunan Foundation change its name if it wanted to stay in Beijing. When the Naunan Foundation refused to do so, it was thrown out of China.[36] Soon after, Jiang Zemin, then CCP Secretary General, made a speech on being careful about foreign foundations. Since the Ford Foundation was so well-known in China, it was assumed to be the target of Jiang's speech.[37] At the same time, the Ford Foundation agreed to sponsor an international workshop on legal reforms; however, MOCA refused to accept the Foundation's grant, even though it meant the cancellation of the workshop.[38]

In another example, since the establishment of the People's Republic of China, even after the reforms, Chinese religious organizations have been under strict official supervision, and they are not categorized as social organizations, nor are they registered with the MOCA. Chinese religious organizations and institutions, as well as foreign religious activities, are the subject of the State Bureau of Management of Religious Affairs. The government implements a detailed and very strict regulation on communications between the foreign and Chinese religious organizations and the foreign organizations and individuals participating in religious activities in China (MOCA 2000a: 1). International religious groups have been entering China since the opening in 1978; yet, they are seriously restricted in pursuing religious activities, although their contributions to and participation in economic and social development are well accepted. Chinese officials are extremely suspicious of attempts to fund Chinese churches, temples, or other religious groups, and it is almost impossible for foreign religious groups to carry this out.[39] As Table 6.7 shows, from 1994 to 1996, the largest proportion of US private foundations' funds went to education and healthcare, areas strongly promoted by the government, while in contrast, social services and religious organizations only received 1.86 percent and 0.46 percent, respectively, of the funding from independent foundations and zero percent from corporations. In 2000, Ford Foundation grants to China-related projects reached US$20 million, only US$50,100 of which went to projects related to religious culture (FF 2000). This was a clear example of "self-censorship" – of not funding programs that meet with Chinese government disapproval.

As mentioned above, the state of Chinese NGOs has proved to be a crucial condition for the INGOs' operations in the country, and it will become more so while the official policy towards foreign organizations is loosening up. The underdeveloped condition of Chinese NGOs has, to a great extent, shaped and limited the international NGOs' role in China, and this is the primary reason why the INGOs have been, as discussed earlier, the leading force behind cross-organization and cross-regional non-governmental operations in China. The lack of general financial support of the non-governmental sector from the Chinese public has been one of the biggest obstacles to the growth of independent NGOs. Independent and grassroots NGOs often are not able to obtain sufficient income for their own programs, let alone operate programs that cross organizational or regional boundaries. Nor do they have the necessary experience, influence, and mechanisms to initiate and carry out large-scale and long-term programs. Furthermore, not many Chinese NGOs know the new trends, methodologies, and technologies that are being adopted in civil societies around the world. This was especially true until recently. While recognizing the contribution of INGO initiatives to the development of the Chinese non-governmental sector, one must note the complicated consequences of this unbalanced relationship between Chinese NGOs and their foreign counterparts.

When Chinese independent and grassroots NGOs depend largely if not entirely on foreign support, their independence becomes questionable. To varying degrees, obtaining grants has become vital to the existence of these organizations, thus for Chinese NGOs raising funds is the first priority. Without diversity of revenue sources, many of them have no choice but to shape their programs and missions around foreign organizations' interests. Some Chinese NGO leaders are strongly opposed to this outcome, arguing that indigenous organizations should devise their own agendas and be assisted by INGOs, rather than simply assisting INGOs in their initiatives and programs.[40] Foreign organizations obviously have their own specific missions and political or cultural orientations that often determine what programs are in their favor and what types of organization they intend to assist. These considerations may not be relevant to China's conditions and needs, and foreign organizations' insufficient knowledge of what is best for the local organizations has further limited what they can accomplish.

Furthermore, most INGOs themselves are grant-seeking organizations and they need projects that are in line with international trends in order to raise their own operating funds. Under such conditions, one can understand why programs or methodologies such as capacity training, participatory approach, micro-credit programs, PRA, eco-tourism, and environmental conservation are the most popular among Chinese NGOs, because they are well received internationally, and these are the types of projects that most INGOs are familiar with. In fact, the "participatory approach" has been so popular in China that even the government has officially announced that this approach is to be "the guiding principle in China's alleviation of poverty" (Young 2002b).

To a large degree, the grant-seeking foreign NGOs are competing with the indigenous NGOs for international funding. It is no exaggeration to say that China's social, environmental, and economic problems provide enormous opportunities for INGOs, whose existence largely depends on good projects. With their well-defined mission and recognizable non-profit status, as well as experience in fundraising and working in developing countries, many international NGOs are in a more advantageous position to receive funding than are China's NGOs. The taxation policy of the Western grant-giving organizations' own countries also put well-established Western NGOs in a more favorable condition. For instance, Boisture concludes that US foundations interested in supporting charitable activities overseas often prefer to give grants to US public charities that can then work in collaboration with one or more non-US charities to conduct the activity. This is especially true of those foundations with limited experience in funding programs in China (Young 2002b). To a great extent, the Ford Foundation's fund distribution supports this conclusion. As Table 6.8 indicates, a large proportion, sometimes even the largest proportion, of the Ford Foundation's money went directly to programs that are run by US and other INGOs.

On the other hand, the preliminary condition of governance and professional operation of indigenous organizations and the negative influence of commercialized culture on the NGO sector in China have hampered them from obtaining more international grants than they do now. Most Chinese NGOs do not have a clear vision of their independent social or political roles in China's reform, and they are also unable to initiate or design programs to fulfill their mission. On top of this, the great majority of Chinese NGOs have not yet established professional and ethical standards as non-governmental and non-profit institutions, and this situation does not benefit either their public image or their fundraising efforts. A serious concern of international grant-distribution organizations about funding Chinese organizations is whether the money would be used for the proposed programs. Under China's current commercialized culture, non-profit operations have become a new business and source of private profit. Foreign foundations and INGOs, well aware of the fact that many so-called NGOs in China are in fact "grant diggers," often tend to support only those that they know or that have established a good reputation.[41] With all the progress INGOs have made in reaching out to the local organizations, their connections with, as well as knowledge of, the latter are insufficient, and this has certainly impeded their ability to fund or cooperate with a wide variety of groups and regions.

This situation has limited the chances of obtaining international aid for organizations that are small, newly organized, or located in remote regions. For example, in the mid-90s the Ford Foundation rejected a grant proposal of a then-unknown organization focusing on AIDS/HIV prevention education at the time when it needed help the most. The leader of that NGO later became well-known, and the Foundation has supported his institution three years in a row.[42] Another example concerns Lijiang, which since the 1990s has become a popular tourist city in Yunnan Province and is now a focus of international attention. It is not only that Yunnan Province has been a major focus of INGOs in China, but also Lijiang's unique ancient architecture and the Naxi minority's rich culture are very attractive to foreigners.

Internationally sponsored programs have crowded into this small region and funds have poured in. In comparison, other remote minority mountain areas in Yunnan Province where transportation is difficult have not been selected by INGOs as program sites, even though they need more help.[43]

The competition among Chinese NGOs over foreign funding often limits rather than opens INGOs' contacts with local organizations. International organizations, eager to enter China, are seeking Chinese partners, especially among the non-governmental organizations. This situation gives indigenous organizations opportunities to raise funds and negotiate terms of cooperation. Yet, the opportunity is not equal for all Chinese NGOs. The "trick" of the game is who gets information about these resources, who knows how to apply for them, and, last but not least, who has the connections with the resources, namely foreign organizations. Not all indigenous groups have knowledge of such resources. In fact, a serious problem in the development of Chinese NGOs is the absence of networks among Chinese NGOs and communication channels between INGOs and indigenous NGOs. The great majority of local and grassroots organizations do not have access to information about all the international resources available. Only those organizations with well-informed leaders who are knowledgeable of INGOs' operations and resources have good chances of getting their proposals funded. Yet, it has become a common practice that Chinese NGOs withhold information about international resources from their peers, in what one Chinese NGO scholar calls the "small peasant mentality."[44] Consequently, this situation prevents Chinese NGOs, small and less well-established ones in particular, from receiving more international assistance.

The distribution of international funds has created two major phenomena: on the one hand, a large proportion of funds have gone to international organizations rather than local organizations; and on the other hand, some high-profile indigenous NGOs have consistently received funds, whereas in general, insufficient funding has become the biggest obstacle to the majority of Chinese NGOs carrying out effective programs. A serious question raised by a Chinese NGO leader was whether "funding foreign NGOs working in China, rather than supporting indigenous organizations, is the best way to help the country?"[45] As China's third sector is rapidly growing, this question is increasingly relevant.

There are other factors at work here, too. First, it is expensive to maintain an office with foreign staff in major Chinese cities, and now more and more INGOs have opened offices in China. The living conditions of foreign staff are considered luxurious by Chinese standards. Some UN officials and INGO staff were even considered by some Chinese NGO leaders as corrupt.[46] In general, investigations and operations conducted by foreign organizations cost much more than similar projects done by local NGOs. Second, it requires a long time for international organizations to understand China's situation and culture, and the frequent change of foreign field officers and staff only makes this more difficult. Furthermore, the personnel change causes replication of investigation and operation. From the local people's point of view, foreign projects are like seasonal birds passing through, because they see neither deep understanding of their situation nor long-term commitment. Programs run by INGOs tend to be short-term, and some are not able to be maintained by the Chinese after these organizations leave. Finally, the cultural difference and language barrier create tensions between foreign and Chinese staff, as well as organizations, and in my interviews with Chinese NGO practitioners, complaints of arrogance and incompetence on the part of foreign NGO staff often appeared.[47]

Of course, complaints from Chinese NGOs are only one side of the story. As discussed above, it is the current low level of China's civil society and third sector, as well as the Chinese government's controversial policy, that have caused serious hesitation on the part of international grant-giving organizations and private foundations to fund Chinese NGOs. This is indeed a dilemma. Theoretically, and in the long run, the Chinese NGOs should be the biggest recipient of private international funds going into China, but for this purpose they need to establish themselves as independent and accountable NGOs with creative programs first. Understandably, INGOs benefit from funding or cooperating with high-profile indigenous organizations that have much influence on the Chinese public and are more likely to meet their proposed goals. Yet, continued support for these high-profile NGOs will not help INGOs to reach out to and raise up the less advanced organizations, the ones that need their assistance even more.

To conclude, the economic and social transformation in China has given INGOs unprecedented opportunities to make an impact in China. The past two decades have witnessed enormous contributions from the international community, and China's non-governmental sector has benefited greatly. The scope and depth of INGOs' involvement in China's social and economic development indicates both a substantial change in the government's attitude towards foreign organizations and the consistent and ever-growing determination and efforts of INGOs in reforming China. At the same time, the country's current political system and cultural conditions have created serious impediments for international organizations to deliver these efforts. The lack of horizontal cooperation among Chinese NGOs and their petty mentality towards their peers are clear hindrances. The INGOs, on the other hand, have a long way to go to establish a balanced relationship with the indigenous organizations. After all, it takes two to tango.

Conclusion

China is no longer a country where the party-state has the power to totally control society and people's lives. From the absence of NGOs in Mao's era to "NGO Heat" (NGO *re*) in the early 2000s, China's associational landscape has changed profoundly. During the last two decades, the most substantial progress in NGO development includes the improvement of the legal and political environment for non-governmental activities, the rapid increase and multiplication of formal and informal associations and non-profit service providers, the deepening and broadening of the NGOs' involvement in social and economic issues, the emergence of the first generation of NGO leaders, and the increase in cooperative activities among NGOs. To a great extent, these NGOs are facilitating a civil society in China. An old Chinese motto says, "It is always very difficult to get things started" (*wanshi katou nan*). In this sense, Chinese NGOs should celebrate their first triumph. In this conclusion, I highlight and compare the major findings and arguments of the book.

The major forces promoting Chinese NGOs

China is still a Communist Party state, and the Chinese people have yet to enjoy full freedom of speech and association. The long-expected political reforms are still indefinitely pending, and the CCP government continues its suppressive policy towards independent political organizations and NGOs' engagement in sensitive political matters. Nevertheless, the NGOs, more and more of them becoming independent, have not only survived but thrived. The simple explanation of this phenomenon is that the economic reforms in the past twenty-odd years and the consequent social changes have created both the environment and the needs for NGOs to grow. With their specific motivations and priorities, the government, the intellectuals, the newly emerged entrepreneurs, and the international NGOs (INGOs) have all played significant roles in advancing NGOs in China.

Today, the party and the government remain the most decisive factor affecting NGOs' current and future conditions. From lifting the total prohibition of non-governmental associational activities in the late 1970s to its most recent efforts in unifying official NGO policy over all non-governmental and non-profit entities in China, the official NGO policy has gone through substantial changes and development. These changes reflect the Chinese government's ability to adjust to new situations and its confidence in its control over society. Yet, the key reason for the policy changes has been the party-state's perception of the functions of social forces and non-governmental efforts in China's economic development and social stability. To achieve its goal of "small government and big society," the government has vigorously promoted certain types of NGOs to take over responsibilities that it can no longer assume. The best example is the transfer of almost the entire mid-tier managerial agencies from the state system into non-governmental intermediary associations. Under China's current political conditions, without the government's approval and encouragement, it would be impossible for the Chinese NGOs to make such dramatic progress.

Yet, the setbacks of China's current polity and the government's strong influence are obvious. The government's intervention in private affairs is not yet the subject of legal limitation. Without legal protection for NGOs from the abuse of official power, NGOs still exist at the state's mercy. The NGOs' growth patterns have thus been considerably shaped by the official reform agenda and its preference for advancing certain types of NGOs while suppressing others. That is evident in the most rapid growth of trade associations and certain service institutions and the strikingly under-developed state of advocacy and political organizations. The official dual registration policy, against the strong opposition of NGOs, and the absence of governmental funding to independent organizations have become the major obstacles for the fast growth of grassroots NGOs. The official discouragement of grassroots NGOs reflects the CCP government's deep fear of the empowerment of democratic forces in society.

Among all social forces promoting non-governmental activities, the intellectuals and entrepreneurs are the most active and significant. Historically, the intellectuals and gentry-merchants/bourgeois were the mainstays of the modernization movement and private associational lives in early twentieth-century China. In many ways, this tradition continues. After the reforms and open policy, the intellectuals were the first group to learn of NGO and civil society concepts and practice, and they were also the most ready to communicate and interact with the international NGO community. Scholarly associations were among the first groups of social organizations to resurface immediately after the Cultural Revolution, and during the 1980s they had a considerable impact on rebuilding educational and scientific research resources that were totally destroyed by that ten-year catastrophe.

Most significantly, the 1990s theoretical discourse of civil society among the mainland intellectuals represented the bottom-up efforts of these people in promoting China's political reforms. They have systematically introduced and translated Western thoughts on civil society, NGOs, the state–society relationship, corporatism, etc., to China, and their proposal of a constructive, interactive relationship between the state and civil society for China's future democratic system carries a great political impact. Because of these efforts, NGO and civil society studies are rapidly expanding in universities, and many scholars have held training workshops for NGO governance, leadership, and sustainable development. Simultaneously, many intellectuals have established independent institutes delivering social services, research, or assistance to marginalized people.

By promoting civil society theories and participating in NGO practice, these intellectuals have expressed their political ideas and fulfilled their moral and cultural values, which are very much what China's traditional educated people pursued. At the same time, because of their education, language skill, knowledge of INGOs' programs and funding, resourcefulness and social connections and, most of all, their devotion and social conscience, the intellectuals have provided leadership in China's growing NGO movement. These criteria also enable them to become the crucial link between the officials, NGO practitioners, and INGOs.

Private entrepreneurs, unlike intellectuals, came from low social and economic positions, and they gained their political and social recognition only recently. To survive and succeed in a market economy, the private entrepreneurs are increasingly recognizing their common interests and the need for self-organization, especially when the officially organized trade associations do not protect the private entrepreneurs' interests, nor provide market services to them. As Wenzhou's case showed clearly, the flourishing of private chambers of commerce since the late 1990s indicates both the increase of entrepreneurs' economic power and their desire for collective expression of their interests. Indeed, the great political potential of this group lies in its rapidly increased population and wealth, and its ever growing importance in China's economy today. As China's economy heads towards further privatization and marketization, the entrepreneurs are becoming more vibrant actors in operating intermediary associations between the state and private businesses.

In comparison with the grassroots organizations led by intellectuals and connected with and supported by INGOs, the entrepreneurs' organizations, in their missions, leadership, and governance, are more identical to traditional chambers of commerce in the late Qing and early Republic. They represent the continuity of China's early modern civic associations, and in many ways the current state of private chambers of commerce also reflects the general conditions of new entrepreneurs. Such individuals often grew up in financial difficulties and social turmoil. A great proportion of these people had little education or professional careers before the reforms. Such backgrounds have undeniably affected the roles of the entrepreneurs as a whole in China's social and political reforms. At present, chambers of commerce and other private economic associations mainly serve the self-interests of their members. While many Chinese NGOs are hoping to generate more support from domestic private resources, the entrepreneurs have not yet lived up to this

204 Conclusion

expectation. Thus, can entrepreneurs play a major role outside of the economic realm and become a core force in political reforms? This is an open question.

INGOs entered China right after the end of Mao's regime, and they have become increasingly active since the mid-1990s. The swift upsurge of global civil society and the associational revolution around the world gave a great momentum to the INGOs' China missions. These organizations have not only launched their own programs from environmental conservation to poverty alleviation, but they also have provided the major support to independent grassroots NGOs. The most valuable input of INGOs' involvements in China are the new visions, ideas, and methods they have pioneered in other countries and that now apply to Chinese NGOs and local communities. Mostly because of the INGOs, Chinese NGO practitioners and scholars have connected with the global civil society and thus become a part of the global campaigns against poverty, environmental degradation, AIDS, drug trafficking, etc. No doubt the funding and grants from foreign grant-giving foundations and governments are crucial to many independent NGOs that have not been able to generate sufficient domestic support. Via the capacity and leadership training programs and funding, INGOs have successfully enlarged their influence among indigenous NGOs. Because of their experience and resources, INGOs have been a key actor in cooperation between the government, business sector, and Chinese NGOs.

All the domestic and international forces involved in advancing China's NGOs are in fact working interactively and jointly, and yet, because of varying purposes and focuses, these efforts have created a diverse and unbalanced NGO landscape. Ultimately, NGO development in China will be decided by China's own political, economic and social conditions and needs. This is especially true because international aid, whether from foreign governments, multilateral funds or the private sector, will surely move from China to other more needy countries as China's economy continues its rapid growth.

Changes in associational landscapes in China

Under the Mao regime, China was a desert for associational life, but now we can see green grassland where young trees are growing. After over two decades of development, the quantitative state of China's associations has the shape of a standing dumbbell. On top, there are a large number of so-called GONGOs (governmentally organized NGOs), and on the bottom, we see a vast sea of loosely associated networks and groups. What is in between is a much smaller number of formally established grassroots NGOs. One can hardly overestimate the significance of these independent NGOs, because their influence considerably exceeds their number and resources. With all their programs and achievements, their most important contribution is their example of what NGOs should be and what NGOs can do. They represent institutional alternatives, and indeed they have challenged the governmental organizations. Organized by visionary and resourceful people, those grassroots NGOs demonstrate initiative, creativity, social responsibility, and courage. These NGOs are platforms where people exchange ideas, make decisions, operate programs; ultimately, these organizations give people an institutional channel in which to participate in public matters and express collective voices. Currently the grassroots NGOs still face political, social, and financial challenges, and most of them are yet to become stabilized and mature. Nevertheless, they have shown great vitality.

In contrast, the GONGOs are a much complicated and controversial group, and in terms of learning how to understand associational behavior against their specific cultural or political circumstances, these GONGOs provide the most interesting cases. The GONGOs as a whole are highly diverse, and they enjoy differing amounts of autonomy. Their relations with the government, their financial conditions, as well as their political influence are so diverse that the term GONGO carries no definite meaning. It is true that the great majority of them continue their ties with the government, for historical, political, and practical reasons. Yet, the key here is that they no longer exist within the state system. This reality forces them to learn how to sustain themselves in the marketplace, which decisively changes their mentality and attitude towards both the government and their constituency. To various degrees, all GONGOs, including mass and people's organizations, demonstrate a clear centrifugal tendency away from governmental control.

Thus, China's unique NGO body explains why autonomy is not a practical and functional criterion to determine the nature of a great many Chinese organizations. To a large degree, maintaining close relations with the government is the NGOs' survival strategy, and many of them continue to depend on the government's resources to sustain them. Only by emphasizing the difference of the GONGOs from the governmental organizations and their predecessors can we have a better understanding of what has happened in the past two decades. This study finds that Chinese NGOs in general enjoy much more autonomy than it seems on the surface, and the majority of GONGOs are now making their own decisions on organizational matters rather than waiting for orders from supervising government administrators. Also, these GONGOs have a much stronger sense of insecurity, and thus they have the motivation to become more effective and efficient than the administrative bureaus. Furthermore, most GONGOs are seeking financial independence, and when they realize financial self-sufficiency, they will have more autonomy in general. This study concludes that the GONGOs are still the most numerous, well-organized, resourceful, and influential organizations among all non-governmental entities; therefore, both their advances and limitations affect the current state of China's NGO sector and its future development greatly.

Along with the improvement of their economic conditions and political environment, the Chinese people have engaged in all kinds of cultural, spiritual, self-help, and public service associations and networks. Yet, the substance of the vast number of informal social networks has long been ignored by the students of modern China, and their extremely pervasive and fluid nature no doubt adds to the difficulty in analyzing them either quantitatively or qualitatively. These networks are important to our depicting China's associational behavior, because they are voluntary, autonomous, can be very political, and, most of all, they are at the community level; thus, in comparison with formally registered organizations, they are the closest to ordinary people's daily lives. The swift resuscitation of social networks reveals both people's enormous needs for associational engagement and the influence of those networks.

The study of a wide variety of associational engagements concludes that it does not really matter if civic associations are registered or not, or whether they devote themselves to the public interest or private interest; such engagements have a positive impact on society because they have increased participants' social capital and civility. Joining in those associations or networks, Chinese people have learned how to interact with each other, to take responsibility and get things done. These associations are also the institutional platforms that have given people opportunities to participate in public affairs and sometimes even in policy making. Together, they are an integrative part of the expansion of society.

Do NGOs facilitate civil society in China?

From Alexis de Tocqueville's fascination with active and pervasive civic associations in early nineteenth-century American social and political life to the recent "global associational revolution," it has become very clear that NGOs play the most critical role in the evolution and function of civil society. Lester Salamon and Helmut Anheier list the characteristics that allow these civil associations to become strategically important in the search for a "middle way" between sole reliance on the market and sole reliance on the state. These include

> their unique position outside the market and the state, their generally smaller scale, their connections to citizens, their flexibility, their capacity to tap private initiative in support of public purposes, and their newly rediscovered contributions to building "social capital."
> (Salamon *et al.* 1999: 5)

Not surprisingly, Goran Hyden declares: "one can argue that civil society is no better than the sum of its associations" (Hyden 1997: 17).

The associational revolution in China in the past twenty-odd years serves as the most powerful evidence of the evolution of civil society in China. The civil society development is along two interrelated fronts: theoretical discourse and civic associational development. This study finds that the Chinese intellectuals' search for civil society has been strongly influenced by their own concerns about China's political reforms and their understanding of China's reality and history. One consequent development is the wide acceptance of the ideas of civil society, rule of law, and the non-governmental sector by many Chinese scholars, reformers, and NGO activists as ideal models for China's future power structure and state–society relationship. Yet, these scholars have adopted these Western concepts with their own interpretation to suit their political ideas and China's circumstances as well; thus, theoretically the evolution of civil society has taken its own path.

As a conceptual framework to analyze the state–society relationship, different normative visions of civil society emphasize the political, economic, social, and cultural aspects of such a relationship differently. Among contemporary Western theorists, a triadic model of state, civil society, and economy that excludes the market from civil society is widely accepted. Disagreeing with this model, the Chinese scholars are in favor of the classical dichotomous model of state vs society (civil society). In this dichotomous model, Chinese intellectuals emphasize that the market economy not only is the major realm of civil society activities; it is also the foundation of civil society's existence and development. They attribute the profound change in China's state–society relationship and expansion of society to the emergence of a market economy.

This study finds that the Chinese intellectuals' contestation of a civil society model, including markets, is in accordance with China's situation. The past two decades have witnessed a most impressive increase of Chinese NGOs in numbers and influence, and the organizations in the economic and social realms are the most vibrant forces in expanding societal space and power and changing China's institutional landscapes. As political scientists generally maintain, the most important and vital composition of civil society is the associational realm that comprises associations initiated by individuals to develop or protect their interests and values and to enjoy a certain autonomy from the state. This is exactly how the Chinese civic associations are functioning, and this study thus concludes that China's civic associations are indeed facilitating the evolution of civil society in the country. On the other hand, this study recognizes the important political role of civil society, even though it does not see civil society as a political society or tie its function entirely to democratization. With all their progress, the Chinese NGOs at this moment have not yet had a substantial political voice, nor can they affect policy-making in major ways.

One distinct feature of NGOs' development in China, relating to their insignificant political role, is their cooperative attitude towards the state. The CCP government continues to see NGOs as assisting and complementing its reform agenda and as a bridge to help the party reach the people. While the NGOs do not necessarily agree with such an opinion, they recognize the fact that they have not yet become an independent force to balance state power or to fight for their own interests in the policy-making process. Political scientists often contend that when a market economy is developing, the private economy and other social forces will push for a democratic political system. In China's case, what we see here is an ambiguous and even contradictory picture. On the one hand, the intellectuals and entrepreneurs are indeed pushing for the expansion of societal space and non-governmental actions, and have already increased citizen participation and self-expression. On the other hand, being the beneficiaries of the state-led reforms, both the intellectuals and entrepreneurs generally support the reform policy and agree with the official view that economic development and social stability are the first priority. Neither of the two groups, with the exception of some individuals, is taking a confrontational approach in pursuing political reforms, believing that such actions would bring social instability.

This non-confrontational policy is clearly expressed by Chinese intellectuals in their vision of a civil society model for China, within which the state and society are in a "constructive interaction" relationship. Accordingly, while in principle the state should not interfere in the affairs of civic society associations, the state's intervention, arbitration, and regulation of the private sphere are indeed rationalized. Facing the state's consistent suppressive policy towards independent political parties or religious organizations, neither theoretical discussions nor NGO practices in the past two decades have addressed the issue of how society and civic associations can protect themselves from the state's intervention and thus achieve the balance between the state and civil society. Under China's one-party state, the NGOs have taken a pragmatic and practical strategy to avoid possible political trouble and stay alive. Therefore, the key features of the evolving civil society in China are the address of society's "constructive interactive relations with the state," the "advancing gradually" style, and the "non-confrontational approach." As a result, the evolution of civil society in China indeed has carried with it Chinese characteristics and is not yet beyond the minimal level.

China is experiencing the most profound transformation in its history. The impressive upsurge of China's non-governmental organizations in the last two decades is one of the most significant and meaningful events in this transformation. It is difficult to exaggerate the long-lasting impact that NGOs have made on China's economic, social, and political development; some scholars even use "revolution" to describe this phenomenon (Li 1998; Wang and He 2004). Though China's party-state continues to perpetuate its control over non-governmental affairs, the growth of NGOs serves as the most convincing evidence of the decline of state power over society. The initiative, creativity, courage, devotion, and resourcefulness demonstrated in the development of NGOs indicate the great potential of Chinese people in fighting for their society and interests; they are the true dynamism behind the growth of civil society in the country. Today an increasingly active and integrative civil society is evolving on China's horizon, and the growing cooperation among the non-profit sectors, domestic and international, the state and the business sector give us great hope for the challenges facing China.

Notes

Introduction

1 Interview with an official in the Division of Administration of Foreign Civil Organizations, BMNGOs, MOCA 2001.
2 Interview with Ding Yuanzhu, a scholar of Chinese NGOs, 2001.
3 The charters of most organizations I interviewed clearly state the organizational role as a bridge between the state and the masses and as an assistant to the government. Similar language also frequently appears in materials related to NGO regulation and management.
4 Interviews with Chinese NGO leaders and activists, 1996–2004. See an example below.
5 In 1998, the party and government issued a document specifically prohibiting current or retired officials, especially high officials, from heading NGOs. CCPD 1998.
6 This is a clear case of an NGO's compromising, because the action went against the will of that organization. To protect both the organization and that person, here I do not provide names.

1 In search of civil society in China: theoretical and historical discourses

1 In 1992, over sixty Chinese, American, French, and Japanese scholars attended an international symposium held by Shanghai Fudan University and University of California in Berkeley, entitled "Historical Inquiry of Social Evolution in Modern China."
2 Since 1992, *Chinese Social Science Quarterly*, a Hong Kong-based journal, has included an impressive number of articles on civil society and China's modernization; and in 1993 it co-hosted with the Shanghai Association of History another symposium on civil society in China in which over forty Chinese scholars participated. Another Hong Kong-based journal, *The Twenty-first Century*, also has published several articles on the topic since 1991. The phrase "civil society" appeared in few articles in mainland journals prior to 1989, yet the articles did not analyze the concept in depth.
3 Quote from Hefner 1998: 22.
4 In his classical studies of citizenship, T. H. Marshall described three permutations of this concept: civil citizenship in the eighteenth century "ensured individual rights to property"; in the nineteenth century a notion of political citizenship underscored the right to participate in the exercise of political power, and in the twentieth century, social citizenship has implied a right to economic welfare and social security. Goldman and Perry 2002: 2.
5 Quote from Ma 1994: 83.

210 Notes

6 On the folk religions in Chinese history and the official suppression of these religions, see Ma and Han 1992. On the PRC's official ban of folk religion groups in the early 1950s, see Ma 1997: 62.
7 For example, Liang Shuming, a renowned scholar in the 1930s–40s, described vividly a traditional China that was nothing like a state in the sense of modern political concepts (Liang 1949).
8 The majority of Chinese publications on civil society during the early 1990s rarely cite the literature on this subject in English or other languages. Since the late 1990s, a profusion of influential Western theories on political science, economics, sociology, philosophy, history, and other humanities fields have been translated into Chinese.
9 The great majority, if not all, of scholars in mainland China participating in the discussion of civil society were young scholars graduating with higher degrees after the Cultural Revolution.
10 Quite a few Chinese studies of this subject make the same assumption. John Keane casts doubt upon this commonplace assumption in his well-known article "Despotism and democracy." He states that "Hegel was neither the first nor necessarily the most important modern thinker to consider the subject of civil society . . . early modern German discussions of the scope and power of the state . . . were the *least* receptive to the democratic political implications of the new distinction between civil society and the state." Keane 1993: 35–71.
11 In fact, both Bobbio and Keane explicate Marx's idea of civil society in a sophisticated way (Bobbio 1993: 73–99; Keane 1993: 35–71).
12 Cohen and Arato express that "[w]e need a theory capable of thematizing both the threat and the promise. Habermas's 'critique of functionalist reason' provides the best available conceptual framework for reconstructing the three-part model of civil society." Cohen and Arato: 426.
13 The first debate was on whether "practice is the sole criterion for testing truth." The second, "Mr Zi vs Mr She (capitalism vs socialism)," was about whether a market economy was capitalism. The third one, "Mr Gong vs Mr Si (State-ownership vs Private-ownership)," debated the nature of non-state businesses. For an elaborate account on the subject, see Ma and Ling 1998.
14 Interview with a senior editor of *History Study*, the most prestigious historical journal in mainland China. He told me how difficult it was for them to publish a group of articles on civil society in a 1996 issue. I had a similar impression of the political sensibility of civil society and NGOs during my 1996 field research in China.
15 Quote from Wakeman (1993).
16 Interviews with Chinese historians Yu Heping, Zhao Shiyu, and Min Jie, 1996.
17 For an elaborate study on *shi*, see Yu Yingshi 1987.
18 Quote from Zhang *et al.* 2000a: 342.

2 "Small government, big society": the Chinese government's NGO policy and its dilemma

1 Interview with a vice-director of Bureau of Management of NGOs (BMNGO) in MOCA 2004.
2 Interviews with former director of Division of Social Organizations (DSO), 1996.
3 Interviews with the secretary general of Shanghai Federation of Industrial and Economic Associations. He was a former high official in Shanghai Bureau of Labor, 2000 and 2001.
4 The term "non-state-owned businesses" includes: collective, joint-venture, stock share companies, foreign investment companies, the Hong Kong/Taiwan/Macau investment companies, private ownership, and individual ownership.

5 Interview with an official in the Federation of the Textile Industry, 1996.
 6 An impressive amount of research on community construction has been published in the last decade, often explaining the meaning of this word by referring to American communities.
 7 Worth noting that the meaning of *shequ* is much narrower than the connotation of community in English, and *shequ* refers mainly to residential districts or compounds.
 8 Interview with a vice-director of BMNGO, 2004.
 9 Ibid, 2001.
10 Ibid, 2004.
11 CSC1950, item 6.
12 Chen is the director of Zhejiang Province Bureau of Civil Affairs.
13 Interview with the founder of NPO Network, 2004.
14 Interview with a vice-director of BMNGO, 2004.
15 The official insisted that China's registration system is similar to Japan's. Interview with a MOCA official, 1996.
16 Interview with Tony Saich, the Ford Foundation's chief representative of its China office (1993–99), 2003. See Chapter 6.
17 For example, the Ford Foundation makes a large grant to its host institution. See Chapter 6.
18 Interview with a vice-director of BMNGO, 2004. He stated clearly that if foreign organizations had difficulty finding mothers-in-law, the government would make special arrangements for them.
19 Interview with the founder of NPO Network, 2004.
20 Interviews with former and current directors of the DSO and BMNGO, 1996, 2001, 2004.
21 See CSC 1998a, items 32–7 and CSC 1998b, items 24–9.
22 Interview with a Chinese scholar on labor laws, 1996.
23 Interviews with private universities and cultural organizations, 1996 and 2001.
24 "The International Conference on the Non-profit Sector and Development" in July; "The International Conference of the Development of the Non-Profit Organizations and the China Project Hope" in October.
25 Interview with an NGO scholar, 2001.
26 Interview with a vice-director of BMNGO, 2001.
27 Ibid, 2004, and with two former directors of DSO, 1996.
28 Ibid, 2004.
29 Interviews with graduates of Peking University, between 1996 and 2003.
30 In China, registered churches are officially controlled, and since the reforms many believers are studying the Bible and worshipping at private settings. They are called house-churches.
31 Interviews with Shanghai YMCA officers, 2001.
32 In the past two decades the real value of government funds to GONGOs has fallen considerably due to serious inflation. Thus, these organizations are under strong pressure to seek other financial resources. Like all SOs (except the foundations), they also are allowed to run for-profit businesses to supplement their incomes. But government funds are still their major revenue. For example, the CCYL is a fully funded people's organization, but the government allows it two for-profit enterprises with 1,150 employees.
33 Interviews with a participant involved in the discussion of the drafting of a "social organization law," 1996, and an official in the BMNGO, 2001.
34 Interviews with the former director of the DSO, 1996.
35 MOCA has been advocating for NGOs' "three selfs": self-management, self-recruiting, and self-sufficiency. Interview with a high official at MOCA, 1996.
36 Ibid.

212 *Notes*

37 Interview with Wang Chun, a vice-director of the Center for Biodiversity and Indigenous Knowledge (CIBK), 2004.
38 Interview with a vice-director of BMNGO, 2004.
39 Interview with a MOCA official, 1996.
40 Interview with a Chinese NGO scholar, 2001.
41 This conclusion is based on my interviews with NGO leaders and a reading of research on Chinese NGOs.

3 NGO landscape in China: classification, scope, and autonomy

1 Interviews with officials of the DSOs in MOCA and Chinese scholars, 1996.
2 Interviews with a former director of the DSOs, 1996.
3 Ibid.
4 Interview with a law professor at Beijing University, 1996.
5 Interviews with Chinese NGO scholars, activists and government officials, 2001, 2004.
6 There are other less frequently used terms.
7 Interviews with a former director of DSOs, 1996.
8 The so-called eight big organizations (the list varies from time to time) normally refer to those that participate in the China People's Political Consultative Conference, and they are: the All-China Federation of Trade Unions, China Communist Youth League, All-China Women's Federation, China Federation of Literature and Arts, All-China Association of Journalists, China Association of Writers, China Association of Science and Technology, and All-China Federation of Returned Overseas.
9 According to the 1950 regulations of social organizations, the people's organizations were exempted from registration with the government. The 1989 and 1998 regulations did not include such an item, yet this practice continued.
10 The Chinese names for these organizations were *"fei zongjiao da tongmeng"* and *"fei jidujiao tongmeng."*
11 In 2004, the MOCA also published data on SOs at provincial and county levels.
12 The MOCA and BOCAs collect such information from applications and annual reports of registered organizations.
13 The MOCA started registering SOs in 1989; however, during the first few years the statistics at the provincial level were incomplete. The NGNCEs' registrations started in 1999.
14 For example, the NGO Research Center at Qinghua University conducted several NGO surveys.
15 Interview with this official, 2004.
16 One reason for the sharp drop of SO total numbers in Sichuan in the 1990s is because its largest city – Chongqing – has been a *zhixiashi* (a city directly under the central government) since 1997.
17 The classification of foundations as SOs is confusing, because all other organizations in the SO category are membership organizations. An explanation is that prior to 1998, all kinds of non-governmental organizations were classified as SOs.
18 Interviews with several national foundations in 1996.
19 The amounts of interest yielded from endowments of many foundations shown in this book were not from a single year but accumulated in years. DNFI 1996.
20 Interview with the vice-director of the DSOs in MOCA, 1996, 2000.
21 Interviews with officials in ACWF and Shanghai Industrial Federation, 1996, 2001.
22 I was told of his speech by a Chinese NGO scholar, 2001.
23 Unpublished Chinese materials about the fourth WCW, collected by the author.

Notes 213

24 Interviews with officials in ACWF, WFs in Beijing and Xi'an, 1996, 2001.
25 Ibid.
26 Interview with a senior WF official in Beijing, 1996.
27 Interview with a young cadre in the ACWF, 1996.
28 This case study is based on my interviews with CYDF leaders 1996, 2001, 2002, 2004. It also relies on CYDF's annual reports, newsletters, and Kang 1997a and 1997b.
29 The education crises at the elementary and middle school levels in indigent rural regions revealed two major problems: poorly funded schools without decent buildings and without enough teaching equipment and teachers, and a high rate of drop out among students due to the 100 RMB fees a year at the low average for books and other fees.
30 According to a statistic of 1987, illiterate and semi-literate people were 25.1 percent of the entire Chinese population, or a total of 250,000,000. The percentage of people with college degrees or with high school degrees were 1.4 percent and 12.3 percent respectively. Guan 1989: 1; Kang 1997a, 101, 106–8.
31 Around 2000, the CYDF decided to end its Hope Project and switch to other programs. This decision was disagreed with by many local Youth Leagues because it would mean they lose their most important program. Interviews with CYDF leaders, 2001, 2002, 2004.

4 Social capital: the significance and dynamics of grassroots NGOs and social networks

1 Interviews with a former vice-director of DSO, 1996, a vice-director of BMNGO, 2004. There are several reasons for the lack of statistics on grassroots NGOs in China: most grassroots NGOs do not register as SOs or do not register, and the official statistics do not distinguish between the grassroots NGOs and GONGOs.
2 Many so-called "voluntary activities" in China are in fact organized by the state-owned institutions, from elementary school students' "cleaning the city" actions to work units' tree planting.
3 About the newly emerged volunteerism, see Ding (2004).
4 An elaboration on Chinese folk religion groups, Ma and Han (1992) and Zhao (2002).
5 This case study is based on materials I collected in my interviews with NFA, 2002.
6 Interviews with officials of NFA, 2001.
7 Interview with an organizer of the association, 1996.
8 Interviews with members of SDFC, 2004.
9 This statement is based on interviews with NGOs and reading of reports or research on these organizations both in English and Chinese.
10 The FON brochure.
11 The GVB brochure; about the Green Home, <hppt://www.greenhome.org.cn>.
12 Interviews with Liang Congjie, 1996, 2001.
13 Interview with Liang Congjie, 2001.
14 Before the FON started this program, some members visited schools in Germany and Holland to study their environmental education programs. *FON Newsletter*, 2, 2001.
15 Interviews with Wang Yu, 2001 and 2004.
16 Interviews with graduates of Peking University, 2002 and 2003.
17 During my years of fieldwork in China on Chinese NGOs, I have interviewed almost all these outstanding individuals or their organizations, and also read a substantial number of publications about their works.
18 The following discussion is based on interviews with scholars in research institutions and universities, from 1996 to 2004.

214 *Notes*

19 Interviews with scholars in universities and China Social Science Academy, 1996, 2000 and 2001.
20 For example, the consistent salary increases for doctors, professors, researchers and other professionals since the late 1990s and the substantial improvement of their housing conditions have rapidly broadened the gap between intellectuals and workers and farmers.
21 Interviews with NGO scholars and NGO leaders, 1996–2004.
22 Interviews with an NGO scholar, 1996 and 2001, and with directors of private schools, nursing homes and research institutes, 1996–2001.
23 This case is based on interview of Tianze's secretary general, 1996, and materials collected by the author.
24 Ibid.
25 Interview with Gao Xiaoxian, the founder of Shanxi Province Research Center for Women Theory, Marriage and Family, 2002.
26 Interviews with some of the scholars, 2001.
27 The following is based on interviews with Liang and materials collected by the author. About Liang and FON, see also Economy 2004a: 145–9.
28 Liang Qichao escaped the pursuit of the Court; however, six of his cormorants were beheaded by the Qing Court.
29 The following is based on interviews with Xu and CBIK program officers, 2002 and 2004, and materials collected by the author.
30 After Xu resigned, there was a legal dispute about whether Xu had the authority to pass on the directorship without the approval of the board of executives of CBIK.
31 The following is based on an interview with Wan Yanhai, 2003, and materials collected by the author.
32 Wan Yanhai's article in *Chinese Journal of Health Education* (1992); I quote from "Awards for Action on HIV/AIDS and Human Rights" <www.aidslaw.ca> (accessed July 29 2003).

5 Corporatism vs civil society: NGOs in the economic realm

1 The trade unions (*gonghui*) do not register with MOCA as other SOs do, and they are mass organizations. See Chapter 3.
2 According to Unger and Chan, "In that [liberal corporatism] the leaders of the peak associations are beholden to their memberships, not the state, and the state is not directly in a position to dictate the terms of agreement between sectors... Under state corporatism, the government may even take charge of creating and maintaining all of the corporatist organizations and may grant itself the power to assign and remove their leaders at will. Often such 'representative organizations' serve a function of pre-empting the emergence of autonomous organizations. The watchword of state corporatism is top-down control" (1996: 97).
3 Interviews with Wenzhou Federation of Industry and Commerce (WFIC) and some women's NGOs, 1996, 2000, and 2001.
4 For example, the Shanghai Federation of Industrial Economy (SFIE) is a member of the China Federation of Industrial Economy. SFIE now has over 300 institutional members, among them 62 trade associations that cover 50 percent of Shanghai's industrial enterprises (over 80,000) (Chen and Xu 1999: 142).
5 Interview with an official in Shanghai Material Industrial Bureau who was also the head of Association of Shanghai Material Industry (ASMI), 2000.
6 For example, by the end of the 1990s, there were over 190 private grouping-companies in Wenzhou, and over sixty of them have capital assets exceeding 100 million RMB (Li, H. 2000: 367).

7 Interviews with ASMI, 2000, 2001.
8 Interviews with the secretary general of the SFIE, 2000, 2001.
9 The government allows NGOs, including trade associations, to run for-profit businesses as part of their revenue.
10 When I interviewed a trade association in Wenzhou, officials there were calculating how much this would cost them and how wrong it was that the government asked them to do things without funding.
11 Besides operating assistance, trade associations, like many other GONGOs, can apply for government funding for specific programs.
12 Interview with Wenzhou Garment Chamber of Commerce (WGCC), 2001.
13 There are two reports on this issue, <http://www.chinanewsnet.com> (accessed April 2003).
14 Currently there are three statuses:

1 Some associations continue receiving both official funding and employment quotas (SO staffs hired under the quota receive salaries and other benefits relatively equal to civil servants, and they can be hired back into governmental organizations) and they are the most closely supervised and usually have certain administrative functions.
2 The majority of top-down associations are moving toward financial independence. Nevertheless, their incomes are not steady and sufficient, and they continue to seek government support.
3 The number of organizations that receive neither governmental funding nor employment quotas is increasing.

15 To ensure that capable people transfer from official bureaus to trade associations, the government has compensated them with certain benefits. For example, in the Ministry of Machines, men above 58 and women above 53 enjoy the same benefits after they transfer to trade associations. Younger workers receive 20,000 RMB from the government for two years, and after that trade associations take responsibility for them. Interview with an official who was in charge of SOs in the Ministry of Machine Industry, 1996.
16 Interviews with SFIE secretary general, 2000, 2001. In Shanghai, the salary for one staff member, plus four insurances (health, pension, unemployment, and maternity), is around 30,000 RMB per year. Also, interviews with WGCC, 2001.
17 Interviews with officials in the Beijing Federation of Industry and Commerce (BFIC), 1996, and with WFIC, 2001.
18 Interviews with BFIC, 1996.
19 This law stipulates in very general terms that companies and individuals are entitled to taxation preferences according to respective administrative regulations.
20 From 1994 to 1999, the Worthy Cause projects did not receive any tax benefits, and after that the tax exemption varied, depending on local tax bureaus' policies.
21 As late as February 2002, a State Council document indicated that all employees of the people's organizations and the FIC were entitled to a health insurance policy similar to civil servants' (*People's Daily*, 28 February 2002).
22 Interviews with officials in the CCA in 1996, 2000 and 2001, and the collections of CCA's publications.
23 Interview with an official at the CSELA, 2004.
24 Interviews with officials in WFIC, 2001.
25 At the national level, the CSELA does not have its own members, and the National Bureau of Industry and Commerce gives CSELA 70 percent of the fees it gets from its local bureaus (CSELA 1994: 86).
26 Interview with a CSELA official, 1996.
27 Interview with a CSELA official, 2004.

216 *Notes*

28 Interviews with the head of the CGCPA, 1996, 2001; also, CGCPA's documents.
29 Interview with the head of CGCPA, 1996.
30 Interview with an official in the Ministry of Machine Industry, 1996.
31 Ibid.
32 No consistent statistics on these categories are available to the public.
33 Interview with Ma Jinlong, the head of the Office of Economic Policy, Wenzhou Municipal Government, 2001.
34 For a comparison of the governance of NGOs today with chambers of commerce in the late Qing and early Republic, see Ma 2004: 26–33; for the patriarch's role, see Yu and Xiao 2004.
35 The following is based on interviews with the president and the secretary general of WGCC, 2001, and on materials collected from WGCC.
36 Interview with the director of the division of social organizations, Wenzhou BOCA, 2001.
37 Others were mostly collective ownership or family businesses. Interview with the director of the Research Division, WFIC, 2001.
38 Interview with Ma Jinlong, 2001.
39 At the outset of the private chambers of commerce, there were serious debates in Wenzhou government on whether the government should recognize these organizations legally. See Qu *et al.* 2003: 84.
40 The following paragraphs are based on materials I collected and interviews with WFIC and WCCs, 2001.
41 Interview with the secretary general of WGCC, 2001.
42 Interviews with the heads of Wenzhou Fashion Industry Chamber of Commerce and Glasses Industry Chamber of Commerce, 2001. These are the most well-known associations of their kind.
43 Interviews with officials in WFIC and several chambers of commerce, 2001.
44 The WFIC's ultimate power belongs to the CCP send-out group (*dangzu*), and all WFIC staffs are on the government payroll. Interviews with officials in WFIC, 2001.
45 There were debates among national and provincial officials about Wenzhou's economic policy during the late 1980s and early 1990s. Interview with Ma Jinlong, 2001.
46 Ibid.

6 "It takes two to tangle": international NGOs in China and their impacts

1 This study recognizes the differences between NGOs based on a single country doing works abroad vs NGOs organized internationally or regionally. It uses the term "international NGOs" to refer to all types of foreign organizations that operate in China, and provides indication of their differences when needed.
2 Interview with a CANGO program officer, 2004. Since 2002, the CANGO has made some substantial efforts to increase financial independence, including obtaining its own bank account and paying for its offices and staff salaries.
3 This conclusion is based on information in Huang 2000: 105–42.
4 Interviews with several INGOs in Kunming, 2002 and 2004. For example, the head of YPINS, who is also the director of Yunnan BOCA, refused my request to interview him when he learned that I came from America, 2004.
5 Interview with Du Xiaoshan, a researcher at the Institution of Sociology in the China Academy of Social Science, 2004. Du was involved in the micro-credit projects for years.
6 Interviews with two renowned Chinese NGO leaders, 2003, 2004.
7 Interviews with Save the Children UK, Salvation Army, and Hong Kong Oxfam in Kunming, 2002, 2004.

Notes 217

8 The final revision of the "Regulations on the Management of the Foundations" in 2004 requires all foreign foundations in China to be formally registered with the civil affairs bureaus (CSC 2004). The vice-director of the BMNGOs confirmed that the revision of the regulations of SOs would include requirements similar to those for all foreign NGOs. Interview, 2004.
9 This was particularly true in the earlier period. Later on, some of these organizations were able to open offices in Beijing or other cities on the mainland.
10 According to Nancy Yuan, vice-president of the Asia Foundation's Washington office, as of 2000, there were 700 grant-making foundations, 70 advocacy groups, 200 humanitarian organizations and 150 faith-based charitable organizations, all foreign, operating in China. Yuan 2003: 40.
11 This was particularly true in the 1980s and early 1990s. For example, Oxfam, Salvation Army, and Save the Children Fund UK all operated in Hong Kong first and opened offices in Yunnan later.
12 Few Chinese scholars specialized in NGO study in the 1990s. Some of those scholars eventually organized their own research or social service organizations. Interviews with NGO scholars in China, 1996–2004.
13 Such examples can be found in He 2000.
14 Unpublished Chinese materials on the fourth WCW, collected by the author.
15 Ibid.
16 Interviews of cadres in the ACWF and Beijing WF, 1996.
17 For example, a comparative survey on five Asian countries' NGO governance is organized by Australian scholars Mark Lyons and Samiul Hasan, among others. The International Center for Not-for-Profit Law in New York has provided advice and information to MOCA on international NGO laws.
18 Interviews with NGO scholars and activists Yang Tuan, Wang Ming, Zhao Liqing, Ding Yuanzhu and Shang Yusheng, among others.
19 For example, Salamon visited China twice to discuss with Chinese scholars the possibility of China joining the Johns Hopkins Comparative Non-profit Sector Project. Nothing resulted from this attempt since the Chinese scholars found it difficult to fit the Chinese non-profit sector into the framework of the Johns Hopkins' inquiry.
20 Interviews with Yang Tuan in 1996 and 2000.
21 For more examples, see <www.npo.com.cn>, <www.chinabrief.org>, <www.pact.org>, <www.audy.org.cn>, <www.wwfchina.org>.
22 The information in the following paragraphs is from <www.wwfchina.org>.
23 The following is based on interviews with the director of the NPO Network, 2001, 2004, and information from <www.npo.com.cn>.
24 Interviews with Yang Tuan, an initiator of the network, in 1999.
25 I obtained the list of these organizations from the NPO Network, 2004.
26 Pact's mission statement, <www.pact.org>.
27 The following is based on interviews with Saich, 1996 and 2003.
28 Ibid.
29 The Ford Foundation's summary on its work in China, <www.fordfound.org>.
30 Ibid.
31 Interview with Saich, 2003.
32 I interviewed five Chinese NGOs that received such grants, 2004.
33 <www.fordfound.org>.
34 <www.chinadevelopmentbrief.org>.
35 This information is provided by the China Medical Board of New York, 1996.
36 Interview with Saich, 2003.
37 I was told about this speech in a 1996 interview with an official.
38 A conversation with Karla Simon, the director of the International Center for Not-for-profit Law, who was involved in the preparation of the workshop, 1996.

218 *Notes*

39 According to the official regulations, only the funds for sponsoring training of Chinese clergy abroad are acceptable, and the funds must be managed by China's national religious organizations (MOCA 2000a).
40 Interviews with NGO activists, 2003.
41 Interview with a program officer of the Ford Foundation's Beijing office, 2001.
42 Interview with the founder of that organization, 2003.
43 Interview with Tami Blumenfield who worked for Lijiang Research Association of Minority Cultures and Gender, 2003.
44 Interview with Zhao Liqing, 1999.
45 Interview with a Chinese NGO leader, 2003.
46 Ibid.
47 Interviews with Chinese NGO staff members and American students who worked for Chinese NGOs, 2001–03.

Bibliography

Ackinan, D. (2002) "Religious freedom in China," Statement at a Roundtable before the Congressional-Executive Commission on China, March 25, Washington DC: US Government Printing Office.
Alford, W. P. and Shen, Y. (1998) "The limits of the law in addressing China's environmental dilemma," in M. B. McElroy, C. P. Nielsen, and P. Lydon (eds) *Energizing China: Reconciling Environmental Protection and Economic Growth*, Cambridge, MA: Harvard University Committee on Environment.
All-China Federation of Industry and Commerce (ACFIC) (1996) Pamphlet.
All-China Women's Federation (ACWF) (1991) 中华全国妇女联合会四十年 (Forty Years of the ACWF), Beijing: China Women Press.
Anheier, H. K. (2001) "Introduction," in H. K Anheier (ed.) *Organisational Theory and the Non-profit Form: Proceedings of a Seminar Series at the LSE Centre for Civil Society*, London: Centre for Civil Society, London School of Economics and Political Science.
Anheier, H. K., Glasius, M. and Kaldor, M. (eds) (2001) *Global Civil Society 2001*, New York: Oxford University Press.
Baker, G. (1998) "Civil society and democracy: the gap between theory and possibility," *Politics*, 18(2): 81–7.
Baum, R. and Shevchenko, A. (1999) "The 'state of the state'," in M. Goldman and R. MacFarquhar (eds) *The Paradox of China's Post-Mao Reforms*, Cambridge, MA: Harvard University Press.
Becker, J. and Howden, D. (2004) "The secret dam: China begins huge project in World Heritage Site, displacing up to 100,000 people and devastating unique tribal societies," October 16. A report I received from Yunnan NGO Forum.
Bell, D. (1976) *The Cultural Contradictions of Capitalism*, New York: Basic Books.
Blecher, M. (2000) "The Dengist period: the triumphs and crises of structural reform, 1979 to the present," in C. Hudson (ed.) *The China Handbook, Prospects onto the 21st Century*, Chicago, IL: Glenlake Publishing Company.
Bobbio, N. (1993) "Gramsci and the concept of civil society," in J. Keane (ed.) *Civil Society and the State: New European Perspectives*, New York: Verso.
Boisture, R. A. (1998) "Options for increasing US support for Chinese nonprofit organizations," *International Journal of Not-for-Profit Law*, 1(2), <http://www.icnl.org>.
Bourdieu, P. (1997) "The forms of capital," in A. H. Halsey (ed.) *Education: Culture, Economy, and Society*, New York: Oxford University Press.

Bibliography

Bourdieu, P. and Wacquant, L. J. D. (1992) *An Invitation to Reflexive Sociology*, Chicago, IL: University of Chicago Press.

Brook, T. (1992) *Quelling The People: The Military Suppression of the Beijing Democracy Movement*, New York: Oxford University Press.

Brook, T. and Frolic, M. B. (eds) (1997) *Civil Society in China*, New York: M. E. Sharpe.

Canadian HIV/Aids Legal Network (CHALN) (2002) "Awards for action on HIV/AIDS," <www.aidslaw.ca> (accessed July 29, 2003).

Cai Lingping (2003) "没有标准的答案" (Answers without standard), *China Development Brief*, 14: 21–2.

Cao Haidong (2004) 怒江大坝搁置后的民间力量 (The nongovernmental force behind shelving the Nujiang Dam), <http://www.yhfh.com> (accessed May 26, 2003).

Cao Haidong and Zhang Peng (2004) "温州商会的惊人力量揭秘" (Discover the striking force of Wenzhou chambers of commerce), *Economy*, 9, <http://www.jlqyw.com/news>.

Central Organizational Structural Committee of CCP (COSC) (1996) 十九个社团组织机构 (The administration of 19 social organizations), Beijing: Huaxia Press.

Chen Baoliang (1996) 中国的社与会 (*China's Organizations and Associations*), Hangzhou: Zhejiang People's Publishing House.

Chen Jiaming (1993) "黑格尔的市民社会及其与国家的关系" (Hegel's civil society and its relationship with the state), *Chinese Social Science Quarterly*, 3: 23–7.

Chen Jingpan (1979) 中国近代教育史 (*A History of Education in Contemporary China*), Beijing: People's Publishing House.

Chen Jinluo (1997) 社团立法和社团管理 (*Legislation and Governance of Social Organizations*), Beijing: Law Publishing House.

Chen Jinwei (2003) "改革和完善社会团体管理体制" (Reforming and improving regulatory system of social organizations), in Xie Lingli (ed.) *NGOs in China*, Shanghai: Shanghai Academy of Social Science Press.

Chen Jixia (1993) "积极发展首都民办高等教育" (Actively promoting the non-governmental higher education, *Beijing Adult Education Journal*, 1: 19–20.

Chen Junxian and Zhou Zengxing (2002a) 温州探秘 (*Understanding Wenzhou*), Beijing: People's Daily Publishing House. <http://peopledaily.com.cn> (accessed November 15, 2003).

—— (2002b) 话说温州 (*Talking of Wenzhou*), <http://www.peopledaily.com.cn> (accessed November 15, 2003).

Chen Mingqian (2002) "试论温州民营经济发展动因与特点" (On reasons and features of Wenzhou Private Economy), *Zhejiang Research*, 3 (from Internet, no page numbers).

Chen Xian and Xu Zhongzhen (1999) 体制转型与行业协会 (*The Transformation of the System and the Industrial Associations*), Shanghai: Shanghai University Press.

Chen Xiaoya (2002) "关于万延海爱知行动" (About Wan Yanhai's AiZhi Action), <http://chinatown.coolfreepage.com> (accessed July 29, 2003).

Chen Yanqing (ed.) (1998) 当代中国社会转型论 (*On China's Current Social Transformation*), Taiyuan: Shanxi Education Publishing House.

Cheng Xinying (2000) 转型时期的当代中国社会发展 (*China's Social Development in the Transitional Period*), Beijing: Contemporary China Publishing House.

China Development Brief (CDB) (2002) *Directory of International NGOs in China*, Beijing: China Development Brief.

China Development Brief (CDB) (English edition, 中国发展简报, Chinese edition).

—— (1999a) "NGOs are 'an inevitable trend of the times'," 2(3): 21.
—— (1999b) "New law promises tax breaks but ducks some key issues," 2(3): 24.
—— (2003) 中国儿童少年基金会2002筹款突破2亿 (the China Teenagers and Children Foundation raised 200 million RMB in 2002).
China Environmental Protection Foundation (CEPF) (1998) "Environmental NGOs in China," an unpublished report, author's collection.
China Grouping Companies Promotion Association (CGCPA) (2001) "工作报告" (Work reports), author's collection.
China Industrial Economic Associations Study (CIEAS) (1998) "中国工业行业协会现状及改革趋势" (The current state and reform trend of China's industrial trade associations), an unpublished research report, author's collection.
China Ministry of Labors (CML) (1999) 中国劳动统计年鉴 (*China Labor Statistics*), Beijing: Statistics Publishing House.
China Self-Employed Laborers' Association (CSELA) (1994) 个体经济与个体劳动者协会 (*Self-Employed Economy and Self-employed Laborers' Association*), Tianjin: Tianjin People's Publishing House.
China Youth Development Foundation (CYDF) (2000) 年报 (*Annual report*).
—— (2004) "国务院新闻发布", *CYDF Newsletter*, April 7.
Chinese Communist Party Document (CCPD) (1998) "关于党政机关领导干部不兼任社会团体领导职务的通知" (An official notice on the CCP and governmental cadres cannot concurrently head the social organizations), in CLRSW (2003) *Collection of Laws and Regulations on Social Welfare*, Beijing: Business and Civil Society.
Chinese State Council (CSC) (1950) 社会团体登记暂行办法 (*Tentative Measures on Registration of Social Organizations*), September 29, author's collection.
—— (1988) "基金会管理办法" (Regulations for foundations), issued September 27, in CLRSW (2003) *Collection of Laws and Regulations on Social Welfare*, Beijing: Business and Civil Society.
—— (1989) "社会团体登记管理条例" (The regulations for registration and management of social organizations), in Chen Jinluo (1997) *Legislation and Governance of Social Organizations*, Beijing: Laws Publishing House.
—— (1998a) "社会团体登记管理条例" (The regulations for registration and management of social organizations), *People's Daily*, October 26: 3.
—— (1998b) "民办非企业单位登记管理暂行条例" (The temporary regulations for registration and management for non-governmental and non-commercial enterprises), *People's Daily*, October 26: 3.
—— (2004) "基金会管理办法" (Regulations of foundations), *People's Daily*, March 18.
CLRSW (2003) *Collection of Laws and Regulations on Social Welfare*, Beijing: Business & Civil Society. (No editor information)
Cohen, J. L. and Arato, A. (1994) *Civil Society and Political Theory*, Cambridge, MA: MIT Press.
Coleman, J. S. (1990) *Foundation of Social Theory*, Cambridge, MA: Harvard University Press.
Dai Qing, Thebodeau, J. G. and Williams, P. (eds) (1998) *The River Dragon Has Come: the Three Gorges Dam and the Fate of China's Yangzi River and its People*, Armonk: M.E. Sharpe.
Deng Xiaoping (1993) 邓小平文选 (*Selected Works of Deng Xiaoping*), Volume 3, Beijing: People's Publishing House.

222 Bibliography

Deng Zhenglai (1994) "中国发展研究的检视：兼论中国市民社会研究" (Examining China development studies: also discussing China's civil society researches), *Modernity and Tradition*, 4: 21–27.

—— (1997) 国家与社会：中国市民社会研究 (*The State and Society: A Study of Chinese Civil Society*), Sichuan: Sichuan People's Publishing House.

Deng Zhenglai and Jing Yuejin (1992) "建构中国的市民社会" (Building a Chinese civil society), *Chinese Social Science Quarterly*, 1: 1–22.

Department of Comprehensive Statistics of National Bureau of Statistics (DCSNBS) (1999) 新中国五十年统计资料汇编 (*Comprehensive Statistical Data and Materials on 50 Years of New China*), Beijing: China Statistics Press.

Dickson, B. J. (2003) *Red Capitalists in China: The Party, Entrepreneurs and Prospects for Political Change*, Cambridge, MA: Cambridge University Press.

Ding, Yijiang (2000) "The conceptual evolution of democracy in intellectual circles' rethinking of state and society," in S. Zhao (ed.) *China and Democracy: Reconsidering the Prospects for a Democratic China*, London: Routledge.

Ding, Yuanzhu (2004) "Volunteering and the third sector in China," in Hasan and Lyons (eds) *Social Capital in Asian Sustainable Development Management: Examples and Lessons*, New York: Nova Science Publishers.

Dittmer, L. and Lü, X. (2000) "Organizational involution and sociopolitical reform in China: an analysis of the work unit," in L. Dittmer, H. Fukui and P. N. S. Lee (eds) *Informal Politics in East Asia*, New York: Cambridge Press.

Division of the Business Policy in the State Economy and Trade Committee (DBP) (1999), 中国行业协会改革与探索 (*China's Trade Associations: Reforms and Exploration*), Beijing: China's Business Publishing House.

Division of Law of the State Council and the Bureau of Nongovernmental Organizations of MOCA (DLSC) (1999) 社会团体登记管理条例，民办非企业单位登记管理暂行条例释义 (*The Explanation of Regulations for Registration and Management of Social Organizations and the Temporary Regulations for Registration and Management of Non-governmental and Non-commercial Enterprises*), Beijing: China Social Publishing House.

Division for Non-bank Financial Institutions of China People's Bank (DNFI) (1996) 中国全国基金会指南 (*A Guide to National Foundations in China*), Beijing: The Central Broadcast and Television University Press.

Du Fangqin (2000) "命运与使命：高校妇女研究中心的历程和前景" (Fate and mission: experience and future of women study centers in universities), *Zhejiang Research Journal*, 3: 90–4.

Duo Wei News (DWN 多维新闻) (2003) "中国民间组织在夹缝中生存" (Chinese NGOs exist in a narrow space), <www.chinanewsnet.com> (accessed January 15, 2003).

Economy, E. C. (2004a) *River Runs Black*, Ithaca, NY: Cornell University Press.

—— (2004b) "The politics and economics of China's environmental challenge." A speech at the workshop "Environment, Culture, and Development in East Asia," Ohio Wesleyan University, October 14–16.

Economy, E. C. and Schreurs, M. A. (1997) "Domestic and international linkages in environmental politics," in Schreurs and Economy (eds) *The Internationalization of Environmental Protection*, New York: Cambridge University Press.

EDF (1995) "China's first environmental leader talks to EDF," *EDF Letter*, March.

Edwards, M., Hulme, D. and Wallace, T. (1999) "NGOs in a global future: marrying local delivery to worldwide leverage," *Public Administration and Development*, 19: 117–36.

Elliott, L. (1998) *The Global Politics of the Environment*, New York: New York University Press.
Engels, F. (1973a) "On the history of the Communist League," in K. Marx and F. Engels, *Selected Works*, Volume 3, Moscow.
—— (1973b) "Ludwig Feuerbach and the end of classical German philosophy," in K. Marx and F. Engels, *Selected Works*, Volume 3, Moscow.
Fan Baojun (ed.) (1995) 中国社会团体大辞典 (*The Encyclopedia of Chinese Social Organizations*), Beijing: Jingguan Education Publishing House.
Fang Zhaohui (1993) "市民社会与资本主义国家的合法性：论哈波马斯的合法性学说" (Civil society and the legitimacy of capitalist countries – on Habermas's legitimacy theory), *Chinese Social Science Quarterly*, 3: 34–41.
—— (1994) "市民社会的两个传统及其在现代的汇合" (The two traditions of civil society and their convergence in modern times), *Chinese Social Science*, 5: 82–102.
Feinerman, J. (February 7, 2002) A statement at roundtable "Hearing on Human Rights in the Context of the Rule of Law" before the Congressional-Executive Commission on China, Washington, DC: US Government Printing Office.
Fewsmith, J. (2000) "Formal stricture, informal politics, and political change in China," in L. Dittmer, H. Fukui, and P. N. S. Lee (eds) *Informal Politics in East Asia*, New York: Cambridge Press.
—— (2001) *China Since Tiananmen: The Political Transition*, Cambridge, MA: Cambridge University Press.
—— (2004) "What type of party is this, anyway?" A speech at the symposium "Understanding the New China," Case Western Reserve University, Cleveland, November 13.
Fiedler, K. (2002) "NGOs and the Challenge of Globalization." A paper presented at "NGOs and Social Transformation under Globalization," an international conference at Shanghai Fudan University, Shanghai, September.
Fisher, J. (1998) *Non Governments: NGOs and the Political Development of the Third World*, West Hartford: Kumarian Press.
Foley, M. W. and Edwards, R. (1996) "The paradox of civil society," *Journal of Democracy*, 7(3): 38–52.
Ford Foundation (FF 1979–2003), *Annual Reports*, New York: Ford Foundation.
Forges, R. V. D. (1997) "States, societies, civil societies in Chinese history," in T. Brook and B. M. Frolic (eds) *Civil Society in China*, New York: M. E. Sharpe.
Friend of Nature (FON, 1999–2002) 自然之友通讯 (FON Newsletters), Beijing: Chinese Cultural Association.
Frolic, M. B. (1997) "State-led civil society," in T. Brook and M. B. Frolic (eds) *Civil Society in China*, New York: M. E. Sharpe.
Gan Yang (1998) "'民间社会' 概念批判" (A critique of the concept of "minjian society"), in Zhang Jing, 国家与社会 (*The State and Society*), Zhejiang: Zhejiang People's Publishing House.
Gao Bingzhong (1999) 居住在文化空间里 (*Living in a Cultural Space*), Guangzhou: Zhongshan University Press.
—— (2000) "社会团体的兴起及合法性问题" (The legitimation of social organizations), *Chinese Social Science*, 2: 100–9.
Ge Yunsong (2003) "非营利组织发展的法律环境" (The legal environment of the development of NPOs), in Xie Lingli (ed.) *NGOs in China*, Shanghai: Shanghai Academy of Social Science Press.
Gold, T. B. (1990a) "Tiananmen and beyond: the resurgence of civil society in China," *Journal of Democracy*, 1: 18–31.

—— (1990b) "Autonomy versus authoritarianism," in George Hicks (ed.) *The Broken Mirror: China after Tiananmen*, Hong Kong: Oxford University Press.

Goldman, M. and MacFarquhar, R. (eds) (1999) *The Paradox of China's Post-Mao Reforms*, Cambridge, MA: Harvard University Press.

Goldman, M. and Nathan, A. J. (2000) "Searching for the appropriate model for the People's Republic of China," in M. Goldman and A. Gordon (eds) *Historical Perspectives on Contemporary East Asia*, Cambridge, MA: Harvard University Press.

Goldman, M. and Perry, E. J. (eds) (2002) *Changing Meaning of Citizenship in Modern China*, Cambridge, MA: Harvard University Press.

Goodman, B. (1995) *Native Place, City, and Nation: Regional Networks and Identities in Shanghai, 1853–1927*, Berkeley, CA: University of California.

Guan Shixiong (1989) "深化教育体制改革，鼓励与支持全民办学" (Further education reform and support education by society), in Beijing Bureau of Adult Education (ed.) 北京社会力量办学概况 (*The State of Non-public Education in Beijing*), Beijing: Education and Science Publishing House.

Habermas, J. (1973) "What does a crisis mean today? Legitimation problems in late capitalism," *Social Research*, 40: 643–67.

Habermas, J. (1989) *The Structural Transformation of the Public Sphere: An Inquiry into a Category of Bourgeois Society*, Cambridge, MA: MIT Press.

Hall, J. A. (1995) "In search of civil society," in J. A. Hall (ed.) *Civil Society: Theory, History, Comparison*, Cambridge: Polity Press.

Hall, P. D. (1992) *Inventing the Nonprofit Sector and Other Essays on Philanthropy, Voluntarism, and Nonprofit Organizations*, Baltimore, MD: Johns Hopkins University Press.

Hao, Y. (1992) "Environmental protection and Chinese foreign policy," in T. W. Robinson (ed.) *The Foreign Relations of China's Environmental Policy*, Washington, DC: American Enterprise Institute.

Harding, H. (1997) "Reflections on China today," *Focus on China*, Asian Perspectives Series, Washington, DC: Asia Foundation.

Hasan, S. and Lyons, M. (eds) (2004) *Social Capital in Asian Sustainable Development Management: Examples and Lessons*, New York: Nova Science Publishers.

He, B. (1995) "The idea of civil society in mainland China and Taiwan, 1986–1992", *Issues and Studies*, 31(6): 24–64.

—— (1997) *The Democratic Implications of Civil Society in China*, New York: St. Martin's Press.

He Liping (2002) "让渡空间与拓展空间：政府职能转变中的半官方社团研究" (Withdrawing from and expanding space: a study on quasi-NGOs during the transformation of governmental function), a Ph.D. dissertation, Peking University.

He Qinglian (1997) 中国的陷阱 (*The Primary Capital Accumulation in Contemporary China*), New York: Mirror Books.

He Yimin (1992) 转型时期的社会新团体：近代知识分子与晚清四川社会研究 (*New Social Groups in the Transitional Period: A Study on Modern Intellectuals and Late Qing Sichuan Society*), Chengdu: Sichuan University Press.

He Zengke (1993) "市民社会与文化领导权：葛兰西的理论" (Civil society and the cultural leadership – Gramsci's theory), *Chinese Social Science Quarterly*, 3: 28–33.

—— (1994a) "关于市民社会概念问题的几点思考" (Several points on the concept of civil society), *Modernity and Tradition*, 4: 41–8.

—— (1994b) "市民社会概念的历史演变" (Historical evolution of the concept of civil society), *Chinese Social Science*, 5: 67–80.

—— (ed.) (2000) 公民社会与第三部门 (*Civil Society and the Third Sector*), Beijing: Social Science Documents Publishing House.
Hefner, R. W. (1998) "Civil society: cultural possibility of a modern ideal," *Society*, 35(3): 16–27.
Ho, P. (2001) "Greening without conflict? Environmentalism, NGOs and civil society in China," *Development and Change*, 32(5): 916.
Howell, J. (1996) "Striking a new balance: new social organizations in post-Mao China," *Capital & Class*, 54: 89–111.
—— (1998) "Trade unions in China: the challenge of foreign capital," in G. O'Leary (ed.) *Adjusting to Capitalism: Chinese Workers and the State*, New York: M. E. Sharpe.
—— (2000) "Shifting relationships and competing discourses in post-Mao China: the All-China Women's Federation and the People's Republic," in S. Jacobs, R. Jacobson and J. Marchbank (eds) *States of Conflicts: Gender, Violence and Resistance*, New York: Zed Books.
Howell, J. and Pearce, J. (2001) *Civil Society and Development: A Critical Exploration*, Boulder, CO: Lynne Rienner Publishers.
Hsia, R. Y. and White, L. T. III (2002) "Working amid corporatism and confusion: foreign NGOs in China," *Nonprofit and Voluntary Sector Quarterly*, 31(3): 329–51.
Hu Angang (ed.) (2002) 中国战略构想 (*Strategy of China*), Hangzhou: Zhejiang People's Publishing House.
Huang Haoming (ed.) (2000) 国际民间组织：合作事务与管理 (*International NGOs: Cooperation and Governance*), Beijing: Foreign Economy and Trade University Press.
Huang, P. C. C. (1993) "'Public sphere'/'Civil society' in China? The third realm between state and society," *Modern China*, 19(2): 216–38.
Human Rights Watch (HRW) (2002) "Detention of Dr. Wan Yanhai," <http:www.hrw.org> (accessed September 11, 2003).
Hyden, G. (1997) "Civil society, social capital, and development: dissection of a complex discourse," *Studies in Comparative International Development*, 32(1): 3–30.
Iriye, A. (1999) "A century of NGOs," in M. J. Hogan (ed.) *The Ambiguous Legacy: US Foreign Relations in the "American Century"*, Boston, MA: Cambridge University Press.
Israel, J. (1971) *Progressivism and the Open Door: America and China, 1905–1921*, Pittsburgh, PA: University of Pittsburgh Press.
Jiang Beni (2002) "中国农村的民间社会" (Folk society in rural China), *China Development Brief* (Chinese version), 13: 5–6.
Jiang Qing (1993) "儒家文化：建构中国式市民社会的深厚资源" (Confucianist culture: a rich resource for building a Chinese-style civil society), *Chinese Social Science Quarterly*, 2: 170–5.
Jing Yuejin (1993) "'市民社会与中国现代化' 学术讨论会述要" (A summary of the symposium "Civil Society and China's Modernization"), *Chinese Social Science Quarterly*, 4: 197–202.
—— (1994) "市民社会研究及其意义" (The study of civil society and its significance), *Modernity and Tradition*, 4: 20–33.
Johnston, A. I. (1998) "China and international environmental institutions: a decision rule analysis," in M. B. McElroy, C. P. Nielsen and P. Lydon (eds) *Energizing China: Reconciling Environmental Protection and Economic Growth*, Newton, MA: Harvard University Committee on Environment.

Kang Xiaoguang (1997a) 创造希望：中国青少年发展基金会研究 (*Create Hope: A Study of the China Youth Development Foundation*), Guangxi: Lijiang Publishing House.
—— (ed.) (1997b) 希望工程调查报告 (*An Investigation Report on the Hope Project*), Guangxi: Lijiang Publishing House.
—— (1999) 权力的转移：转型时期中国权力格局的变迁 (*Power Shifting: The Change of China's Power Structure During a Time of Transition*), Zhejiang: Zhejiang People's Publishing House.
—— (2000) "转型时期的中国社团" (Chinese social organizations in the time of transition), a conference paper, International Conference of the Development of the Non-profit Organizations and the China Project Hope, October, Beijing.
Keane, J. (1984) *Public Life and Late Capitalism: Toward a Socialist Theory of Democracy*, New York: Cambridge University Press.
—— (1993) "Despotism and democracy: the origins and development of the distinction between civil society and the state 1750–1850," in J. Keane (ed.) *Civil Society and the State: New European Perspectives*, New York: Verso.
Koll, E. (2003) *From Cotton Mill to Business Empire: The Emergence of Regional Enterprises in Modern China*, Cambridge, MA: Harvard University East Asian Press.
Kuhn, P. A. (1991) "Civil Society and Constitutional Development." A paper for the American–European Symposium on State vs Society in East Asian Traditions, Paris.
Lardy, N. R. (2002) *Integrating China into the Global Economy*, Washington, DC: Brookings Institution Press.
Law Documents (LD) (1992) 中华人民共和国工会法 (*The PRC's Union Law*), author's collection.
—— (LD) (1999) 中华人民共和国公益事业捐赠法 (*The People's Republic of China Law of Donations to Public Causes*), Beijing: Law Publishing House.
Lee, C. D. (2000) "Legal reform in China: a role for nongovernmental organizations," *The Yale Journal of International Law*, 25: 363–434.
Lieberthal, K. (1998) "China's governing system and its impact on the environmental policy implementation," in A. Frank (ed.) *China Environmental Series*, Washington, DC: Woodrow Wilson Center.
Li Fan (1998) 静悄悄的革命：中国当代市民社会 (*A Silent Revolution: Becoming Civil Society in China*), Hong Kong: Mirror Publishing House.
Li Haoran (2000), 现代化与温州的发展 (*Modernization and the Development of Wenzhou*), Wenzhou: Science Publishing House.
Li Xiaoji (2000) "引入市场机制" (Bring in market mechanisms), *People's Daily*, April 13: 10.
Li Xiaojiang (ed.) (2000) 身临 "奇境" (*Being in a "Wonderland"*), Nanjing: Jiangsu People's Publishing House.
Liang Congjie and Liang Xiaoyan (eds) (2000) 为无告的大自然 (*For the Voiceless Great Nature*), Tianjin: Baihua Press.
Liang, S. (2003) "Seeds of change," *China Rights Forum*, no. 3. <www.hrf.org>.
Liang Shuming (1949) "中国文化要义" (The essence of Chinese culture), in Cao Jinqing (ed.) (1994) 梁漱溟文选 (*Selected Works of Liang Shuming*), Shanghai: Yuandong Publishing House.
Liang Zhiping (2000) "法治：社会转型时期的制度建构" (Rule of law: the system establishment in the period of social transformation), *Contemporary China Studies*, 2: 18–67.

—— (2001) "'民间', '民间社会', and Civil Society – Civil Society 概念再探讨" ("Social space", "Non-governmental society", and civil society – a re-examination of the civil society concept), *Contemporary China Studies*, 72(1): 63–89.
Liao Hong (2000) "1999年民政事业发展报告" (The report on the development of civil affairs in 1999), in Zhengxin Shi (ed.) 中国社会福利与社会进步报告2000 (*The Report on China's Social Welfare and Social Progress, 2000*), Beijing: Social Science Documents Publishing House.
Liao Xiaoyi (2004) A speech at the Third Green China Forum, <http://www.gvbchina.org> (accessed April 8, 2004).
Lieberthal, K. (1998) "China's governing system and its impact on the environmental policy implementation," in A. Frank (ed.) *China Environmental Series*, Washington DC: Woodrow Wilson Center, available online, <http://wwics.si.edu/index.cfm>.
Lin Cha (ed.) (1998) 后改革中国：交锋后的交锋 (*Post-reform China: Confrontations After the Confrontation*), Beijing: Red Flag Publishing House.
Lin Han (2001) "为重视生态建设呐喊引导" (Advocating and guiding eco-construction), *News Front*, 1.
Lin, N. (2001) *Social Capital: A Theory of Social Structure and Action*, New York: Cambridge University Press.
Liu, A. P. L. (1996) *Mass Politics in the People's Republic: State and Society in Contemporary China*, Boulder, CO: Westview Press.
Liu Bohong (2000) "中国妇女非政府组织的发展" (The development of women NGOs in China), *Zhejiang Research Journal*, 4: 109–14.
Liu Guogung, Wang Luolin and Li Jingwen (1996) 1996年中国经济形势分析与预测 (*China's Economic Situation in 1996: Analysis and Prediction*), Beijing: China Social Science Press.
Liu Ningyuan, Ma Chentong and Chen Jing (eds) (1994) 北京的社团 (*Social Organizations in Beijing*), Beijing: Zhishi Publishing House.
Liu Rongcang (1999) 中国：走向二十一世纪的公共政策选择 (*China: Choice of Public Policy Towards the 21st Century*), Beijing: Social Science Documents Publishing House, Volumes I and II.
Liu Zhiguang and Wang Suli (1988) "从'群众社会'走向'公民社会'" (From "mass society" moving towards "civil society"), *Political Research*, 5: 9–12.
Lü Dong (1999) "贯彻'纲要'，把协会工作推上一个新台阶" (Carry on the "guideline," promoting the associational work to a new height), in the Division of Business Policy in the State Committee of Economy and Trade (ed.) 中国行业协会改革与探索 (*China's Trade Associations: Reforms and Exploration*), Beijing: China's Business Publishing House.
Lu Feng (1989) "单位：一种特殊的社会组织形式" (The work units: a special social form), *Chinese Social Science*, 1: 71–88.
Lu Pinyue (1994) "中国历史进程与市民社会之建构" (China's historical progress and the building of civil society), *Chinese Social Science Quarterly*, 8: 173–8.
Lü, X. and Perry, E. J. (eds) (1997) *Danwei: The Changing Chinese Workplace in Historical and Comparative Perspective*, New York: M. E. Sharpe.
Lyons, M. (2001) *Third Sector: The Contribution of Nonprofit and Cooperative Enterprise in Australia*, Crows Nest: Allen & Unwin.
McCormick, J. (1989) *The Global Environment Movement*, London: Belhaven Press.
Ma Changshan (2001) "市民社会与政治国家：法治的基础和界限" (Civil society and political state: the foundation and boundary of rule of law), *The Science of Law Study*, 3: 19–41.

Ma Jinlong (1998) "温州模式的形成条件与创新过程" (The pre-conditions and creating process of the Wenzhou Model), *Wenzhou People*, 7: 24–8.

Ma Licheng and Ling Zhijun (1998) 交锋- 当代中国三次思想解放实录 (*Confrontation – Three Liberations of Mind in Contemporary China*), Beijing: Jinri Zhongguo Publishing House.

Ma Min (1995) 官商之间：社会巨变中的近代绅商 (*Between Officials and Merchants: Modern Gentry-merchants in Profound Social Transformation*), Tianjin: Tianjin People's Publishing House.

Ma Min and Zhu Ying (1993) 传统与近代的二重变奏 (*The Double Variation between Tradition and Modernity*), Chengdu, Sichuan: Bashu Publishing House.

Ma, Q. (1997) "Chinese non-governmental and non-profit organizations since the late 1970s," a Research Report, Washington, DC: The Aspen Institute Working Paper Series.

—— (1999) "The current status of nongovernmental organizations in China," in ISTR (ed.) *The Third International Conference of the International Society of the Third-Sector Research*, Washington, DC: The International Society of the Third-Sector Research.

—— (2002a) "The governance of NGOs in China since 1978: how much autonomy?" *Nonprofit and Voluntary Sector Quarterly*, 31(3): 305–28.

—— (2002b) "The Peking Union Medical College and the Rockefeller Foundation's medical programs in China," in W. H. Schneider (ed.) *Rockefeller Philanthropy and Modern Biomedicine: International Initiatives from World War I to the Cold War*, Bloomington, IN: Indiana University Press.

—— (2003) "Non-governmental and non-profit organizations and the evolution of Chinese civil society," a statement at a Roundtable before the Congressional-Executive Commission on China (March 24), in *To Serve the People: NGOs and the Development of Civil Society in China*, Washington, DC: US Government Printing Office.

—— (2004) "Classification, regulation, and managerial structure: a preliminary inquiry into the governance of Chinese NGOs," in Hasan and Lyons (eds) *Social Capital in Asian Sustainable Development Management: Examples and Lessons*, New York: Nova Science Publishers.

Ma Rong and Guo Jianru (2000) "中国居民在环保意识与环保态度方面的城乡差异" (Differences in awareness and attitude towards environmental protection among China's urban and rural populations), *Social Science Front*, 1: 201–10.

Ma, S. (1994) "The Chinese discourse on civil society," *The China Quarterly*, 137: 180–93.

Ma Xisha and Han Bingfang (1992) 中国民间宗教史 (*A History of China's Folk Religions*), Shanghai: Shanghai People's Publishing House.

Mao Zedong (1968) "论人民民主专政" (On people's democratic dictatorship), in 毛泽东选集 (*Selected Works of Mao Zedong*), Beijing: People's Publishing House.

Marshall, P. D. (2002) "Religious freedom in China," statement at a Roundtable before the Congressional-Executive Commission on China, March 25, Washington, DC: US Government Printing Office.

Marx, K. (1973) "The German ideology", in C. Marx and F. Engels, *Selected Works, Volume 1*, Moscow.

Mas, S. (1999) "The role of social organizations in China and their contribution to the emergence of a civil society," MA thesis, University of Bremen, ENRO.

Min Jie (1995) "戊戌学会考" (A verification of associations during the 1898 Reform Movement), *Modern History Research*, 3: 39–76.

Min Qi and Li Yingming (1995) 转型期的中国：社会变迁 (*China in Transition: Social Changes*), Taipei: Time Publishing House.

Ministry of Civil Affairs (MOCA) (2000a) "涉外社会调查活动管理暂行办法" (A temporary stipulation on the management of social investigations that involve foreign individuals or organizations), issued July 16, 1999, in the Department of Finance and Administration, MOCA, 中国民政统计年鉴 (*China Civil Affairs' Statistical Yearbook*), Beijing: China Statistics Press.

—— (MOCA) (2000b) 民间组织管理最新法规政策汇编 (The collection of the most recent regulations and policies on management of NGOs), Beijing: Bureau of NGOs of the Ministry of Civil Affairs.

Moore, T. G. (2002) *China in the World Market: Chinese Industry and International Sources of Reform in the Post-Mao Era*, New York: Cambridge University Press.

Nathan, A. J. (1997) *China's Transition*, New York: Columbia University Press.

National Bureau of Statistics (NBS) (1990, 1993, 1995, 1998a, 1999–2003) 中国民政统计年鉴 (*China's Civil Affairs Statistical Yearbook*), Beijing: China Statistics Publishing House.

—— (1998b) 98中国发展报告 (*China Development Report, 1998*), Beijing: China Statistics Publishing House.

Naughton, B. (1997) "*Danwei*: the economic foundations of a unique institution," in X. Lü and E. J. Perry (eds) *Danwei: The Changing Chinese Workplace in Historical and Comparative Perspective*, New York: M. E. Sharpe.

Nevitt, C. E. (1996) "Private business associations in China: evidence of civil society or local state power?," *The China Journal*, 36: 25–43.

Newsletter of Yunnan NGOs (NYNGOs) (2003) "对境外民间组织有效管理的设想和建议" (Plan and suggestion on effectively managing foreign NGOs), vol 34(7–8).

Newton, K. (1999) "Social capital and democracy in Modern Europe," in J. W. Deth, M. Maraffi, K. Newton and P. F. Whiteley (eds) *Social Capital and European Democracy*, New York: Routledge.

O'Brien, K. J. (2003) "Neither transgressive nor contained: boundary-spanning contention in China," *Mobilization*, 8(1): 51–3.

O'Brien, M. (1998) "Dissent and the emergence of civil society in post-totalitarian China," *Journal of Contemporary China*, 7(17): 153–66.

O'Neill, M. (1989) *The Third America: The Emergence of the Nonprofit Sector in the United States*, San Francisco, CA: Jossey-Bass.

Pan Ni (2002) "梁从诫：为无告的大自然流泪" (Liang Congjie: crying for the voiceless great nature), <http://www.greeweb.com.cn> (accessed June 5, 2003).

Pearson, M. M. (1994) "The Janus face of business associations in China: socialist corporatism in foreign enterprises," *Australian Journal of Chinese Affairs*, 30: 25–46.

Perrow, C. (2001) "The rise of non-profits and the decline of civil society," in H. K. Anheier, (ed.) *Organisational Theory and the Non-profit Form: Proceedings of A Seminar Series at the LSE Centre for Civil Society*, London: Centre for Civil Society, London School of Economics and Political Science.

Perry, E. J. (1994) "Trends in the study of Chinese politics: state–society relations," *China Quarterly*, 139.

Pomfret, J. (2003) "Environmentalists keep up fight over Chinese dam," *Washington Post Foreign Service*, June 22, A15.

Portes, A. and Mooney, M. (2002) "Social capital and community development," in M. F. Guillen, R. Collins, P. England and M. Meyer (eds) *The New Economic Sociology: Developments in an Emerging Field*, New York: Russell Sage Foundation.

Bibliography

Pu Xingzu (ed.) (1993) 当代中国行政 (*The Contemporary China's Administration*), Shanghai: Fudan University Press.

Putnam, R. D. (1993), with R. Leonardi and R. Y. Nanetti, *Making Democracy Work: Civic Traditions in Modern Italy*, Princeton, NJ: Princeton University Press.

—— (1995) "Bowling alone: America's declining social capital," *Journal of Democracy*, 6: 65–78.

Pye, L. W. (2001) "Civility, social capital, and civil society: three powerful concepts for explaining Asia," in R. I. Rotberg (ed.) *Patterns of Social Capital: Stability and Change in Historical Perspective*, Cambridge: Cambridge University Press.

Qu Hongxiang, Tong Long, and Wang Minglan (eds) (2003) 行业协会发展理论与实践 (*Theories and Practices of the Development of Trade Associations*), Beijing: Economic Science Publishing House.

Rankin, M. B. (1986) *Elite Activism and Political Transformation in China*, Stanford, CA: Stanford University Press.

—— (1990) "The origins of a Chinese public sphere: local elites and community affairs in the late Imperial period," *Etudes Chinoises* IX(2): 13–60.

—— (1993) "Some observations on a Chinese public sphere," *Modern China*, 19(2): 158–82.

—— (2000) "Social and political change in nineteenth-century China," in M. Goldman and A. Gordon (eds) *Historical Perspectives on Contemporary East Asia*, Cambridge, MA: Harvard University Press.

Ren Yuan and Chen Dan (1995) "城市社区就业发展的基本背景" (The background of increasing employment in the urban community), <http://social_policy.info>.

Resource Alliance (RA) (2003) *Report on NPO Governance and Fundraising Training, Beijing, 20–24 March 2003*, <www.resource-alliance.org>.

Risse-Kappen, T. (ed.) (1995) *Bringing Transnational Relations Back In: Non-State Actors, Domestic Structures and International Institutions*, Cambridge: Cambridge University Press.

Rockefeller Foundation (RF) (1914) "The Record of China Conference of the Rockefeller Foundation," January 19–20, North Tarrytown: Rockefeller Foundation Archive Center, RF Collection.

Rong Wenzuo (ed.) (1996) 从部门管理转向行业管理 (*From Departmental Management to Trade Management*), Beijing: Economic Science Publishing House.

Rowe, W. T. (1984) *Hankow: Commerce and Society in a Chinese city 1796–1889*, Stanford, CA: Stanford University Press.

—— (1989) *Hankow: Conflict and Community in a Chinese City, 1796–1895*, Stanford, CA: Stanford University Press.

Saich, T. (2000) "Negotiating the state: the development of social organizations in China," *The China Quarterly*, 161: 124–41.

—— (2001) *Governance and Politics of China*, New York: Palgrave.

—— (2003) "Closing China's welfare gap," *South China Post*, August 15.

Salamon, L. M. (2001a) "Scope and structure: the anatomy of America's nonprofit sector," in J. S. Ott (ed.) *The Nature of the Nonprofit Sector*, Boulder, CO: Westview Point Press.

—— (2001b) "Toward civil society: the global associational revolution and the new era in public problem-solving," in L. Zhao and C. L. Irving (eds) *The Non-Profit Sector and Development: Proceedings of the International Conference in Beijing in July 1999*, Hong Kong: Hong Kong Press for Social Sciences.

Salamon, L. M. and Anheier, H. K. (1992) "In search of the non-profit sector I: the question of definitions," *Voluntas*, 3(2): 125–51.
Salamon, L. M., Anheier, H. K., List, R., Toepler, S. and Sokolowski, S. W. (eds) (1999) *Global Civil Society: Dimensions of the Nonprofit Sector*, Baltimore, MD: The Johns Hopkins Center for Civil Society Studies.
Sang Bing (1995a) 清末新知识界的社团与活动 (*New Academic Social Organizations and their Activities During the Late Qing*), Beijing: Sanlian Publishing House.
—— (1995b) 晚清学堂学生与社会变迁 (*School Students During the Late Qing and the Social Changes*), Shanghai: Xuelin Publishing House.
Schmitter, P. C. (1974) "Still the century of corporatism?," in F. B. Pike and T. Stritch (eds) *The New Corporatism: Social–Political Structures in the Iberian World*, Notre Dame: University of Notre Dame Press.
Schmitter, P. C. and Grote, J. R. (1997) "The fate of corporatism: the past, present, and future," *Politische Vierteljahresschrift*, summer issue. This article was translated into Chinese by Zhang Jing in Jhang Jing (1998) 法团主义 (*Corporitism*), Beijing: China Social Science Publishing House.
Schreurs, M. A. and Economy, E. C. (eds) (1997) *The Internationalization of Environmental Protection*, Cambridge: Cambridge University Press.
Serrano, I. R. (1994) "Civil society in the Asia-Pacific region," in M. D. D. Oliveira and R. Tandon (eds) *Citizens Strengthening Civil Society*, Washington, DC: World Alliance for Citizen Participation.
Shang Yusheng (2002) "关于非政府民政系统管理的NPO的讨论" (On NPOs outside of MOCA regulatory system), unpublished paper, author's collection.
Shen Yue (1990) "市民社会辨析" (An analysis of townspeople's society), *Philosophy Study*, 1: 44–51.
Shi Yuankang (1991) "市民社会与重本抑末—中国现代化道路上的障碍" (Civil society and the policy of "zhongben yimo" – obstacles on China's road to modernization), *The Twenty-first Century*, 6: 105–20.
Shi Zhengxin (ed.) (2000) 中国社会福利与社会进步报告 (*2000*) (*A Report on China's Social Welfare and Social Progress, 2000*), Beijing: Social Science Documents Publishing House.
Shue, V. (1995) "State sprawl: the regulatory state and social life in a small Chinese city," in D. S. Davis, R. Kraus, B. Naughton and E. J. Perry (eds) *Urban Spaces in Contemporary China: The Potential for Autonomy and Community in Post-Mao China*, New York: Woodrow Wilson Center Press and Cambridge University Press.
Simon, K. (2003) A statement at Roundtable before the Congressional-Executive Commission on China (March 24), in *To Serve the People: NGOs and the Development of Civil Society in China*, Washington, DC: US Government Printing Office.
Solinger, D. J. (1992) "Urban entrepreneurs and the state: the merger of state and society," in A. L. Rosenbaum (ed.) *State and Society in China: The Consequences of Reform*, San Francisco, CA: Westview Press.
Song Jian (1996) "依法保护环境，实现可持续发展" (Protect environment lawfully and accomplish sustainable development), *China Environment Newspaper*, July 25: 2.
State Bureau of Religion (SBR) (2000) "The details on management regulation of foreigners' religious activities in the People's Republic of China," *People's Daily Overseas Edition*, September 27: 1.
Stevis, D. and Assetto, V. J. (eds) (2001) *The International Political Economy of the Environment: Critical Perspectives*, Boulder, CO: Lynne Rienner Publishers.

Strand, D. (1990) *Rickshaw Beijing: City People and Politics in the 1920s*, Berkeley, CA: University of California Press.

Su Li, Ge Yunsong, Zhang Shouwen and Gao Bingzhong (1999) 规制与发展：第三部门的法律环境 (*The Regulations and Development: The Third-sector's Legal Environment*), Zhejiang: Zhejiang People's Publishing House.

Sullivan, L. R. (1990) "The emergence of civil society in China, Spring 1989", in T. Saich (ed.) *The Chinese People's Movement, Perspective on Spring 1989*, Armonk: East Gate Book.

Tang Jun (2002) "关于天津市下岗女工小额贷款项目的报告" (A report on micro-credit programs for unemployed female workers in Tianjin), <http://social-policy.info>.

Taylor, C. (1991) "Civil society in the Western tradition," in E. Groffier and M. Paradis (eds) *The Notion of Tolerance and Human Rights: Essays in Honour of Raymond Klibansky*, Ottawa: Carleton University Press.

Tong Shijun (1993) "'后马克思主义'视野中的市民社会" (Civil society in the perspective of "post-Marxism"), *Chinese Social Science Quarterly*, 4: 189–96.

Unger, J. (1996) "'Bridges': private business, the Chinese government and the rise of new associations," *The China Quarterly*, 147: 795–819.

Unger, J. and Chan, A. (1996) "Corporatism in China: a developmental state in an East Asian context," in B. L. McCormick and J. Unger (eds) *China after Socialism: In the Footsteps of Eastern Europe or East Asia?*, Armonk: M. E. Sharpe.

Verba, S., Schlozman, K. L. and Brady, H. E. (1995) *Voice and Equality: Civic Voluntarism in American Politics*, Cambridge, MA: Harvard University Press.

Wakeman, F. Jr. (1993) "The civil society and public sphere debate," *Modern China*, 19(2): 108–38.

Walzer, M. (ed.) (1995) *Towards a Global Civil Society*, New York: Cornell University Press.

Wang Di (2001) 跨出封闭的视野：长江上游区域社会研究 1644–1911 (*Out of a Closed World: A Study of Society in Upper Valley Yangzi River, 1644–1911*), Beijing: Zhonghua Publishing Bureau.

Wang Dongjiang (1998) 中国国有企业改革二十年 (*Twenty-years Reform of China's State Owned Enterprises*), Zhengzhou: Zhongzhou Guji Publishing House.

Wang Jun (2003) 城记 (*A memoir of the city*), Beijing: Sanlian Publishing House.

Wang Licheng (1992) "近代中国现代化进程的探索" (Search for modernization in modern China), *Fudan Journal*, 4: 85–9.

Wang Ming (2000) 中国 NGO 研究：以个案为中心 (*Case Studies on China's NGOs*), Nagono: UN Centre for Regional Development.

Wang Ming, Liu Guohan, He Jianyu (2001) 中国社团改革：从政府选择到社会选择 (*China's NGO Reform: From the Governmental Choice to Societal Choice*), Beijing: Social Science Documentation Press.

Wang Ming, Jia Xijin and Song Ruosi (2003) "中国转型时期NGO的发展" (The NGO development in China's transformation time), in Xie (ed.) *NGOs in China*, Shanghai: Shanghai Academy of Social Science Press.

Wang Shaoguang (1991) "关于'市民社会'的几点考虑" (Several considerations on "civil society"), *The Twenty-first Century*, 6: 102–14.

—— (2003) "促进中国民间非营利部门的发展" (Promoting the development of China's nonprofit sector), in Xie (ed.) *NGOs in China*, Shanghai: Shanghai Academy of Social Science Press.

Wang, S. and He, J. (2004) "Associational Revolution in China: Mapping the Landscapes." A paper at the 1st International Korean Studies Workshop on Civil

Society & Consolidating Democracy in Comparative Perspective, May 21–22, Seoul, Korea.
Wang Ying, Zhe Xiaoye, Sun Bingyao (1993) 社会中间层：改革与中国的社团组织 (*The Middle Stratum of Society: Reforms and China's Social Organizations*), Beijing: China Development Publishing House.
Wang Yongxi (ed.) (1992) 中国工会史 (*A History of China's Trade Unions*), Beijing: Publishing House of History of Chinese Communist Party.
Wenzhou Dictionary Committee (WDC) (1995) 温州词典 (*Wenzhou Dictionary*), Shanghai: Fudan University Press.
Wenzhou Federation of Industry and Commerce (WFIC) (1999) "发展同业公会：发挥商会在市场经济中的作用" (Promoting chambers of commerce: generating the role of chambers of commerce in a market economy), unpublished paper, author's collection.
Wenzhou Garment Chamber of Commerce (WGCC) (2000a) "温州服装商会章程" (The charter of Wenzhou Garment Chamber of Commerce), unpublished document, author's collection.
—— (WGCC) (2000b) "温州服装商会年度财政报告" (Annual financial report of the Wenzhou Garment Chamber of Commerce), unpublished document, author's collection.
White, G. (1993) "Prospects for civil society in China: a case study of Xiaoshan City," *The Australia Journal of Chinese Affairs*, 29: 63–87.
—— (1996) "Civil society, democratization and development," in R. Luckham and G. White (eds) *Democratization in the South: The Jagged Wave*, New York: Manchester University Press.
White, G., Howell, J. and Shang, X. (1996) *In Search of Civil Society: Market Reform and Social Change in Contemporary China*, Oxford: Clarendon Press.
Whiting, S. H. (1991) "The politics of NGO development in China," *Voluntas*, 2(2): 16–48.
Whyte, M. K. (1992) "Urban China: a civil society in the making?," in A. L. Rosenbaum (ed.) *State and Society in China: The Consequences of Reform*, San Francisco, CA: Westview Press.
Wong Jiming, Zhang Ximing, Zhang Tong and Qu Keming (1996) 1996–97年中国发展状况与趋势 (*The State and Trend in China's Development during 1996–1997*), Beijing: China's Social Publishing House.
World Wide Fund for Nature (WWF) (2000) *Annual Report*, <www.wwfchina.org>.
World Summit on Sustainable Development (WSSD) (2002) *The Civil Society Declaration*, Johannesburg, South Africa, August.
Wu Zhongze and Chen Jinluo (1996) 社团管理工作 (*The Management of Social Organizations*), Beijing: China Social Press.
Xia Weizhong (1993) "市民社会：中国近期难圆的梦" (Civil society: a dream that will not become true in China in the near future), *Chinese Social Science Quarterly*, 4: 176–82.
Xia Zaixing (1996) "试析我国教育投资存在的问题及原因" (On the problem and the causes of our country's education investment), *Xianning Teachers College Journal*, 1: 4–9.
Xiang Biao (2000) 跨越边界的社区：北京浙江村的生活史 (*A Community Crossing the Border: Living History of a Zhejiang Village in Beijing*), Beijing: Sanlian Publisher.
Xiao Gongqin (1993) "市民社会与中国现代化的三重障碍" (Three obstacles in civil society and China's modernization), *Chinese Social Science Quarterly*, 4: 183–8.

—— (2002) "新左派与当代中国知识分子的思想分化" (The New Left and the split up of China's intellectuals today), *Contemporary China Studies*, 1: 82–105.

Xie Lingli (ed.) (2003) *NGOs 在中国 (NGOs in China)*, Shanghai: Shanghai Academy of Social Science Press.

Xin, C. and Zhang, Y. (1999) "China," in T. Silk (ed.) *Philanthropy and Law in Asia*, San Francisco, CA: Jossey-Bass Publishers.

Xiong Yuezhi (1994) 西学东进与晚清社会 (*Western Learning Coming to the East and the Late Qing society*), Shanghai: Shanghai People's Publishing House.

Xu Dingxin and Qian Xiaoming (1991) 上海总商会史1902–1929 (*A History of Shanghai General Chambers of Commerce, 1902–1929*), Shanghai: Shanghai Social Science Publishing House.

Xu Jialiang (2003) "社会团体与公共政策制定：全国妇联个案研究" (Social organizations and the making of public policy: a case study of the All China Women's Federation), PhD dissertation, Peking University.

Xu Yong and Chen Weidong (2002) 中国城市社区自治 (*China's Urban Community Self-governance*), Wuhan: Wuhan Publishing House.

Xue Delin (2003) "坚持服务宗旨，促进行业振兴" (Insisting service mission and promoting the development of trades), in Xie (ed.) *NGOs in China*, Shanghai: Shanghai Academy of Social Science Press.

Ya Li (2004) "互联网：现实中国VS.网络中国" (Internet: reality China vs internet China), <http://www.boxun.com> (accessed November 22, 2004).

Yang, G. (2005) "Environmental NGOs and institutional dynamics in China," *The China Quarterly*, 3: 46–66.

Yang Nianqun (1995) "近代中国研究中的'市民社会'：方法及限度" (Civil society in the study of contemporary China: method and limitation," *The Twenty-first Century*, 32: 29–38.

Yang Rongxin (1996) "中国扶贫基金会工作报告" (China Foundation for Poverty Alleviation (CFPA) work report), in *CFPC Newsletter*, 95, September 15.

Yang Tuan (2000) "中国社区非营利组织发展的研究报告" (A report on the development of China's community NPOs), in Shi Zhengxin (ed.) *The Report on China's Social Welfare and Social Progress*, Beijing: Social Science Documents Publishing House.

Yang Xuedong (2000) "社会资本：对一种新解释方式的探索" (Social capital: an exploration of a new interpretation mold), in Li Huibin and Yang Xuedong (eds) 社会资本与社会发展 (*Social Capital and Social Development*), Beijing: Social Science Documentary Publishing House.

Ye Zhengkang (2000) "在促进中小型企业发展中如何发挥工商联作用" (How to play the role of federation of industry and commerce in promoting medium and small businesses), unpublished paper, author's collection.

Young, D. R. (2001) "Third party government," in J. Steven Ott (ed.) *The Nature of the Nonprofit Sector*, Boulder, CO: Westview.

Young, N. (2001) "Searching for civil society," in CDB, *Civil Society in the Making, 250 Chinese NGOs*, Beijing: China Development Brief.

—— (2002a) "Three 'C's: civil society, corporate social responsibility, and China," in *The China Business Review*, 29(1): 34–8.

—— (2002b) "Participate decision-making on environment," *China Development Brief*, No. 13, <www.chinadevelopmentbrief.org>.

—— (2004) "Business elite is unlikely to push for political reform," *China Development Brief*, VI, No. 1: 45.

Yu Heping (1993) 商会与中国早期现代化 (*Chambers of Commerce and China's Early Modernization*), Shanghai: Shanghai People's Publishing House.

Yu Keping (1993) "马克思的市民社会理论及其历史地位" (Marx's civil society theory and its historical importance), *Chinese Social Science*, 4: 59–74.

Yu Li and Xiao Hua (2004) "解密温州商会：政府与市场之间的粘合剂" (Discover the secrecy of Wenzhou chambers of commerce: the adhesive between the government and market), *Southern Weekend*, April 15.

Yu Yingshi (1987) 士与中国文化 (*Shi and Chinese Culture*), Shanghai: Shanghai People's Publishing House.

Yuan, N. (2003) A statement at Roundtable before the Congressional-Executive Commission on China (March 24), in *To Serve the People: NGOs and the Development of Civil Society in China*, Washington, DC: US Government Printing Office.

Yuzo, Mizonuchi (Goukou Xongsan) (1994) "中国与日本'公''私'观念之比较" (A comparison of Chinese and Japanese conceptions of 'public' and 'private'), *The Twenty-first Century*, 3: 85–97.

Zhan Guoshu and Zhang Xiaoguo (2002) "神秘的温州人" (Mysterious Wenzhou people), in Chen Junxian and Zhou Zengxing (eds) *Understanding Wenzhou*, Beijing: People's Daily Publishing House, <http://www.peoplesdaily.com> (accessed June 15, 2003).

Zhang Guo (1999) 中国：大趋势 (*China: The Great Trend*), Beijing: Contemporary China Publishing House.

Zhang Jing (ed.) (1998) 国家与社会 (*The State and Society*), Hangzhou: Zhejiang People's Publishing House.

Zhang Jingru and Liu Zhiqiang (1992) 北洋军阀统治时期中国社会之变迁 (*China's Social Changes During the North Warlords Period*), Beijing: Chinese People's University Press.

Zhang Kaiyuan (1985) 辛亥革命与近代社会 (*The 1911 Revolution and the Modern Chinese Society*), Tianjin: Tianjin People's Publishing House.

Zhang Kaiyuan and Liu Zengping (1980) 辛亥革命史 (*A History of the 1911 Revolution*), Beijing: People's Publishing House, Volume 2.

Zhang Kaiyuan, Ma Min and Zhu Ying (2000a) 中国近代民族资产阶级研究 (*A Study of China's Modern National Bourgeoisie*), Wuchang: Huazhong Normal University Press.

—— (2000b) 中国近代史上的官绅商学 (*Officials, Gentry, Merchants and Intellectuals in China's Modern History*), Wuhan: Hubei People's Publishing House.

Zhang Shuguang (2002) "中国非营利研究机构的成长与21世纪的中国" (The growth of nongovernmental and nonprofit research institutions and the 21st century China), <http://www.chinanewsnet.com> (accessed, July 5, 2002).

Zhang, T. (2004) "Challenges and Opportunities for Environmental Protection and Historic Preservation in Chinese Cities." A speech at the workshop "Environment, Culture, and Development in East Asia", Ohio Wesleyan University, October 14–16.

Zhang Xiaojin (1994) "市民社会研究在中国" (Civil society study in China), *Modernity and Tradition*, 4: 34–40.

Zhang, Y. (1996) "Chinese NGOs: a survey report," "Foundation in China: a survey report," in T. Yamamoto (ed.) *Emerging Civil Society in the Asia Pacific Community: a 25th Anniversary Project of JCIE*, Tokyo: Institute of Southeast Asian Studies and Japan Center for International Exchange.

Zhang Zhenhai (1999) "温州市行业协会试点情况" (Wenzhou's experiment of trade associations), in DBP, *China's Trade Associations: Reforms and Exploration*, Beijing: China's Business Publishing House.

Zhang Zhigang (1999) "目前中国工业协会的状况" (The current state of China's industrial trade associations), an unpublished speech, April 27, author's collection.

Zhang Zuye (1999) "中国政治改革的总体目标：建立宪政民主体制" (The general goal of China's political reform: establishing a constitutionalist democracy), *Contemporary China Studies*, 3: 54–77.

Zhao, L. and Irving, C. (eds) (2001) *The Non-Profit Sector and Development*, Hong Kong: Hong Kong Press for Social Sciences.

Zhao Shiyu (2002) 狂欢与日常：明清以来的庙会与民间社会 (*Celebration and Daily Routine: Temple Festivals and Folk Societies Since the Ming and Qing Dynasties*), Beijing: Sanlian Publishing House.

Zheng Yi (2001) 中国之毁灭：中国生态崩溃紧急报告 (*China's Extermination: An Urgent Report on China's Ecology Collapse*), Hong Kong: Mirror Publishing House.

Zheng, Y. (2004) *Globalization and State Transformation in China*, New York: Cambridge University Press.

Zhu Ying (1991) 辛亥革命时期新式商人社团研究 (*A Study on New Merchant Organizations During the 1911 Revolution*), Beijing: Chinese People's University Press.

—— (1997) 转型时期的社会与国家：以近代中国商会为主体的历史透视 (*Society and the State in the Time of Transformation: A Historical Approach of Modern Chambers of Commerce in Contemporary China*), Wuhan: Central China Normal University Press.

Zou Tianxing (1989) "试论社会力量办学" (On education by social forces), in Beijing Bureau of Adult Education (ed.) 北京社会力量办学概况 (*The State of Education Run By Social Forces in Beijing*), Beijing: Education and Science Publishing House.

Index

Page numbers in italics refer to figures and tables

academic associations *88*, 92, *93*
AiZhi Action 133–5
All-China Federation of Industry & Commerce (ACFIC) 83, 146–9
All-China Federation of Trade Unions (ACFTU) 67, 71–2, 82, 84
All-China Women's Federation (ACWF) 67, 71–2, 82, 96, 98–101, 126–7, 182
Allen, Young 45
Amity Foundation 71
Anhier, Helmut K. 170
anti-competition rule 67
Arato, Andrew 31
Asia Foundation 177, 178
associations, modern *see* modern associations
autonomy 95–8

Baogang He 96
Beidahuang 58th Regiment Friendship Association 111
Bell, Daniel 31
Bergere, Marie-Claire 41
biodiversity 130–3
Blecher, Marc 70
bottom-up organizations 144–5, 165–6, *see also* Wenzhou chambers of commerce
Bourdieu, Pierre 107, 109, 122
bourgoisie 41–2, 202
British Petroleum (BP) 186
businesses: individually owned *54*

Cecil, Lord 39
Center for Biodiversity and Indigenous Knowledge (CBIK) 130–3

chambers of commerce: late Qing/early Republic 35–7, 43–4
Chan, Anita 139, 142
Chen Kuide 106
China: distrust of West 171–2, history and culture 25–8, *see also* late Qing/ early Republic
China Association for NGO Cooperation (CANGO) 174, 191–3
China Charity Federation (CCF) 51–2
China Consumers' Association (CCA) 149
China Development Brief 178
China Elementary and Middle School Green Education Action 186
China Foundation for Poverty Alleviation (CFPA) 51
China Grouping Companies Promotion Association (CGCPA) 143, 153–5
China Teenagers' and Children Foundation (CTCF) 51
China Youth Development Foundation (CYDF) 101–4
Chinese Communist Youth League (CCYL) 67, 71–2, 82, 101–3
Chinese People's Political Consultative Conference (CPPCC) 82, 130
Christian population 70
civic associations 146, 149–53
Civil Affairs Statistical Yearbooks 86–7
civil society: approach 142–5; Chinese history and culture 25–8, 33–5; Chinese phrases for 18–22; and corporatism 137, 165–6; debates in China 17–18, 33, 183; debates in West 16–17; early 20th C 43–6; global 168–71, 184–5; introduction

238 Index

of Western ideas 23–4, 202–3;
  models 28–35, 207; and NGOs
  206–8; reinterpretation of Marxism
  22–5; and social capital 106–7
CLEE *see* US-China Committee for
  Legal Education Exchange
Clinton, President Bill 130
Cohen, Jean L. 31
Coleman, James 107
commercialization culture 125
community construction 58–61
competition *see* anti-competition
  rule
Confucianism 27–8
constitutionalism movement 43
constructive interaction 29–30, 208
corporatism: in China 138–42; and
  civil society 137, 165–6; concept
  137–8
cultural organizations *88*
Cultural Revolution 49–50, 62, 111,
  113, 129, 202

danwei 58–60
democratic governance 38
democratic movement (1989) 63, 67,
  70
Deng Xiaoping 23, 33, 48, 57, 98, 102,
  112, 125, 161, 172
Deng Zhenglai 21, 22–3, 29, 32
departmental management: and
  macromanagement 53–6
Dickson, Bruce 145
Directory of INGOs in China 178
Division of Social Organizations
  (MOCA) 62–3
dual registration 64–6

early Republic *see* late Qing/early
  Republic
economy: and civil society 31–3;
  independent research institutes
  125–6; individually owned *54*;
  privatization 53–6
Economy, Elizabeth 117
education 39–40; CYDF involvement
  101–2; private sector involvement
  49–51
*Encyclopedia of Chinese Social
  Organizations* 78, 86–7
enemy, the 82–3
Engels, Friedrich 20–1
entrepreneural interests 144–5,
  203–4

environmental leadership: in Third
  World 172
environmental movement 185–6
environmental NGOs 116–21, 130–3

Falun Gong 70–1
Fang Zhaohui 20, 24
federations *88*, 92, *93*
federations of industry and commerce
  (FIC) 146–9
Fewsmith, Joseph 123
Fiedler, Katrin 118
Fisher, Julie 9
folk organizations *81*, 85
Ford Foundation 131, 177, 178, 181,
  182–3, 188–95, 196
foreign foundations 65–6
foundations 92–3; foreign 65–6,
  177, 178–9, 189, 194; funding
  93–4, 197–9; statistics *88*, 92, *93*,
  see also Amity Foundation; Asia
  Foundation; China Foundation for
  Poverty Alleviation; China Youth
  Development Foundation; Ford
  Foundation; international NGOs;
  Naunan Foundation
Friends of Nature (FON) 116, 119,
  121, 129–30
funding: foundations 93–4, 197–9;
  government 72–3, 143

Gan Yang 21
Gao Xiaoxian 122
gentry-merchants 39, 41–2, 46, 202
Global Village of Beijing (GVB) 116,
  119–20, 121
globalization 168–71
GNP, industrial, by ownership *54*
gongmin shehui 20, 22
government organized non-
  governmental organizations
  (GONGAs) 58, 64, 73, 75, 86, 204;
  autonomy 96–7, 205
government policy 47–8, 74–5, 201–2;
  administrative downsizing 56–8;
  community construction 58–61;
  contradictions 69–75; funding
  72–3, 143; macromanagement
  53–6; motivation 48–9; political
  organizations 70, 71–2; religious
  organizations 70–1; social welfare
  49–53; tax relief 73
grassroots organizations 109, 111;
  advocating for public interest

116–21; dynamics/leadership 121–5; environmental NGOs 116–21, 130–3; and foreign foundations 195; fulfilment of personal needs 113–16; social conscience raising 116–21; traditional associational values, rejuvenation 111–13; trust/reciprocity 113–16
Green Earth Volunteers (GEV) 116, 121
Gu Xiaojin 103
Guang Xu, Emperor 39
Guo Jianmei 121

Habermas, Jürgen 31–2, 34, 45
Hao Yufan 172
Harding, Harry 169
He Zengke 25, 32
He Zhonghua 121
Heffner, Robert 18
hierarchy *80*
history and culture 25–8
HIV/AIDS 133–5
Hong Kong 24; NGOs 179; Red Cross 178
Hope Project 102–3
Howell, Judy 17, 84
Hu Jintao 72, 144
Hu Yaobang 72
Huang Haoming 73, 121
Huang, Philip 26, 35
Hyden, Goran 95, 206

independent research institutes 125–6
informal organizations *see* grassroots organizations
intellectuals: associations 35–7, 42–3, 46, 202; independent research institutes 125–6; role 121–5, 128–9, 202–3; and women's NGOs 126–8
international NGOs (INGOs) 167–8, 200 by organization *180*; country origins *179*; current state 176–80; and global civil society 168–71, 184–5, 204; government policy 171–6; historical role 176–7; intermediaries 174; legal operational status, methods 177–8; limitations 195–200; and NGO study in China 181–4; role 180–1; staffing 199–200, *see also* non-governmental organizations
Internet use 105–6
Iriye, Akira 77–8

Jiang Zemin 22, 33, 58, 70, 85, 87, 144, 148, 156–7, 196
Jing Yuejin 17

Kang Xiaoguang 9, 48
Kang Youwei 39
Kuhn, Philip 34

Lai Ruoyu 84
late Qing/early Republic 33–5; chambers of commerce 35–7; constitutionalism movement 43; evolving civil society 43–6; and features of modern associations 37–43; intellectual associations 35–7, 42–3, 46
leading classes 83
legal education 182
Li Lisan 84
Li Xiaojiang 126–7
Liang Congjie 119, 121, 129–30
Liang Qichao 129
Liang Sicheng 129
Liang Zhiping 21, 30
Liao Xiaoyi 119, 121, 130
Lin Huiyin 129
Lü Dong 55–6
Lyons, Mark 151

Ma Changshan 30
Ma Min 45
macro-management: and departmental management 53–6
Mao Zedong 28, 33, 48, 82, 84, 98, 129, 204
Marx, Karl 20–1, 22–5, 33; reinterpretation 22–5
mass organizations *81*, 82–4
masses, the 83
medical associations 40
micro-credit projects 175
Ministry of Civil Affairs (MOCA) 62–3, 64, 65, 66, 67, 68, 69, 82, 85, 92, 94, 117, 156, 157
minjan shehui 21–2
modern associations 37–43, 204–6; democratic governance 38; and education 39–40; government relations 40–1, 45; networks 44; newspapers/publications 44–5; Western influence 38–9
mother-in-law agencies 64–6, 157

Nan Lin 108
Naunan Foundation 196
new authoritarianism 22–3, 27
Newton, Kenneth 107, 109
Ningbo Fellows' Association (NFA) 112–13
non-governmental and non-commercial enterprises (NGNCEs) 68–9; legal classification 79–80; and private non-profit service providers 183–4; role/data 94
non-governmental organizations 85–6, 104; social organizations: autonomy 95–8; and civil society 206–8; definitions 77–8; development factors 201–4; geographical spread 90–2; legal definitions 78–81; statistics 86–93; as top-down organization 146–9; typological data *88*, 92, *93*; use of term *81*, see also international NGOs
non-profit organizations (NPOs) *81*, 85; Network 180–1, 185, 186–8
non-profit service providers 183–4

O'Brien, Kevin 118
oriental totalitarianism 27

Pei Shengji 131–3
Peking Opera Fans Club 111, 113–14
Peking Union Medical College (PUMC) 177
people, the 82–3
people's organizations *81*, 82–4
personal needs: fulfilment 113–16
political organizations 70, 71–2
poverty alleviation 51–2
Private Entrepreneurs' Association 150, 203–4
private non-profit service providers 183–4
privatization of economy 53–6
professional associations *88*, 92, *93*, 146, 153–5
public interest advocacy 116–21
Putnam, Robert 44, 107, 108, 109, 110

Qing see late Qing/early Republic

Rankin, Mary 34
reciprocity 113–16
Red Cross 40
registration-regulation 61–9; anti-competition rule 67; dual registration 64–6; foreign foundations 65–6; mother-in-law agencies 64–6, 157; official administrative structure 62–5; relevant official documents *64*; rules 66–8; under party state 61–2
religious organizations 70–1, 196
residents committees 60–1
Rockefeller Foundation 177
Rowe, William 34
rule of law 30–1

Saich, Tony 10
Salamon, Lester 9, 77, 78, 206
Schmitter, Philippe 138, 139
self-employed laborers *150*
Self-Employed Laborers' Associations (SELAs) 150–3; government control 153
self-sufficiency 143
Serrano, Isigani R. 9
Shang Yusheng 121
Shen, Yue 20
shequ 58
Shi Yuankang 27
shimin shehui 20–1, 22
Sina Drivers' Friendship Club (SDFC) 114–15
social capital 105–7, 135; concept 107–11; significance for China 107–11
social conscience raising 116–21
social organizations 85–6; and CCP 74, 82; equivalent organizations *81*; expansion 56–8, 62–3; growth and decline *157–8*; hierarchy *80*; legal classification 79–81; registration-regulation 68–9, 72; running for-profit businesses 73; use of term 81–2
social services see social welfare
social welfare 49–53; and social control 58–61; societalization 52
Socialist Reform of Industry and Commerce, 1950s 146–7
societalization of social welfare 52
Song Jian 117
Soong Ching Ling Foundation 93
State Bureau of Religious Affairs 70
State Economic and Trade Commission 157
state-association relationship 143, 207–8
state-enterprises, intermediaries 53–6
state-owned enterprises 58–61

state-society relationship 26–7, 30–2
students organizations 62–3, 67, 70, 155
Sun Yat Sen 93

Taiwan 82
Taylor, Charles 137–8
Third World, environmental leadership 172
Tiananmen demonstrations 23, 155
Tianze (Unirule) Institute of Economics 125–6
Tocqueville, Alexis de 206
top-down associations 139–42, 165–6; categories 146; characteristics 145–6
townspeople's society 20–1
trade associations *88*, 92, *93*; as intermediaries 53–6, 58; mission 156; as NGOs 157; as top-down associations 139–42, 146, 155–9
trade unions 84
traditional associational values, rejuvenation 111–13
trust/reciprocity 113–16

Unger, Jonathan 139, 142, 147–8, 153
unions *see* trade unions
united front, the 83
United States 178–9, 189, *190*
university teachers 123–4
US-China Committee for Legal Education Exchange (CLEE) 182

Verba, Sidney 108

Wan Yanhai 121, 133–5
Wang Huning 22
Wang Shaoguang 108
Wang Xingjuam 121
Wang Yongchen 121
Wang Yu 119
Wang Zhaoguo 148
Weber, Max 34

Weller, Robert 18
Wen, Premier 121
Wenzhou chambers of commerce (WCCs) 159–65; bottom-up characteristics 159–60; historical/cultural environment 161–3
Wenzhou Garment Chamber of Commerce (WGCC) 160
White, Gordon 139, 142
Whiting, Susan 138–9
women's NGOs 40, 98–101, 181–2; and intellectuals 126–8
work units 58–60
World Conference for Women (WCW) 78, 85, 99, 100, 101, 116, 127, 181–2
World Trade Organization (WTO) 169–70
World Wide Fund for Nature (WWF) 180, 185–6
Wu Dengming 121

Xiao Gongqin 23, 27
Xu Jianchu 121, 130–3
Xu Yongguang 101, 103, 121

Yan Mingfu 51–2
Yang, Guobin 118
Yang Tuan 94
YMCA/YWCA 71
Yongjia School 161–2
Young, Dennis 11
Young, Nick 49, 71, 144
Yu Heping 35
Yu Keping 24, 25, 28

Zhang Jian 36
Zhang Jing 26
Zhang Kailin 121
Zhang Kaiyuan 37
Zhang Shuguan 126
Zheng Guanyin 39
Zheng, Yongnian 169
Zhu Ying 43